PRINCIPLES AND POSSIBILITIES IN COMMON LAW

TORTS, CONTRACTS, AND PROPERTY

Shawn Bayern
Larry & Joyce Beltz Professor
Florida State University

CONCISE HORNBOOK SERIES™

WEST ACADEMIC PUBLISHING

The publisher is not engaged in rendering legal or other professional advice, and this publication is not a substitute for the advice of an attorney. If you require legal or other expert advice, you should seek the services of a competent attorney or other professional.

860 Blue Gentian Road, Suite 350
Eagan, MN 55121
1-877-888-1330

Printed in the United States of America

ISBN: 978-1-68561-242-9

Preface

This book is meant to help demystify American common law by covering three of the typical first-year subjects in American law schools: tort law, contract law, and property law. It assumes no prior knowledge and shows readers the underlying structures that make these subjects easier to understand. It's aimed mainly at law students in the United States who are looking for a sophisticated, substantive guide to the subjects—one that aids learning but isn't just a study guide filled with "tips" and "tricks." It should also be useful to students in other disciplines who want an introduction to law, to lawyers and law students in other legal systems who want to learn more about how American lawyers think about the common law, and to general readers who are curious about how modern law works. I have also kept in mind general readers with an interest in common law, as well as undergraduate students, in crafting various explanations of legal rules. Law need not be an alien discipline; because it reflects social morality and social policy, it should be accessible, even at a relatively sophisticated level, to interested nonspecialists.

An unusual feature about modern American common law is that everyone needs to come to their own understanding of it. Civil law—the legal system of other countries like France and Germany—is often taught in a top-down fashion, with general theoretical principles treated as a consensus position and taught from the outset.[1] By contrast, common-law teaching doesn't proceed that way in part because common law does not have, or even purport to have, the same sort of consensus. People need to reach their own understanding of the common law precisely because every feature of it is subject to question, debate, and reanalysis—including the foundational principles of law and even including how legal subjects should be organized. Similarly, it is hard or impossible to analyze or even apply the common law without evaluating its soundness, considering new principles and possibilities; in the common law, it is very difficult to produce a single clear statement of what the law "is" without an understanding of what the goals of judges have been, what the law has been in the past, how it has changed, *why* it has changed, and where it is heading. Like US law schools generally, this book treats the common law as an animated subject rather than as a

[1] *See* JOHN HENRY MERRYMAN & ROGELIO PÉREZ-PERDOMO, THE CIVIL LAW TRADITION 70–81 (4th ed. 2019).

collection of "rules." Law school could be much shorter but would not be nearly as interesting if the law were as static and simple as that.

Because law isn't just a collection of rules to memorize or look up, the book often includes arguments about the common law—again, what it is, what it is moving toward, and what it should be—not because these arguments are the final word on the subject but because that is the most natural way to talk about the common law. In other words, in the common law, there is no way to avoid that sort of debate. One reason that American professors teach law through the Socratic method is that we equate learning the common law with questioning it. Every case is an opportunity for the law to change, and it's also an opportunity to reconsider how the doctrine fits together.

General discussions about this book or its subjects over the years with Rob Atkinson, Nancy Benavides, Larry Garvin, Erin O'Hara O'Connor, David Landau, Mark Seidenfeld, Joseph Singer, Don Weidner, and Sam Wiseman have been very helpful. Kat Klepfer at Florida State's library was very helpful, too, in responding to my often unusual library queries.

I also owe an immense debt of gratitude to my own professors, particularly Mel Eisenberg and the late Steve Sugarman. In fact, I'm occasionally embarrassed by how much of my own thinking, particularly in overall approach to the law, follows theirs. (When I mentioned this concern years ago to Professor Eisenberg, who taught me contract law, he responded with Tolstoy's opening line from *Anna Karenina*: "All happy families are the same.") I have cited the scholarship of my teachers throughout, but attributing particular thoughts doesn't capture their full contributions to my approach generally and in this book—which is dedicated to them.

Summary of Contents

Table of Contents

PRINCIPLES AND POSSIBILITIES IN COMMON LAW

TORTS, CONTRACTS, AND PROPERTY

Chapter 1

INTRODUCTION

Contents

It's too easy when learning the law to focus on the details and miss the big picture. Law is much harder to learn if it's just a pile of disconnected rules. Memorizing and applying the law mechanically without understanding its structure is neither fun nor productive.

That is true of most subjects, but it's particularly true of law because law is designed to be useful—it's supposed to serve important social goals. The law isn't imposed on us by aliens. The common law in particular is a living system, responding and adapting to a changing society. As an example, most of the rules of contract law from a hundred years ago have changed extensively since then—which is fortunate because most of those rules were terribly wrong: they weren't fair, weren't useful to contracting parties, weren't efficient generally, and aimed to serve no other particular policy. Christopher Columbus Langdell, the dean of Harvard Law School in the late 1800s and one of the architects of what we now call *classical contract law*, responded to an argument against one of his ideas in contract law as follows:

> It has been claimed that the purposes of substantial justice, and the interests of contracting parties as understood by themselves, will be best served by [a particular rule of contract law]; and cases have been put to show that the contrary view would produce not only unjust but absurd results. The true answer to this argument is, that it is irrelevant . . . .[1]

In other words, around a century ago the dean of Harvard Law School could say with a straight face that it was "irrelevant" that a rule of

---

1 C.C. LANGDELL, A SUMMARY OF THE LAW OF CONTRACTS 21 (2d ed. 1880).

contract law was unjust, would not serve the interests of contracting parties, and might even have "absurd" consequences.

Fortunately, that is not the view any longer, although it may be useful to know that there are still a few professors in contract law, tort law, and property who seem to be dedicated to the idea that we got everything in these subjects right a century ago. And in full disclosure, it may be worth adding that whether a rule is just, useful, or absurd might or might not matter much in constitutional law today, because the state of that area of law is much like that of common-law subjects a hundred years ago, and there are still many professors and commentators in those areas who adopt entirely *conceptualistic* or *formalistic* views. Many professors speak as if the point of the law is to make law professors happy by allowing their concepts to line up neatly—or to serve the abstract goals of one theoretical philosopher or another.

That is less often the case in the common-law subjects like contract law, tort law, and property. Much of the study of law in these areas is in fact specifically the study of change—and of the messiness of change. For example, in many areas of contract law, there is an older rule that is still in the process of being eroded; it is hard to learn contract law without learning (1) the old rule, (2) the reasons it is a bad rule, and (3) the direction in which the law has been moving. Lawyers, particularly in common-law subjects, often have that kind of thinking in mind when discussing legal rules or giving legal conclusions. It's part of the reason lawyers so often describe results as "likely" rather than certain. In the end, in a common-law system, every case is an opportunity to make the law a little better. The alternative is to freeze the law, distill it into fixed rules, and make it nonresponsive to (changing conceptions of) justice and policy. That would perhaps be easier for lawyers, and it would certainly be cleaner to teach, but it would cause the law to fail to serve the *functional* ends of social morality and social policy. When that approach to the law has been tried, it has not lasted.

Because common law is a dynamic system—because it exhibits, perhaps, an institutional version of what some psychologists have called a "growth mindset" as opposed to a "fixed mindset"[2]—it is impossible to understand any particular rule of common law without understanding where it has been and where it seems to be going. This book's title refers to "principles and possibilities" because both are necessary to understand the common law. Features of some legal rules may represent zero-sum games, but the law as a whole is not zero-sum in the same way, and thoughtful new ideas to analyze

---

[2] *See, e.g.*, Carol S. Dweck & David S. Yeager, *What Can Be Learned from Growth Mindset Controversies?*, 75 AM. PSYCH. 1269 (2020).

doctrine can work like any other development in technique, technology, or art; the law can certainly improve over time. This sort of change is one reason that law school in the United States takes three years; students are not just learning a collection of rules but are learning how to think about the boundaries of those rules, in view of how and why those boundaries have already changed.

The specific legal subjects in this book have in fact changed dramatically in the last century or so. "It would cut up the doctrine of consideration by the roots," wrote Oliver Wendell Holmes in 1884, "if a promisee could make a gratuitous promise binding by subsequently acting in reliance on it."[3] But that (as we'll see in chapter 3) is precisely what happens under today's law. Similarly, in tort law, Holmes wrote somewhat dismissively in 1881 that "The state might conceivably make itself a mutual insurance company against accidents, and distribute the burden of its citizens' mishaps among all its members. There might be a pension for paralytics, and state aid for those who suffered in person or estate from tempest or wild beasts. . . . The state does none of these things, however."[4] Yet the federal government developed Social Security around fifty years later, and the tort system (as we'll see in chapter 2) has changed in many ways that Holmes didn't envision—or did envision but specifically rejected.

1.1 What to Focus on in the Study of American Law

When I say that it's too easy to focus on the details in studying law, I don't mean that all details are problematic; many details are in fact quite important in deciding cases. The key, of course, is focusing on the right details. Machine-learning researchers have developed the notion of *attention* for artificially intelligent systems—essentially, the ability for a software system to focus on useful features of data when processing it.[5] A very similar ability is important in the study of law, and it is something that is rarely taught, except maybe by example in some classrooms.

---

3 Commonwealth v. Scituate Savings Bank, 137 Mass. 301, 302 (1884).

4 OLIVER WENDELL HOLMES JR., THE COMMON LAW 94–96 (1881).

5 *See, e.g.*, Kyunghyun Cho et al., *Describing Multimedia Content Using Attention-Based Encoder-Decoder Networks*, 17 IEEE TRANSACTIONS ON MULTIMEDIA 1875 (2015) ("Attention mechanisms are employed for two purposes. The first is to reduce the computational burden of processing high dimensional inputs by selecting to only process subsets of the input. The second is to allow the system to focus on distinct aspects of the input and thus improve its ability to extract the most relevant information for each piece of the output, thus yielding improvements in the quality of the generated outputs.").

For instance, in *Farwell v. Keaton*,[6] a case commonly taught in Torts courses, a sixteen-year-old named Siegrist is out with a slightly older friend causing minor trouble, taunting others and the like. They are attacked, and Siegrist sees his friend get badly beaten up. Siegrist is unreasonable in failing to provide aid to his friend, whose medical condition deteriorates rapidly. When his friend dies, the friend's estate (more concretely, an administrator who becomes responsible for all his financial affairs, including potential lawsuits against others) sues Siegrist because of his negligence in failing to help. Siegrist defends by relying on a well-known rule, which we'll cover in more detail in the next chapter, that under the common law people have no duty to rescue others in distress. To be clear about the "no duty to rescue" rule, it lets people off the hook even if they fail to make extremely easy, essentially riskless "rescues" like making a phone call or pulling a fire alarm when someone's life is in danger (see section 2.3.2).

The court refuses to apply that rule to this case on two different grounds. First, Siegrist started to rescue his friend, taking some steps that began a rescue—like applying an icepack to his head—and those who start a rescue need to act reasonably in continuing or aborting the rescue. Second, Siegrist was out on a "social venture" with his friend, and being on such a venture is a relevant "special relationship" that constitutes an exception to the "no duty to rescue" rule. The particular special relationship here was something like "being a common participant in a night out on the town, causing a little trouble." So Siegrist is liable for failing to rescue his friend.

There are several different levels of learning that the case offers, and it's very easy to get stuck on the wrong things. First, of course, in reading any case, students have to figure out what's going on, often following legal terminology that might simultaneously be new to them and significantly outdated. Next is to focus on the particular "rule" of the case: people have duties to rescue those in a common "social venture," whatever that is, and once people start rescuing others they need to act reasonably in handling or aborting the rescue. Too many people stop there—a rule has been extracted, so they think they're done. Stopping there, however, is exactly what's important to avoid. If the goal were simply to give students a list of special relationships for which the law requires reasonable rescue efforts, the professor or casebook could simply supply that list. In reading common-law cases, it's important to go deeper.

A small further step in understanding *Farwell v. Keaton*—and its role in helping to teach tort law—is that it provides an *example* of

6 240 N.W.2d 217 (Mich. 1976).

the kinds of "special relationships" that can matter when considering whether there's a duty to rescue. So, for example, if you saw a case that were broadly similar to *Farwell*—maybe three experienced coworkers are traveling together in an airport, one slips and falls in an otherwise empty terminal, and the others just laugh and leave him there—you'd be able to draw an analogy. I say this is only a small further step because many students and even some professors make too much of it. Whole books have been written about how the common law depends on analogy,[7] but it is very easy to overemphasize the role of analogy to the point where people think the common law has no principles and is just a matter of drawing comparisons and distinctions among cases. Analogy does play a role in some legal reasoning, but it is not very useful on its own.

For example, lawyers need to know what facts are important to cases, and it is impossible to do that without understanding the principles that animate the cases. For instance, is my hypothetical case involving three coworkers at an airport really "similar" to the facts of *Farwell*? There's no way to answer that question in the abstract without understanding the *reasons* we're drawing comparisons. There are some similarities between the cases (people see someone they know get injured and don't do enough to help) but a lot of differences: two bystanders instead of one; a professional rather than a social relationship; older people rather than teenagers; an accident rather than an attack by a third party; and no common history of causing the injury together, in *Farwell*'s case by taunting others and thereby perhaps increasing the likelihood of an attack. In any event, analogies can be useful but their role should not be overstated—and more importantly, the analysis of *Farwell* is still not complete even after a student uses the case as an example or data point about what "special relationship" means or about how to draw analogies to the facts of the case.

The really important steps in learning from a case like *Farwell* are deeper than just treating the case as an example. Instead, they involve recognizing that *Farwell* shows a court *generalizing* the notion of special relationships—that is, choosing to expand it to a new set of facts. In earlier law, the special relationships that mattered were relatively limited; they included relationships like *ship captain to crewmember* and *shopkeeper to customers*, but the categories were small and focused.[8] Nobody who had seen only the term "special relationship"—and indeed not even lawyers who had read the old cases about ship captains and shopkeepers—would have predicted on

---

7 *E.g.*, EDWARD H. LEVI, AN INTRODUCTION TO LEGAL REASONING (1949).

8 W. PAGE KEETON ET AL., PROSSER AND KEETON ON TORTS § 56, at 376–77 (5th ed. 1984).

that basis alone that a court in Michigan in 1975 would apply it to two friends hanging out together. Recognizing that the court has made a decision to extend the duty to rescue others teaches us several things. First, it shows that the category of "special relationship" is vague and manipulable—easily the subject of argument, narrowing, or expansion. Every two people in a tort case have *some* relationship, even if it's just that they were in the same place, using the same road, interacting on the same computer network, and so on. This alone suggests that the existence or absence of a "special relationship" doesn't really drive the cases; the question is why the courts are choosing to call some relationships "special" (so that there is a duty to rescue).

That brings us to the final step: to try to find a principle on which courts are narrowing or expanding a category like "special relationship." To be fair, it would be impossible to do that with just one case, but for example in the context of a full Torts course—or while reading chapter 2 of this book—you may well recognize that the *Farwell* court was motivated to impose liability here rather than to tolerate a sort of immunity from liability. After all, Siegrist—the person who left his friend to die—behaved in a morally wrongful fashion, and the "no duty to rescue" rule would exempt him from liability when justice and perhaps other values would require otherwise. The final step, then, is to see that *Farwell* is part of a *pattern* under which courts and other lawmakers have been eroding the "no duty to rescue" rule—to the point where no sophisticated lawyer would, if asked in advance, tell someone as a general matter that it's fine for them not to rescue others.

And because with learning there's never really a "final step," a further level of analysis worth considering is that reading *Farwell* and understanding it in this way helps you see similar kinds of patterns in other areas of law too. For example, the no-duty-to-rescue rule in tort law is eroding in much the same way as several of the more formalistic applications of the consideration doctrine have eroded in contract law.

The actual modern line of rules that *Farwell* is a part of, in any event, is much more complicated than it might seem at first. Every US law student learns that there's "no duty to rescue" in tort law, but that rule has so many exceptions—and the exceptions have expanded so far—that it's hard to say that the no-duty-to-rescue rule has really survived intact. Why has it eroded? Chapter 2 will discuss the topic more fully, but the simple answer is probably that most people who encounter it find the no-duty-to-rescue rule morally outrageous. There are cases suggesting, as two leading tort commentators of the 1900s put it, that an "expert swimmer, with a boat and a rope at hand, who sees another drowning before his eyes, is not required to do anything at all about it, but may sit on the dock, smoke his cigarette, and watch the man drown."[9] As the same commentators noted, "Such decisions are revolting to any moral sense. They have been denounced with vigor by legal writers."[10] The law does not ignore that sort of problem, even if it takes a while for it to correct itself.

In any event, the long-term pattern that *Farwell* is a part of is the expansion of the duty of care in tort law. Finding that kind of pattern and then applying it to new cases is exactly what many Torts courses ask students to do. It is also what the leading professors, practitioners, and judges at the American Law Institute do in writing their *Restatements of the Law*, treatises that try to make sense of the cases. For example, on a topic related to *Farwell*, the Restatement says: "The law appears . . . to be working slowly toward a recognition of the duty to aid or protect in any relation of dependence or of mutual dependence."[11] Written almost sixty years ago, that is a somewhat narrower, more cautious version of the general direction of the law I just suggested above.

Again, there's no way to figure all that out by reading *Farwell* alone. Much of the work of learning the law is in reading widely enough—usually with professors as a guide—so that you can begin to see patterns and the principles that underlie them. But the important idea to recognize for now is that it is important to pay attention not just to the rules of the cases but to *why* the cases have been assigned and *how* they add to your general understanding of the law. In addition to asking what the case's rule is, you need to ask whether the rule is the right rule (which is to say whether it's consistent with social morality and social policy), why the courts have applied the rule they way they have, and how the case interacts with other cases. If you don't do that, then you're just making lists and drawing analogies, and that's an easy way to get the law wrong. For example, a lawyer who did that would not have predicted the outcome correctly in *Farwell*.

Note that while *Farwell* is in many Torts casebooks and is interesting because it did something a little new with tort duty, it is not on its own a case that many people will need to cite, reread, or directly apply. It is in the casebooks because it shows how the law develops, as well as exhibiting a few particular details of the law of duty in tort law (e.g., social venturers, starting but not finishing a rescue). In courses like Civil Procedure and Constitutional Law that

---

[9] *Id.* at 375.

[10] *Id.* at 376.

[11] RESTATEMENT (SECOND) OF TORTS § 314A cmt. b. (1965).

depend on pronouncements by the Supreme Court of the United States, many cases *are* "the law" nationwide and have to be learned accordingly. In other words, the goal in studying those subjects may well simply be how to apply those cases: given its decisions in three particular cases, how would the Supreme Court decide a fourth case? The whole enterprise—the whole structure of learning and analysis—is different in the common-law subjects. Many cases in the common-law casebooks are included precisely because they're wrong or because they reflect an unusual position adopted by only a few states (sometimes called a *minority rule*). Or they're included to help students see broader patterns, as I have been describing.

In that sense, legal cases in law school are like educational case studies—much like students in business schools see—but they are also more than that. They are ways for you to build up principles in the law and then test those principles to see if they survive exposure to the real world. One of the nice things about law is that it forces us to answer questions, so principles aren't merely abstract and can often be tested with new facts.[12]

Throughout all these steps, it is important to recognize that everything is open to debate and critique, and it's rare to find two common lawyers who will see cases in exactly the same way. Nothing I have said about *Farwell* is the final word on the matter. Perhaps you think the no-duty-to-rescue rule has better policies in its favor than I do; perhaps you analyze the trend in cases differently from the way I do. That sort of disagreement and ongoing discussion is all part of the process that leads the common law to develop.

1.2 Social and Doctrinal Justifications for Legal Rules

In common law, *doctrine* refers to the rules that can be found in cases. Doctrine is ordinarily a sufficient reason for a lower court to apply a rule: the court is bound by the decisions of higher courts in its jurisdiction. Doctrine is often a persuasive reason even for high courts to keep a rule in place; reversing precedent too readily can lead to confusion about what the law is, and it may undermine parties' specific reliance on the rule and general confidence in the stability of the law. As a result, if a doctrinal rule is good enough, courts might keep it around even if it's imperfect.[13] Old cases are often called

---

[12] *Cf.* Lon L. Fuller, *On Legal Education*, *in* THE PRINCIPLES OF SOCIAL ORDER: SELECTED ESSAYS OF LON L. FULLER 271, 278 (Kenneth I. Winston ed., 1981) ("The secret of the success of American legal education, in comparison, say, with undergraduate instruction, lies in the fact that it centers about problems.")

[13] For more information on the general features of common-law precedent, overruling, and similar topics, see MELVIN ARON EISENBERG, THE NATURE OF THE COMMON LAW (1991).

precedent, and the rule that courts need to follow old cases is sometimes called the *doctrine of precedent* or *stare decisis*, Latin for "to stand with what has been decided."

Even when the common law changes, as the last section described, it can often be slow to change. Significant processes in common law are explained by the constraints that judges feel themselves under—usually against changing the law too sharply or too quickly. Sometimes, courts will keep a rule in place but erode it with exceptions; this is what we saw with *Farwell*. The court didn't impose a general duty to rescue; it kept the no-duty-to-rescue rule in place but held that it didn't apply to friends who went out together to cause trouble. Sometimes, in order to reach sound results, courts will change a rule while purporting to apply an old rule. Justice Benjamin Cardozo was an expert at this; many of his opinions are impressive examples of how a judge can purport to follow doctrine while making significant improvements to the law.[14] To be clear, however, that is not the best way for the common law to proceed. Honesty is better, but honesty may not always be possible.

Fundamentally, doctrine needs to be justified by social propositions—mainly notions of morality and notions of policy.[15] This is probably what most people expect; moral values (what is right and wrong) and instrumental values (what leads to good consequences versus bad consequences) are the kinds of values that animate most decisions in other practical endeavors (government, business, personal career decisions), and it would be surprising if law ignored them. When doctrine is no longer sound enough in view of social propositions, that is when it changes. Often and maybe usually, when people read a case they have a sense of who "should" win; that sort of intuition often rests on moral propositions which, if formed and expressed, can be the basis of a legal argument. Similarly, it is clear that some rules can be productive and others can be unproductive; all else equal, judges would prefer productive rules.

If doctrine is neither moral nor productive, it becomes hard to justify keeping it static, and the common law works accordingly. Lawyers in civil-law systems (and indeed many lawyers in common-law systems) sometimes say they prize "certainty" as a paramount virtue of the law, but clearly certainty overall is not a prime social goal, or else we'd (for example) outlaw all technological and social change. *Pointless* legal uncertainty is a problem, but nobody argues in favor of that, and it is usually easy to avoid; improving a legal rule over time is not pointless uncertainty, because it brings an improvement. Change in doctrine may have downsides if people have

---

14 *Cf.* MELVIN A. EISENBERG, LEGAL REASONING 106–10 (2022).

15 *See* EISENBERG, *supra* note 13.

relied on the old rule, but those downsides can be weighed against the benefits of improvement.

Moreover, certainty for *lawyers* is not the most important kind of certainty. I have heard people say things like, "lawyers must always know what the result in a case will be." First of all, that is plainly untrue; if lawyers always knew the result in advance, there would never be litigation. Second, it is very common for people to act without legal advice. What's more important than certainty for lawyers is that the law be predictable for people in general—for business parties, for example, planning to enter into contracts. Often making sure the law is adaptable and responsive to business norms is a better way to achieve that kind of certainty than simply to prevent doctrine from changing. Third, while legal certainty can be quite important, it is not important for its own sake; it is usually just a proxy for some other value—like people's interest in having relied on an old rule.

Take an example: suppose there is an unproductive rule of contract law that prevents parties from renegotiating a debt.[16] A lawyer who is familiar with that rule might argue that it will throw lawyers' certainty into doubt if the courts change the rule; maybe details of doctrine have built up around the old rule, and the new rule could have gaps and invite misunderstandings. This may be true, and it is certainly one factor to consider when determining whether to change the rule—that is, one factor to be weighed against the value of letting people renegotiate their debts, if that is a socially useful thing for them to do. But that factor may not carry much weight in a world where debts are commonly renegotiated informally by individuals, without detailed advice from lawyers. Those individuals will follow current business norms, not outdated ones, and may not be aware of the older rule. Note also that in such a world, business parties are unlikely to have relied on the old rule, so that it would not be unfair to change it. In this example, changing the rule to one that incorporates current business norms may well *increase* the predictability of law for the parties. If parties or their lawyers had relied on the old rule and the rule had continued to underlie business or financial activity, that would be a different and more difficult matter.

In any event, the rules of common law should not feel alien to you; if they do, then, again, you have at least the start of a legal argument against them. Some research has suggested that unhappiness among practicing lawyers is increased when they work in fields where the rules have started to feel alien or external to them,

16 *Cf.* Foakes v. Beer, 9 App. Cas. 605 (1884). Section 3.1.6 discusses *Foakes*, and the general argument in the text about uncertainty in cases like it, in more detail.

as if they are just applying rules mechanically that have no relation to social morality or social policy. That is not supposed to be the case under modern law, and recognizing the discrepancy between a rule and its justifications is a good start toward understanding and then potentially reforming a rule. Some of the best lawyers in the country are actively engaged in "law reform" efforts to update, clarify, simplify, and generally improve the common law.

1.3 Common Law in the United States

Common law is distinct from civil-law systems, which are legal regimes said to be based primarily on statutes and which are dominant in most countries. Common-law systems don't avoid statutes and are in fact often have extensive statutes; for example, California has adopted statutes for tort and contract law, although they don't change the background common-law system very much. The primary difference between common-law systems and civil-law systems is cultural and historical, rather than depending specifically on the presence of statutes or on specifically different substantive legal rules in subjects like contract law, tort law, or property law.[17] Common law tends to have several practical, operational differences from civil law: previously decided cases are recognized in at least some contexts and in some ways as binding on courts; judges tend to be senior lawyers rather than people who adopt a separate judicial career path early in their studies; many statutes are overtly understood as incomplete and in need of development; courts are overtly recognized to be able to develop the law.[18]

Common law in the United States in particular is distinct from common law in most other jurisdictions in a variety of important ways. Legal education in the United States is always postgraduate; students typically study some other subject for their first higher-education (baccalaureate) degrees, and in fact the subject they study may be entirely unrelated to law because "majors" in US university education are generally of less significance than they are in much of the world. This may in part explain the greater *realism* of American law, or (very broadly speaking) the widespread notion that law is responsive to morality and policy rather than operating as its own formal system. Students are not taught legal principles from a young age but instead bring perspectives from other disciplines to bear on the law, and law students in the US tend to be older than law students in other countries.

---

[17] *Cf. generally* JAMES GORDLEY ET AL., AN INTRODUCTION TO THE COMPARATIVE STUDY OF PRIVATE LAW (2d ed. 2021).

[18] For more background on civil-law systems, see JOHN HENRY MERRYMAN & ROGELIO PÉREZ-PERDOMO, THE CIVIL LAW TRADITION (4th ed. 2019).

More importantly, particularly in the traditional common-law subjects that involve the personal relationships between individuals, American law lacks a central authority. The Supreme Court of the United States has developed itself over time, for better or worse, as the final authority on interpreting the United States Constitution, and it is typically the final answer on matters of federal law. But most common-law subjects aren't federal; though federal courts frequently hear contract and tort disputes, they do so under rules that require them to apply the law of a particular US state law rather than federal law.[19] As it happens, these rules may slow down the development of the common law because federal courts, in applying the law of another jurisdiction (an individual US state), are less likely to develop or change law that is not their own. Federal courts may *certify* questions to state supreme courts—that is, simply ask a state high court to answer a question of the state's own law—and the life of US common law would probably be served if federal courts did this more often.[20]

Each of the fifty US states has its own comprehensive common law (except perhaps Louisiana, which draws significantly from the civil-law tradition), as do other jurisdictions like the District of Columbia. Nothing coordinates perfectly among the states, so the tort

---

19 *See* 28 U.S.C. § 1332 (allowing private disputes that could arise under state law to end up in federal courts); Erie Railroad Co. v. Tompkins, 304 U.S. 64, 78 (1938) (the classical case laying out that federal courts in such cases apply the law of the state in which they are located, rather than "federal general common law").

20 The practice of certification may seem indirect and dilatory, and Charles Dickens is said to have criticized similar practices in *Bleak House*, a famous novel about intractable litigation:

> All through the deplorable cause, everything that everybody in it, except one man, knows already is referred to that only one man who don't know, it to find out—all through the deplorable cause, everybody must have copies, over and over again, of everything that has accumulated about it in the way of cartloads of papers (or must pay for them without having them, which is the usual course, for nobody wants them) and must go down the middle and up again through such an infernal country-dance of costs and fees and nonsense and corruption as was never dreamed of in the wildest visions of a witch's Sabbath. Equity sends questions to law, law sends questions back to equity; law finds it can't do this, equity finds it can't do that; neither can so much as say it can't do anything, without this solicitor instructing and this counsel appearing for A, and that solicitor instructing and that counsel appearing for B; and so on through the whole alphabet, like the history of the apple pie. And thus, through years and years, and lives and lives, everything goes on, constantly beginning over and over again, and nothing ever ends.

CHARLES DICKENS, BLEAK HOUSE 67–68 (1853). But that sort of endless referral and circuitousness is not implicated by modern *certified question* doctrine; in either case (direct appeal within the federal system or certification of a question by a federal court to a state court), an appellate court simply decides, after reviewing the facts of a case, a question of common law. My suggestion in the text is that the legal jurisdiction that sees itself as having the power to carefully apply, reconsider, and develop its own law is a better institution to apply law to facts than an institution like the federal courts that, in cases governed by state common law, are applying another jurisdiction's law.

law of North Carolina can be different from the tort law of South Carolina. Courts in one state can of course read the judicial opinions in other states and find the judges' reasoning persuasive, but for practical purposes there is single high court in the subjects that this book covers. "Common" law is, then, something of a misnomer in the modern United States.

Because of the absence of a singular high court, US law can be quite messy. To understand the current state of US law on a particular common-law topic, a student may need to read cases from a variety of jurisdictions and then piece them together. As we'll see on many particular legal questions, often the state of the law is captured not so much by a particular statement of a rule but by a trend or tendency in the courts. Learning US law, then, requires a comprehensive picture and, perhaps even more than in most other legal systems, demands a kind of active reading and assimilation of large amounts of information. Even a lawyer who is litigating a nontrivial case in a single jurisdiction would be wise not to read cases only from that jurisdiction, although they would of course focus on those cases. The need to read and piece together a wide variety of cases is present in all common-law systems, but without a single high court on matters of contract, tort, or property, it is particularly important in the United States.

The decentralization of US law may also explain the American legal "realism" discussed briefly above and the prominence of interdisciplinary approaches to US law. If there were a single court stating rules of contract law or tort law, as there is in most national jurisdictions, academics could focus on the pronouncements from that particular court. They could debate trends in that one court, perhaps spend a lot of time comparing the court's opinions in contract law with those in the court's other subjects, aim criticism at specific opinions that the academic and legal communities could all be assumed to have read and understood, and so on. That is not the case in the United States. Instead, the law is often discussed and critiqued at a much more general level, which may explain why (for example) movements like "law and economics" are especially popular in the United States. Most law teaching of tort, contract, and property in the United States aims to capture general national principles and trends rather than targeting the law of a single jurisdiction.

The absence of perfect coordination among US jurisdictions does not mean that there is *no* coordination.[21] Because of their focus on national principles, casebooks and other student-oriented books serve some role in the national coordination and development of law.

---

[21] *See* Melvin A. Eisenberg, *The Concept of National Law and the Rule of Recognition*, 29 FLA. ST. U. L. REV. (2002).

And an important institution in the United States is the American Law Institute, founded in 1923 to try to help organize, clarify, and improve the law. The American Law Institute publishes the various *Restatements* that are commonly at least part of the basis of law teaching in the United States. Restatements are books, very similar to law treatises produced by individuals or small teams of authors, but they are subject to a much more deliberative process that involves teams of leading lawyers, judges, and legal academics. They therefore reflect considerable thought, attention, and some degree of agreement as to what the law currently is. That said, the Restatements are not ordinarily themselves "the law": they are not statutes and are not binding on courts, although many courts have voluntarily said things like "if there's no rule of law in this state, you can perhaps assume we'll rely on the Restatement."[22] Courts frequently cite the Restatements, but it is not uncommon for them to reject a Restatement rule or provide their own elaboration of it. The American Law Institute also has other output that has been influential in US law generally, like the Model Penal Code and (as a joint project with the Uniform Law Commission) the Uniform Commercial Code (UCC).

There is one particular rule of procedure that distinguishes US law from most other legal systems and may be worthwhile to keep in mind when considering US legal rules. In most countries' legal systems, the loser of a lawsuit pays the winner's legal fees. This is not true in the United States. The loser in US litigation pays courts "costs," but these are only small administrative fees paid to courts. In some cases, like those involving civil rights,[23] courts may award attorney's fees to a plaintiff who prevails, but that is not the general rule in the United States. This may lead US courts and commentators, appropriately or not, to be very concerned about opening the so-called "floodgates of litigation"; the idea is that the wrong rule might invite large numbers of opportunistic lawsuits with no risk of paying the other side's legal costs. US courts, like many

---

[22] *E.g.*, Innerimages, Inc. v. Newman, 579 S.W.3d 29, 46 (Tenn. Ct. App. 2019) ("In the absence of a controlling statute or guidance from the Supreme Court, this Court has the authority to adopt provisions of a Restatement in order to further the development of the common law in this state."); Tierra Ranchos Homeowners Ass'n v. Kitchukov, 165 P.3d 173, 179 (Ariz. Ct. App. 2007) ("Arizona courts look to the Restatement for guidance in the absence of controlling authority"). *See also* 1 V.I.C. § 4 (2019) (in the US Virgin Islands, "[t]he rules of the common law, as expressed in the restatements of the law approved by the American Law Institute, and to the extent not so expressed, as generally understood and applied in the United States, shall be the rules of decision in the courts of the Virgin Islands in cases to which they apply, in the absence of local laws to the contrary.").

[23] *E.g.*, 42 U.S.C. § 1988(b) ("[T]he court, in its discretion, may allow the prevailing party, other than the United States, a reasonable attorney's fee as part of the costs . . . .").

others, have rules in place to prevent and penalize frivolous lawsuits, however.

1.4 This Book's Approach

This book aims to help you see the kind of thing that law schools in the United States are trying to teach their students. It covers quite a bit of tort law and contract law (and a moderate amount of property law) but is not meant to be a complete substitute for hornbooks in those areas. It could not, in any reasonable length, cover every topic in three broad subjects—and indeed the subjects are taught very differently, in their details, around the country. But in building up principles and in showing relationships between the main private-law subjects, the book can give you a vantage point on the law that is sometimes hard to build up from the study of the subjects separately.

This book's approach is practical and functional. Though discussing "principles" that underlie the cases may at first sound somewhat abstract, the book never engages in what we might think of as high theory. For example, I don't explain or defend any of the rules in the common law by referring to the nature of liberal democracy or by quoting John Locke. The common law did not even originate in a liberal democracy, and the specific problems of tort and contract law—proximate causation, whether to enforce donative promises, and so on—do not go away in a monarchy. They instead are simply about how humans have to live with each other, usually on a relatively small scale. Explanations of common-law rules that depend on grand pronouncements of political theory or rest on the values that the law "communicates" tend to be tautologies: just-so stories that can explain anything.

My sense is that this approach is at least broadly consistent with most professors in common-law courses. Political theory may have something to say about the institutional competence of courts to resolve disputes, but morality and small-scale notions of efficiency and incentives drive the common law much more than grand theories of government do.

1.4.1 Pluralism in the Common Law

Relatedly, this is a *pluralist* book. What that means is that it rejects the idea that any single, comprehensive theory of law is sufficient to explain the richness of the common law. Law doesn't rest on a particular philosophical school's conception of justice, a single economic school's conception of efficiency, or a single approach to policymaking. Philosophy, economics, science, institutional and human experience, and politics can all feed into the way that common-law rules develop. The common law often has to make difficult tradeoffs precisely when these different ways of approaching the world are in conflict—when, for example, moral philosophy conflicts with economic efficiency.

Some scholars have criticized pluralism—again, the notion that multiple ways of analyzing legal problems can matter—by saying that pluralistic approaches are unsatisfactory because they provide the least guidance in the most difficult cases.[24] It is more accurate, however, to say that pluralist approaches avoid pretending that there are easy answers to the law's difficult questions. When lawmakers pretend that are easy answers and try to distill them into formalistic legal rules, the attempt is not durable; the rigid rules get eroded precisely because they don't do justice and aren't useful. Some legal problems are hard and will likely remain hard—and disputed—for years to come. As Mel Eisenberg, a leading scholar of the common law, once wrote, "It is . . . clear that law generally [has] too many rooms to unlock with one key."[25]

1.4.2 Connections Across Legal Subjects

An important part of this book's approach, in trying to help you learn the common law by seeing the bigger substantive picture, is to draw connections and comparisons across the three legal areas it covers—tort law, contract law, and property law. Too often, professors of these subjects don't even talk to each other about the details of the law that they teach. Much as with comparative law across different legal jurisdictions, however, comparing the law within US legal subjects can be a fertile source of ideas. For example, as we'll see over the next few chapters, principles of comparative negligence in tort law could be, but usually aren't, applied to analogous problems in contract law. Is there any reason for that, or is that a way the law could develop in the future? As another example, though the difference between principles of negligence and of strict liability comes up primarily in tort law, using that conceptual difference to analyze problems in other subjects can be a helpful in understanding the policy choices behind the law's answers to those problems.

Sometimes recognizing the correspondences across legal subjects is helpful in determining the role that legal doctrine plays. For example, "no duty" rules in tort law (see section 2.3) serve a very similar role to rules in contract law that refuse to enforce promises that have "no consideration" (see section 3.1): they both exempt

---

[24] *E.g.*, Alan Schwartz & Robert E. Scott, *Contract Theory and the Limits of Contract Law*, 13 YALE L. J. 541, 543–44 & n.2 (2003) ("[P]luralist theories . . . tend to be least helpful when they are most needed.").

[25] Melvin Aron Eisenberg, *The Responsive Model of Contract Law*, 36 STAN. L. REV. 1107 (1984).

morally wrongful conduct from legal liability, and they rest on similar types of policies. Teachers rarely focus on connections like that between tort law and contract law, but seeing those connections and patterns can be very useful in learning those subjects and in arguing about the their development and future possibilities. This book often draws attention to that kind of correspondence.

1.5 Notes on Learning the Common Law

A few other general notes about learning the common law may be helpful before moving on to particular legal subjects, like torts and contracts.

1.5.1 What Courts "Do" Versus What They "Say"

In general it is helpful to pay attention to what courts *do*, rather than only what they *say*. This too often isn't taught explicitly enough, although it lies behind a lot of what professors are looking for students to figure out. What courts say they are doing is of course important, and student should not ignore it. But it is important to approach the text of court opinions with a healthy skepticism. Does what the court says match or serve as a useful predictor of its results? Does it even make sense? Why are the judges writing what they're writing (rather than something else, or a much shorter and perhaps unpublished opinion)? Why do they report some facts and not others? What are they looking to achieve?

As a small example, the contract doctrine of unconscionability (the notion that extremely unfair contracts should not be enforced) is often said to depend on two types of unconscionability: *procedural* (there wasn't really a contract because the bargaining process was defective) and *substantive* (the terms of the contract are extremely unfair). Some courts say that they require that a party show both procedural and substantive unconscionability to demonstrate that a contract is unconscionable. But a discernable pattern in the cases is that courts almost always either find *both* procedural and substantive unconscionability or *neither* procedural nor substantive unconscionability. So the distinction between the two types of unconscionability—or a disagreement among courts about whether both types are required before the court declares a contract unconscionable—might not really drive the outcome of cases. Good courts can see patterns like this and use it to adjust their doctrines.

As a different sort of example, the state of the actual law is not always easily reduced to a straightforward "rule" or set of them. It is possible to learn landowner duties in tort law or consideration in contract law by listing dozens of separate doctrinal rules, but it is easier and more insightful to step back and see why those rules are arranged in the way they are. For example, often a collection of detailed rules serve as a series of inconsistent exceptions to an underlying rule that the courts disfavor. It is more helpful to understand that the courts disfavor the underlying rule than to learn mechanically that there is an underlying rule with fourteen exceptions. This book points out those sorts of patterns in the common law whenever it can.

1.5.2 The Difference Between Definitions and Legal Rules in Action

Relatedly, it is important not to be misled by definitions. At a simple level, an important skill in learning and applying the common law is learning which words are *terms of art*—words that don't have their casual meaning but instead carry a specific meaning for lawyers. For example, *reliance* in contract law does not mean that someone "relied" on a promise in the sense that they hoped for or psychologically counted on it; it means they changed their position in some definite way in response to the promise. *Intentional infliction of emotional distress* is the name of a tort, but that tort does not include all cases where someone intentionally inflicts emotional distress on another. *Duty* in negligence means nothing like what it sounds like (see section 2.3). This sort of discrepancy is very common, so it is a bad idea to try to guess what legal terms mean just by considering their usual meanings outside law.

At a deeper level—and this is also an example of paying attention to what courts do rather than what they say—the labels for or descriptions of legal rules do not stand in for deeper judgment, analysis, and caselaw. For example, a supreme-court case in Utah, *Birkner v. Salt Lake Cty,*[26] laid out three elements that need to be true for an employer to be responsible for an employee's negligence:

> First, an employee's conduct must be of the general kind the employee is employed to perform. . . . Second, the employee's conduct must occur within the hours of the employee's work and the ordinary spatial boundaries of the employment. . . . Third, the employee's conduct must be motivated, at least in part, by the purpose of serving the employer's interest.[27]

In a later Utah case, *Christensen v. Swenson,*[28] a security guard on a tight work schedule at a steel plant took a lunch break, drove to a restaurant, and negligently caused a car crash on the way back. The

---

[26] 771 P.2d 1053 (Utah 1989).

[27] *Id.* at 1056–57.

[28] 874 P.2d 125 (Utah 1994).

employee was not hired to get lunch, was off the site of the workplace (i.e., not within its "spatial boundaries") at the time of the accident, and was not in any familiar sense motivated to serve her employer when she drove negligently and caused the accident.

The *Christensen* court analyzed all these factors differently from the way a casual or naive reader of *Birkner* might have done—and certainly differently from the ordinary meaning to laypeople of the simple text of that opinion. As a result, the Utah Supreme Court reached exactly the opposite result that someone would have predicted if they had only (1) read *Birkner* and (2) followed its basic definitions uncritically.

For the first factor—was the employee hired to do what she did?—the court considered the employee's course of conduct at a high level of generality rather than a more particular one: had the employer "tacitly sanctioned [the] guards' practice of obtaining lunch"[29] in a hurry, given the rushed lunch schedule they imposed on employees? As to this factor, the court also accepted a transparently ridiculous argument: that part of this guard's job function was to get lunch in uniform and thereby strike fear into the hearts of people nearby by alerting them to the fact the steel plant had security. This is silly because surely the typical reaction of a potential thief to seeing a steel plant's security guard getting lunch would be to think "the steel plant is less guarded at the moment" and not "the steel plant is a hard target, so we should look for easier, unguarded victims." The guards worked at gates and would have been visible to potential thieves anyway.

For the second element, the court asked whether the nearby lunch destination was within the "ordinary spatial boundaries"[30] of the employee's actual routine—rather than the literal boundaries of the land—which again was largely dictated to her by her employer. For the third, the court again recognized that the employer imposed—and benefitted from—a tight schedule. In other words, the guards were motivated, at least in part, to serve their employer by rushing to get lunch—rather than to have a leisurely lunch. On the third element, the court again accepted a transparently ridiculous argument: "Employees must occasionally eat meals and use the restroom, and employers receive the corresponding benefit of productive, satisfied employees."[31] I have never thought that my eating or use of a restroom was for the benefit of my university; I doubt my university's Board of Trustees would see it that way either, although admittedly I have never asked. In any event, if an

[29] *Id.* at 128.

[30] *Id.*

[31] *Id.* at 129.

employee's basic bodily functions are for an employer's benefit, it's hard to think of anything that isn't—so it's hard to think of anything that wouldn't satisfy the third *Birkner* element.

The above discussion lays the groundwork for two related points. First, the descriptions or definitions of the test in *Birkner* would lead an uncritical reader to get the result in *Christiansen* exactly wrong—or, more accurately, to get the result right in lower courts but then to be overturned by the state's supreme court. Predicting the right result requires a broader sense of the doctrine of employer liability (see section 2.8.2). Second, the *Birkner* elements themselves appear to be under pressure, because the acceptance of ridiculous arguments to fit a case into those elements suggests that the court isn't really being driven by the elements but instead by a broader policy. *Christensen* doesn't overrule *Birkner*, and it formally maintains *Birkner*'s basic framework. But that framework doesn't seem to be doing much work. Instead, the *Christensen* court seems to be doing something that would be hard to predict from the *Birkner* elements alone: perhaps recognizing that employers should be liable for employees' torts when employers could reasonably expect employees to engage in the conduct that caused the torts, and the torts are a result of the employer's workplace policies and conditions. Here, the employer knew that guards had to rush to get lunch and nonetheless set up their schedules that way. Getting lunch in a rush at the closest restaurant is therefore not, at least according to *Christiansen*, necessarily outside the scope of the employees' job.

Again, it would be hard to know all that from reading a single case, but reading *Christensen* alone is sufficient to see that interpreting the older *Birkner* case too literally would be a mistake.

1.5.3 A Single Reason Isn't Sufficient

In a famous study, psychologist Ellen Langer found that in least in many situations, people seem to be remarkably easily persuaded by *any* reason, even if the reason adds no new information to the situation.[32] At least in many situations, "We should adopt a legal rule because . . ." may be persuasive even if the reason that's given isn't particularly forceful.

For example, the costs of administering the legal system, or the risk that there will be too many legal cases if we adopt a particular rule (thereby opening the so-called floodgates of litigation) can be important, and are certainly valid arguments to consider. But it's too

---

[32] Ellen Langer et al., *The Mindlessness of Ostensibly Thoughtful Action: The Role of "Placebic" Information Interpersonal Interaction*, 36 J. PERS. & SOC. PSYCH. 635 (1987) (known sometimes as the "photocopier" study because the experiment involved people about to use an office photocopier).

easy to use the mere threat of administrative costs or generalized institutional considerations to (for example) deny claims that can, in fact, relatively easy be remedied. It is useful in the study of the common law to remember that while all arguments for and against legal rules are important to consider, simply counting them up or noting their presence is not enough.

Similarly, as I suggested when I discussed "pluralism" above, legal academics frequently try to import methodologies from other subjects as if the mere presence of some theory or technique elsewhere is sufficient to drive legal outcomes. It is not. Of course, applying methodologies from other subjects in law is frequently interesting and helpful, but it needs to be done sensitively and with expertise. For example, as someone with a mathematical background I've always been skeptical when I hear people casually try to apply Gödel's incompleteness theorems to problems of contract interpretation. It is unlikely that abstract principles of mathematical logic will provide a solution for the rich, practical problems of contract interpretation, which have long been among the most litigated questions of contract law and which have resisted a single comprehensive solution. More practically, however, sometimes commentators find a single abstract economic argument or model to be much more persuasive than it should be (see, for example, section 3.6.4).

1.5.4 The Accessibility of Common Law

The law can seem, and be, complex, with intricate rules and sometimes impenetrable terminology—and with the multiple US jurisdictions discussed above and the lack of a central coordinating authority or single high court. But fundamentally, common-law judges are applying mainly (1) doctrine, or past cases; (2) social morality, or the prevailing sense of what is right and wrong in society; or (3) social policy, or the prevailing sense of what is useful and productive in society. Students have direct access to these three factors, just as the judges do. At least, most students do; in a typical classroom of law students, there are likely to be at least one or two sociopaths who may lack direct access to a moral sense, although they can at least observe it in others. Judges have more experience applying these factors, but those who learn the common law should recognize that there is nothing that needs to be mysterious about it. As I mentioned earlier, if you read a case and the result offends your moral sense or seems to create unproductive or dangerous incentives, that is the start of a legal argument against the case's result.

To be clear, *social morality* and *social policy* are informal and widespread social phenomena.[33] Social morality is conceptually distinct from the morality discussed by academic philosophers—which may not reflect that of society. For example, academic philosophers may be committed to exploring the consequences of particular abstract or theoretical ideas, or the writings of particular past thinkers, rather than explaining the operational morality of any particular society. (As it happens, there is also some evidence to indicate that, in the real world, academic philosophers are not even especially ethical! A researcher in 2009 conducted an empirical study and published it under the title *Do Ethicists Steal More Books?*; the study's answer to that question was essentially "yes.")[34] The point isn't that academic philosophers are wrong or aren't doing something useful; it is just that when judges apply notions of morality, they are not doing so directly in consultation with academic philosophers but instead asking what society regards as right or wrong.[35] That understanding of morality is something law students have access to even if they haven't studied Kant or Bentham. Similarly, social policy is not dictated to courts by economics or political-science departments. In making decisions, judges—and law students—often need to assimilate information from many social sources. But because they live in a society, that information is all ordinarily accessible to them and not alien to their own experiences.

1.5.5 What "Question Everything" Means

Professors and lawyers often tell law students that they should "question everything" when, for example, they read a case or learn a new area of law. This is useful advice in every discipline—for example, students should always try to figure out how we know the things we think we know, why people have written what they have written, whether alternative views of the subject would be better, and so on—but it is particularly valuable in learning the common law for at least a few reasons.

First, litigators and even judges are trying to convince their audiences that their view of the law is correct. This sort of convincing runs through all levels of legal materials, including judicial opinions: it involves choosing what facts to report, framing them, identifying what law applies to them, interpreting and applying that law, and responding to counterarguments. Lawyers do this at every stage of their work because, in an adversarial system like that of the common law, making good choices at each of those steps is an important part

33 *Cf.* EISENBERG, *supra* note 13, at 16–19, 26–31.

34 Eric Schwitzgebel, *Do Ethicists Steal More Books?*, 22 PHIL. PSYCH. 711 (2009).

35 *Cf.* EISENBERG, *supra* note 13, at 19–21, 160.

of representing their clients' interests. Judges do it because they usually want their opinions to be persuasive as a matter of values and reason (or at least rhetoric), rather than merely compulsive as a matter of authority or raw power. Students should read cases similarly to the way they would read argumentative briefs, rather than taking them as authority—particularly in common-law courses like Torts and Contracts where those cases are rarely widespread legal authority in the first place (see section 1.1).

Second, there is no universal consensus about even the basic structure or nature of the common law. There has long been a debate about the fundamental nature and purpose of law; for example, Roscoe Pound, around a hundred years ago, laid out no fewer than twelve "ideas of what law is for."[36] There is of course significant debate about what particular legal rules should be. Between those two levels of generality—the domains of grand theories and specific rules—there is also debate about the structure and organization of legal doctrine and legal subjects. As we'll see several times throughout this book, just because a doctrine exists doesn't mean it needs to exist; some old doctrines serve no useful role and get eroded, and others add only confusion to the law. It is useful to approach anyone's view of legal doctrine and its organization with healthy skepticism—and that of course includes your own analysis of the material in this book!

1.5.6 Scholastic Assessment of Common-Law Learning

This book is focused on the substance of the common law and how to learn it, not on how to take US law-school exams, but because features of the common law may influence the way that law professors assess student learning a short note may on law exams may be worthwhile. Many US law students, because of their undergraduate background in other subjects, are used to exams where it is their responsibility to supply a clear, correct answer. Most professors in law schools are not looking for students to do this. Just as the point of reading a case is not simply to extract a rule from it, the point of law-school exams is not simply to apply a definite law to the facts of a case. Too many students freeze up on exams because of this misconception: they see a difficult question and panic because they don't know the answer and don't see any way to identify a clear right answer from what they regard as the course's "material."

Though law sometimes does have a single clear answer, the point of law exams is often not to ask students to recite the easy parts of the law. Often the best exam answers are those that identify the

[36] ROSCOE POUND, AN INTRODUCTION TO THE PHILOSOPHY OF LAW 59–68 (1922).

difficult questions, explain why they're difficult, and actively try to reason toward a solution using the principles and possibilities that have arisen in class reading and discussion. Just as a practicing lawyer may not immediately know a complete answer upon hearing a difficult set of facts, a law student may actually learn something while taking (and thinking about) a law exam. To put it differently, the student's job is often to explain why the easy parts of the exam are easy and the difficult parts of the exam are difficult. Indeed, on a particular set of facts the current state of the law may well be something like "there is no clear or uniform answer to this question, but there's an old rule that has been significantly eroded for good reasons, and courts are likely to take one of two or three approaches in trying to resolve a question like this"—rather than the simple recitation of a rule. Lawyers often say things like that, and law students often should as well on exams.

A separate skill that law students are expected to learn is sometimes called *issue spotting*, although I think that term misstates and perhaps trivializes the practice. An important feature in applying law is that lawyers—at least, sophisticated lawyers or those who are working without guidance from other lawyers—need to determine the area of law to apply to any particular set of facts. Clients don't normally walk into a law office and say, "I have a consideration question in contract law" or "Can you help me with my 'no duty' problem in tort law?" They say "An employee of mine was injured near the worksite; will I be liable?" or "How can I enforce this contract?" It is the lawyer's job to figure out how the law applies to those facts. Consequently, lawyers are not frequently asked "Tell me everything you know about causation in tort law," so students are not typically prompted to do that either. Law students with experience in other disciplines may have come to see learning as reading and remembering, and maybe additionally as solving a particular type of puzzle. Learning the law involves all those things—reading, memory, and problem-solving—but when professors give law exams, they rarely ask for a comprehensive dump of static information or a walk-through of a previously given narrow problem. Students who learn the law by practicing how to recite rules tend to find themselves surprised by their first round of law exams, which don't have questions like "Explain how 'scope of liability' works in tort law."

To express this same idea differently, applying law to facts requires an imaginative or creative spark, even if in many cases just a small one. A lawyer or law student hears some facts, and it is up to them to figure out possibilities like, "On these facts, I think there could be a promissory estoppel claim." That step—making sense of the facts in view of the law—is a significant part of legal skill and judgment, and people don't learn how to do it only by studying the black-letter rules of promissory estoppel.

I have few educational gimmicks to offer, but one that is relevant here might be termed "studying in the right direction." For example, a student learning vocabulary in a Latin course may find themselves ill-prepared for an exam if they study a list of Latin words and their English translations; this may, depending on how they learn and access their memory, make it easy for them to translate Latin words to English but difficult for them to translate English words to Latin on a timed exam. Students need to prepare for the task that will be asked of them. The task that is normally asked of students in courses on tort law, contract law, and property law is not specifically to recite the law but to figure out how the law applies to complex factual scenarios. I certainly would not go as far as Wordsworth in saying

> One impulse from a vernal wood
> May teach you more of man;
> Of moral evil and of good,
> Than all the sages can.[37]

However, walking around a park and asking yourself who, if anyone, might be liable (and why) if you tripped on a badly maintained bridge—and anything else that starts with facts and moves toward law, rather than the other way around—could well be worth far more than trying to memorize the sections of the *Restatement (Second) of Torts* on landowner liability.

---

[37] William Wordsworth, *The Tables Turned; an Evening Scene, on the Same Subject, in* WILLIAM WORDSWORTH & SAMUEL TAYLOR COLERIDGE, LYRICAL BALLADS, WITH A FEW OTHER POEMS 186, 188 (1798).

Chapter 2

TORT LAW

Contents

Tort law is simpler than it appears—or at least learning its general structure is. The components of what we now call tort law assembled over hundreds of years in messy and complicated ways, and it is easy to look at the subject as a student or teacher and despair. I have known at least one teacher at a leading US university who gave up teaching the first-year Torts course because, they said, the subject never ended up making sense.

There is some truth to the idea that tort law is complicated. It is an extremely broad field, without even a clear definition that everyone agrees on. The term *tort* just means "wrong"—with an origin in the notion of twisting (as if things that are "twisted" are somehow "wrong"), so it shares a root with words like *torque*. It is often defined to include any non-contractual civil wrongs, although that definition is imprecise: modern tort law imposes liability for many actions that are not "wrongful," for example, and the definition of *tort* usually happens to exclude many non-contractual civil wrongs (like non-criminal underpayment of taxes and many types of unjust enrichment).[1] Tort law covers everything from accidental injuries in a car crash to complex, intentional financial fraud affecting

[1] *Cf.* RESTATEMENT (THIRD) OF RESTITUTION AND UNJUST ENRICHMENT § 1 (2011) ("The identification of unjust enrichment as an independent basis of liability in common-law legal systems—comparable in this respect to a liability in contract or tort—was the central achievement of the 1937 Restatement of Restitution. That conception of the subject is carried forward here.").

thousands of victims. Moreover, courts don't always apply the subject's concepts and doctrines consistently. Tort law has seen no shortage of attempts at grand, theoretical explanations—usually reductive applications of legal formalism, philosophy, or economics—but none of them has succeeded.[2] As we'll see, courts aren't even fully consistent when they use basic terminology in tort law, such as *duty* or *causation*.

All this is true in many areas of law, though, and it needn't be a significant barrier to learning a legal subject. The main task in learning tort law is to try to see enough of a pattern that the overall structure of the topic makes sense and allows you to tune out the irrelevant details. While doing this, however, it is important not to oversimplify the subject like some of the more reductive academic theories do. The goal of this chapter is to help you see the overall patterns of the subject and to focus on the right details.

Like most areas of the law, the general goals of tort law include some combination of policy-related goals and moral goals. The policy-related goals of tort law may include (1) *deterrence*, or the law's practice of discouraging dangerous behavior and reducing the likelihood and severity of accidental injuries; (2) *compensation*, or trying to restore, as well as possible, a victim to the situation they were in before an injury occurred—often with an eye toward making sure that people's basic needs are covered after a disabling injury has occurred; and (3) *cost internalization*, or causing parties to pay for the harms they cause so as to move society closer to an efficient allocation of resources. These instrumental goals may also correspond to moral goals; for example, maybe it is *right* rather than just useful that businesses pay their way, and maybe morality requires us to pay due attention to the need to reduce physical injuries. Other moral goals of tort law may include *punishing wrongdoers*. Theorists have supplied many other candidates for moral-philosophical goals for tort law, such as implementing classical notions of "corrective justice" or "restorative justice," providing an institutionalized substitute for private vengeance (which may also be a policy goal), communicating social values (likewise), providing an outlet for victims, and so on. In the caselaw, the clearest goals for tort law are probably deterrence and compensation, with cost internalization providing a rationale for some of the development of strict liability in the US caselaw of the 1900s (see section 2.8.1).

The chapter, like many Torts courses in the United States, spends most of its time on a legal claim (or *cause of action*) known as

---

[2] *Cf.* Fuller, *supra* ch. 1, note 12, at 279 ("It is remarkable how many people in this world [particularly those with "positions of influence"] . . . go about deciding things with only the slightest notion of what it is they are really deciding.").

negligence. There are two reasons for this focus. First, just practically, negligence is far more important than most other torts. Sadly, most of us know people who have been injured or killed in car crashes or who have needed to file insurance claims resulting from them—whereas few of us know people who have filed a claim for false imprisonment. Cars have gotten safer over the years, but a striking modern estimate is that any individual in the United States still has about a one percent chance of dying in a car crash.[3]

Second, as an educational matter, the negligence claim gives us a template for understanding the rest of tort law—and indeed much of law in general. Negligence is broken up into several conceptually distinct *elements* that the plaintiff, at least in theory, has to prove: *duty, breach, causation,* and *scope of liability* (or *proximate causation*). Each of these elements has a role to play in deciding whether a plaintiff should be able to recover damages from a defendant. As we will see, understanding each of those elements will help you structure your overall understanding of tort law.

2.1 The Principles of Negligence and Strict Liability

A fundamental question that most nonlawyers haven't considered is whether legal liability—that is, the ability for a plaintiff to recover from a defendant—should depend on *wrongfulness* or not. In other words, does a lawsuit arise only because the defendant has behaved *badly* or was *at fault* in some way, or can a plaintiff prevail even if a defendant has done nothing wrong? This has proved to be a surprisingly subtle and difficult question for the law to resolve.

Just as a matter of terminology, we use several terms to describe bad behavior: it might be *wrongful, blameworthy, negligent, unreasonable, at fault,* or in *breach* of a legal duty. These terms all mean much the same thing in this context, as do various other descriptions of unreasonably unsafe decisions, like "the defendant did not show due care" or "the defendant did not act with ordinary care." Some actions can be *more* wrongful than others (for example, intentionally hurting someone is morally and legally worse than doing so carelessly), but there is a basic category of behavior that all these terms are getting at: it is behavior of which social morality and law do not approve—behavior in which someone *should not* have engaged. We won't see exactly how the law determines whether behavior falls into the category until the next section, but the core

---

[3] National Safety Council, *Odds of Dying*, https://injuryfacts.nsc.org/all-injuries/preventable-death-overview/odds-of-dying/ [https://perma.cc/F5BK-T59V].

idea behind the category is disapproval—that someone *should* have done something differently.

Though legal history on the matter is unclear and disputed,[4] it is commonly understood that the traditional view of accident law is that plaintiffs don't win unless they show that the defendant behaved badly in some way. Under that view, the conception of a lawsuit was to "right" a "wrong"—to hold someone to account for harm they had inflicted in violation of moral rules. We might call that view the *fault principle* or the *negligence principle* today.

The negligence principle stands in contrast to a different sort of principle, which is that sometimes it is appropriate to require people to pay even if they haven't done anything wrong. Taxation is a clear example of that principle; when someone is taxed, the Treasury is not saying "you have been wrongful in accumulating money, so you must turn it over to us." It is simply applying rules that apportion social costs based on people's activities without regard to whether they are morally right or not.[5] We call this a principle of *strict liability*—that is, just as a matter of terminology, liability is said to be *strict* when it does not depend on fault.

Tort law, and indeed the rest of the law, uses both of these principles; it does not consistently choose one to the exclusion of the other. (As we will see in section 2.8.1, both principles have strong arguments in their favor.) Most of tort law operates on a fault principle, requiring a showing of negligence or some other wrongfulness before a plaintiff can recover from a defendant, but there are particular areas where it does not. In those particular areas, tort law imposes liability even on people who have done nothing wrong.

Another way to consider the difference between negligence and strict liability is to say that moral norms are usually a direct justification for negligence rules—not necessarily the only justification, but usually an important one. For example, if someone gets drunk and drives recklessly, their wrongful behavior is at least one strong reason to make them pay for what they have done. If someone hasn't done anything wrong, usually features of instrumental policy—notions of the spreading of costs, the general incentives created by legal rules, and the goal of compensating some

---

4 *See* Robert L. Rabin, *The Historical Development of the Fault Principle: A Reinterpretation*, 15 GA. L. REV. 925 (1981); Gary T. Schwartz, *Tort Law and the Economy in Nineteenth-Century America: A Reinterpretation*, 90 YALE L.J. 1717 (1981); Charles O. Gregory, *Trespass to Negligence to Absolute Liability*, 37 VA. L. REV. 359 (1951).

5 The federal income-tax code taxes both rightful and wrongful income. *See* James v. United States, 366 U.S. 213 (1961).

injuries regardless of how they were caused—are the motivations behind liability. Those same instrumental reasons of policy may underlie negligence liability too, but the negligence principle is additionally bolstered by a traditional sort of social morality: if you wrongfully hurt others, you should pay.

As a matter of policy, it is surprisingly difficult to decide whether law should depend on negligence or strict liability. For example, the law-and-economics movement has never decisively favored one over the other on grounds of efficiency. Section 2.8.1 will explain why in more detail.

For now, however, it is important to understand that tort law's general approach is one of negligence, as the name of the negligence cause of action (discussed in the next several sections) suggests. In the usual case, if a customer slips and falls on a supermarket's floor, the basis of the customer's legal claim against the supermarket is a negligence claim, and this means that the customer needs to show not only that the supermarket left the floor in an unsafe condition but that it was *unreasonable* or otherwise *wrongful* to have done so.

2.2 Negligence: Breach and Unreasonableness

Legal claims—more formally speaking, *causes of action*—all have *elements* (sometimes called *essential elements*) that plaintiffs need to prove. Though it sometimes doesn't make much difference, formally the plaintiff has the *burden* to plead and prove the elements of their claim. When a plaintiff establishes all those elements, we say that the plaintiff has established their *prima facie* case—an archaic Latin term that just means, for these purposes, that without any further showing the plaintiff would win. Note that to establish their case, the plaintiff needs to prevail on *all* the essential elements of the case.

The plaintiff doesn't *necessarily* win after establishing their (prima facie) case, because the defendant has an opportunity to prove *defenses* to the plaintiff's claim. Though again it doesn't always make much of a difference, the defendant is said to have the burden to prove their defenses, just as the plaintiff needed to establish the elements. Some defenses are general, like the *statute of limitations,* which causes claims to expire. Others are particular to individual types of claims (like *comparative negligence* or *assumption of risk* for negligence claims—see sections 2.7.1–2.7.2). Defenses can be partial (reducing the defendant's liability) or full (eliminating their legal responsibility entirely). If a defendant prevails on *any* of the defenses, their liability is reduced or eliminated.

In general, when lawyers research an unfamiliar type of legal claim in a particular jurisdiction, they first look to familiarize themselves with the claim's elements and possible defenses. Similarly, it is commonplace in law teaching for teachers to organize material about legal claims by their elements and defenses.

The elements of a negligence claim are *duty*, *breach*, *causation*, *scope of liability* (*proximate causation*), and *damages*. Breach is the perhaps the central element in negligence claims and involves a determination specifically of whether the defendant's behavior was wrongful or not. The plaintiff needs to show the other elements to recover damages from a defendant, but those elements are not about wrongfulness but rather some other feature of the situation, like whether the defendant's wrongful behavior made any difference or whether the defendant is legally exempt even though their actions were morally wrong.

In other words, in a negligence case, the plaintiff must prove that the defendant did something wrong, at fault, unreasonable, blameworthy, etc.—again, courts can use many different terms here, but they much the same thing. The case does not get off the ground unless the plaintiff can prove that the defendant behaved badly in some way. The element of breach is where the law situates and resolves questions about the defendant's wrongfulness. Confusingly, sometimes the very element of breach is itself called, or referred informally to as, *negligence*—or a defendant who has behaved wrongfully is said to have behaved *negligently* regardless of whether the plaintiff has proved the other elements of the negligence cause of action. But again, for the plaintiff to recover damages against the defendant, those other elements must be proved.

Because of the wide range of possible facts in negligence case—which can run from toxic pollution to car crashes, from slip-and-fall accidents to insufficient railings at the edge of a dangerous construction site—there is no single rule that can mechanically resolve whether a defendant has behaved wrongfully. This is true also because social norms, technology, medical awareness, and other factors important to technology all change over time. Precautions that are available to prevent injuries are always evolving, as are people's senses of which risks are tolerable and which aren't. Smoking cigarettes was once an acceptable social practice; in many places, now, it is not. People once regarded seatbelts as intrusive or at least commonly neglected to wear one; now, it is unusual for a driver on a public road not to wear a seatbelt. Kids used to bicycle and ski without helmets; now, at least for many parents, that would be an unacceptable risk. Because socially appropriate safety is a moving target and because it is difficult to make grand pronouncements about wide varieties of cases, the common law's general approach to addressing negligence is to treat it largely as a question of fact—it is sometimes called a *mixed question of law and fact*—that a factfinder determines. Because of the prevalence of juries in the US legal system, this ordinarily means that the general rule in the US tort system is that a jury determines breach—that is, determines whether a defendant has behaved wrongfully.

In areas where juries are so important, rules in a legal subject often serve two different kinds of roles. First, they prevent some cases from getting to the jury. That is largely what the *duty* element of the negligence cause of action does, for example. Second, they structure the analysis for the jury: they set up the problem, are the basis for the *jury instructions* that the judge reads to the jury, and provide for how the jury's decision can be set aside by judges (for example, for not resting on sufficient evidence).

2.2.1 Breach and the "Reasonable Person"

The most general legal rule about breach—which, again, for these purposes is synonymous with reasonableness, wrongfulness, and fault, or with the idea that the defendant *should not* have acted the way they acted—is that it is to be judged against the standard of a *reasonable person*. Referring to a *reasonable person* may not seem to add much to a general definition that a defendant behaves wrongfully if they behave unreasonably, but the idea of a reasonable person at least gives factfinders a hypothetical person to consider. The reasonable person is an ideal, not an average: the reasonable person behaves in the way that an ordinary member of society, acting prudently and with fair concern for other people's safety, would behave. This is clearly not a mechanical concept, and maybe it does little more than very generally guide a jury's deliberations.

The outer bookends that the concept of the reasonable person provides are probably clear enough as a consensus matter. The driver of a car who obeys the speed limit and other normal safety precautions is probably not unreasonable just because they lose control over their car briefly while driving over a portion of the road that was maintained poorly in a way that was not visible to drivers. A city that has left the road in that condition for weeks, even though it has already caused two accidents, is probably unreasonable.

The concept of reasonableness is often tied to particular decisions that parties have made to fail to take a precaution.[6] An unreasonable actor may have made no specific *decision*—perhaps they just acted carelessly without ever thinking about it—but we

---

6 *See* Mark F. Grady, *Untaken Precautions*, 18 J. LEGAL STUD. 139 (1989).

don't say their actions were unreasonable unless those actions were, at a minimum, voluntary. For example, a car driver is not unreasonable for having an epileptic seizure while driving,[7] but a driver who drives despite knowing they very frequently have such seizures probably is.

The reasonableness standard is *objective* rather than *subjective* in the sense that it's not judging the defendant's mental state. A defendant doesn't escape liability for negligence just because they meant well or had a pure intent. The negligence standard judges conduct, not thoughts.

Someone is not unreasonable just because they were the most obvious cause of an accident. For a finding of breach, there ordinarily needs to be a particular feature of someone's behavior that a factfinder can identify and criticize by saying, "You should not have done this, or you should have done this differently."

Even reasonable people don't take *all* precautions. We could have a very different world, in which nobody left their houses and indeed lined their houses with mattresses and other soft surfaces to reduce the impact of potential falls or other unexpected events. The speed limit could be four miles per hour, if we had cars at all. Indeed, in some sense negligence law takes the world at least broadly as it finds it; the question in a negligence case is not normally whether driving a car in the first place is unreasonable, even if that question is interesting to consider in the abstract because of the number and seriousness of car crashes and cars' other potentially negative effects on the world.[8] Common lawyers and judges do not see the negligence cause of action as a suitable vehicle to cause that kind of widespread or rapid social change.

Because reasonable people take only some precautions, courts' analysis of breach has long depended on a notion of proportion between precautions and their safety benefits. For example, in *Adams v. Bullock*,[9] a child was playing with a long wire in 1916—when there was not much else for children to do for fun—and happened to swing it so far that it went underneath a pedestrian bridge and contacted electrified trolley wires, causing the child to suffer an electrical burn. After a trial, a jury found that the defendant trolley company was negligent. Justice Cardozo overruled the jury as a matter of law, essentially holding that no reasonable jury could have reached that result:

---

[7] *See* Hammontree v. Jenner, 97 Cal. Rptr. 739 (Cal. Ct. App. 1971).

[8] *See, e.g.*, Alfred E. Kahn, *The Tyranny of Small Decisions: Market Failures, Imperfections, and the Limits of Economics*, 19 KYKLOS 23 (1966).

[9] 125 N.E. 93 (N.Y. 1919).

> There was, of course, a duty to adopt all reasonable precautions to minimize the resulting perils. We think there is no evidence that this duty was ignored. The trolley wire was so placed that no one standing on the bridge or even bending over the parapet could reach it. Only some extraordinary casualty, not fairly within the area of ordinary prevision, could make it a thing of danger. Reasonable care in the use of a destructive agency imports a high degree of vigilance. But no vigilance, however alert, unless fortified by the gift of prophecy, could have predicted the point upon the route where such an accident would occur. It might with equal reason have been expected anywhere else. At any point upon the route, a mischievous or thoughtless boy might touch the wire with a metal pole, or fling another wire across it. If unable to reach it from the walk, he might stand upon a wagon or climb upon a tree. No special danger at this bridge warned the defendant that there was need of special measures of precaution. No like accident had occurred before. No custom had been disregarded. We think that ordinary caution did not involve forethought of this extraordinary peril.[10]

Cardozo, in other words, is attuned to the proportion between a precaution's difficulty and its likely benefits. This particular accident could have been prevented with some guard that wasn't electrically conductive, but there was no reason in advance to think this accident would happen where it did. So to prevent accidents like this one, the trolley company would have needed to shield its lines much more thoroughly and over long distances—which would be very difficult in general and particularly difficult because overhead electrical trolley lines need to be accessed by the trolleys that they power.[11] (This was before wireless transmission of power or use of traction batteries in motorized vehicles.) Asking the trolley company to do that would not be a reasonable demand.

Again, Cardozo is not imposing a specific rule; he is analyzing the rich factual context. He points out that no similar accident had occurred before. If one had, that might have changed the result. Certainly, if everyone in the neighborhood knew a family or two who had tragically lost a child to electrocution by predatory trolley wires, it is hard to imagine that any factfinder would consider it reasonable

---

10 *Id.* at 93.

11 *Id.* at 94 ("There is, we may add, a distinction, not to be ignored, between electric light and trolley wires. The distinction is that the former may be insulated. Chance of harm, though remote, may betoken negligence, if needless. Facility of protection may impose a duty to protect. With trolley wires, the case is different. Insulation is impossible.").

to allow that situation to continue. But a single hard-to-prevent injury doesn't mean the trolley company should have done anything differently. Note that Cardozo is willing to say this even though personal injury to children is at stake; it is not as if he is putting a particular value on the life or health of a child, but he is clear that it would be unreasonable to ask the trolley company to stop functioning (or to radically increase its expenses by coming up with some barely workable electrical shielding for its necessarily exposed wires) just because of the possibility of such an injury. In much the same way, we don't lower the speed limit to four miles an hour even though we know that children (and many other people) will statistically die as a result.

We can of course question any judicial opinion. Why not, for example, say that the trolley company in *Adams* was unreasonable for failing to post clearer warning signs on a pedestrian bridge that it knew its wires ran underneath? That wouldn't be very expensive and could reduce injuries. There's no clear answer to that question in the case, but it is ordinarily up to plaintiffs' lawyers to help frame cases by identifying the precaution that a defendant should have taken but didn't.[12]

Note that Cardozo overrules a jury judgment in the case; today we would say that he finds, as a *matter of law*, that the defendants could not have breached their duty of reasonable care in view of the factual record of the case. The distinction between *matters of fact* and *matters of law* has never been clear and is always artificial. It is more accurate to say that when a judges say that they decide a question as a matter of law, that means they reserve the question for themselves—as they might do when they believe all reasonable juries would decide the question in the same way. It isn't uncommon to see judges take control of litigation in this way, because they and the parties to the lawsuit may regard juries as unpredictable; even the possibility of a jury trial may mean that a negligence case will settle for large amounts of money when the underlying injury is serious. Though courts often directly decide that there was or wasn't breach in a particular case, they sometimes do this indirectly or confusingly by saying, instead, that the defendant didn't even owe a duty to behave reasonably in that case (see section 2.3.3).

In general, judges' efforts to specify in advance behaviors that count or don't count as breach has not been successful. One of the most prominent and telling examples is a pair of cases that the Supreme Court of the United States decided at a time when it developed general tort principles that would be left to state courts

---

12 *See generally* Grady, *supra* note 6.

today (see section 1.3). In the first case, Justice Holmes, who had never driven a car himself,[13] decided in 1927 that the Supreme Court could determine on its own what counted as unreasonable behavior for automobile drivers when they crossed railroad tracks:

> In such circumstances it seems to us that if a driver cannot be sure otherwise whether a train is dangerously near he must stop and get out of his vehicle, although obviously he will not often be required to do more than to stop and look. It seems to us that if he relies upon not hearing the train or any signal and takes no further precaution he does so at his own risk.[14]

One leading Torts casebook[15] presents this case, commonly referred to as *Goodman*, alongside earlier academic writing by Holmes, in which he suggested that juries are useful in setting standards of conduct but that judges can learn from them and render them less important over time as facts recur:

> But supposing a state of facts often repeated in practice, is it to be imagined that the court is to go on leaving the standard to the jury forever? Is it not manifest, on the contrary, that if the jury is, on the whole, as fair a tribunal as it is represented to be, the lesson which can be got from that source will be learned?
>
> . . .
>
> . . . . A judge who has long sat at *nisi prius* [i.e., trial court][16] ought gradually to acquire a fund of experience which enables him to represent the common sense of the community in ordinary instances far better than an average jury. He should be able to lead and to instruct them in detail, even where he thinks it desirable, on the whole, to take their opinion. Furthermore, the sphere in which he is

---

13 G. EDWARD WHITE, OLIVER WENDELL HOLMES JR. 122 (2d ed. 2006) ("His life, by the 1920s, had settled into a routine that included comparatively few social engagements and a great deal of reading and correspondence. He enjoyed being driven in a car that Fanny had convinced him to buy, but he never learned to drive himself. In 1927 he wrote a unanimous opinion for the Court in a case, *Baltimore & Ohio Railroad v. Goodman*, that laid down an impractical set of rules for car drivers when they approached railroad crossings . . . .").

14 Baltimore & O.R.R. v. Goodman, 275 U.S. 66 (1927).

15 MARC A. FRANKLIN ET AL., TORT LAW AND ALTERNATIVES: CASES AND MATERIALS 65–66 (11th ed. 2021).

16 The phrase *nisi prius* means simply "unless before" in Latin; it is part of a longer phrase that was part of an archaic command like a summons to present oneself at a particular court "unless beforehand" the judges show up locally. The phrase, pointlessly, is still used today in some US jurisdictions instead of the English phrase "trial court."

> able to rule without taking their opinion at all should be continually growing.[17]

Strikingly, however, in *Goodman* Holmes—sitting as a Supreme Court justice—overrode a jury, a lower-court judge, and a federal court of appeals when he laid out his particular view of what the driver of an automobile should do when crossing railroad tracks.[18]

His opinion didn't last a decade. In a 1934 case,[19] Justice Cardozo held that while the earlier case was "no doubt . . . correct in its result"[20]—a commonplace but usually meaningless statement of deference to earlier opinions—Holmes's further statement was unnecessary and incorrect:

> Standards of prudent conduct are declared at times by courts, but they are taken over from the facts of life. To get out of a vehicle and reconnoitre is an uncommon precaution, as everyday experience informs us. Besides being uncommon, it is very likely to be futile, and sometimes even dangerous. If the driver leaves his vehicle when he nears a cut or curve, he will learn nothing by getting out about the perils that lurk beyond. By the time he regains his seat and sets his car in motion, the hidden train may be upon him.[21]

Cars were of course relatively new devices in the 1920s, and early attempts to set particular negligence standards for their drivers didn't work. As Cardozo suggests, courts have mostly abandoned the impulse, although there are many individual cases in which courts declare some set of precautions as reasonable "as a matter of law." We will see this pattern in section 3.5.2 as well in our discussion of contract law; though interpreting contracts, like judging reasonableness, requires an open-ended, context-sensitive inquiry in which any new fact may matter, judges still sometimes try to retain control over litigation by imposing particular standards of conduct as if they were rules of law.

A different sort of attempt to formalize the notion of reasonableness has come from the law-and-economics movement. In *United States v. Carroll Towing Co.*,[22] Judge Learned Hand—that

---

[17] HOLMES, *supra* ch. 1, note 4, at 123–24.

[18] Perhaps, as we will see in section 2.7.1, Holmes was motivated here to enforce strictly a rule of *contributory negligence* that was often undermined by judges and jurors because of its injustice and arbitrariness.

[19] Pokora v. Wabash Ry., 292 U.S. 98 (1934).

[20] *Id.* at 102.

[21] *Id.* at 104.

[22] 159 F.2d 169 (2d Cir. 1947).

was his real name[23]—laid out a pseudo-mathematical formula for trying to determine reasonableness. A ship sank in part because of the lack of a *bargee* or attendant to monitor it. Judge Hand first noted that "there is no general rule to determine when the absence of a bargee or other attendant" constitutes negligence.[24] He then tried to explain *why* there was no general rule:

> Since there are occasions when every vessel will break from her moorings, and since, if she does, she becomes a menace to those about her; the owner's duty, as in other similar situations, to provide against resulting injuries is a function of three variables: (1) The probability that she will break away; (2) the gravity of the resulting injury, if she does; (3) the burden of adequate precautions. Possibly it serves to bring this notion into relief to state it in algebraic terms: if the probability be called P; the injury, L; and the burden, B; liability depends upon whether B is less than L multiplied by P: i.e., whether B less than PL.[25]

This formulation is still commonly taught and discussed in commentary today. Often the formula is put more concisely: given a particular precaution that wasn't taken, an actor is negligent if and only if $B < PL$. This is commonly known as the *Hand formula*, and the law-and-economics movement seized on it as a way to help them try to explain tort law in economic terms.

The specific symbols and use of algebra in the formula don't really help, though Hand's underlying concept may be useful at least in trying to conceptualize breach or to discuss it academically. Hand simply could have said that reasonable people take cost-justified precautions—that is, those whose benefits outweigh their costs. The formula itself is constructed a little haphazardly and limited to one particular kind of case. For example, there is no reason to consider injuries as probabilistic but burdens as definite; in many cases, when a business adopts a safety policy, both the costs of the precaution and the safety benefits are probabilistic, particularly when played out over a long period of time. Moreover, precautions don't usually have just one safety benefit, so that *PL* really means

$$p_1L_1 + p_2L_2 + p_3L_3 + \ldots$$

---

[23] At least, Learned was his middle name. It is not the oddest use of regular English words in a name among historical US figures; that distinction goes to Preserved Fish, a nineteenth-century New York businessman. *See Sketch of the Late Preserved Fish*, 15 MERCHANTS' MAG. & COM. REV. 583, 584 (1846) ("The integrity of Preserved Fish was never impeached . . . ."); Wikipedia, *Preserved Fish*, https://en.wikipedia.org/wiki/Preserved_Fish.

[24] 159 F.2d at 173.

[25] *Id.*

For example, in *Adams v. Bullock*, the case where the boy swung a wire into a trolley's electrical lines, installing physical guards or warning signs would prevent direct physical injuries to those who swing wires, prevent sudden stops by trolleys (and the resulting injuries) from unexpected disruptions to electrical service, reduce the risk of electrical fires, and so on.

Taking all these recognitions together, it would probably be better for learning and communication simply to state the formula more generally: if a precaution wasn't taken, an actor is negligent if $C < S$, where C is the expected cost of the precaution and S is the overall expected safety benefit of the precaution.

The idea behind the Hand formula may be a helpful way for students, teachers, and commentators to try to give form to their intuitions about reasonableness. The general spirit of the formula can be useful as a guiding principle. For example, in *Adams v. Bullock*, Cardozo clearly cared about the feasibility of widescale precautions to prevent the kind of harm that occurred in the case; to economists, "feasibility" is just another way to say "costs." And at least half of the Hand formula's effect is probably uncontroversial: anyone who fails to take a cost-justified precaution is ordinarily negligent because it is reasonable to prevent injuries at a cost less than the injuries. The other half is perhaps more controversial: to say that any actor is *not* negligent just because their costs were a little more expensive than the injuries from their activities might not match people's sense of what is reasonable. Perhaps the reasonable person is a little risk-averse, for example, because of the general importance of safety. And many people are uncomfortable with the idea of exonerating unsafe conduct by reducing the "cost" of human injuries to specific (and, as we will see, mostly made-up) numbers.

Hand's idea has influenced the *Restatement (Third) of Torts*, which defines breach as follows:

> A person acts negligently if the person does not exercise reasonable care under all the circumstances. Primary factors to consider in ascertaining whether the person's conduct lacks reasonable care are the foreseeable likelihood that the person's conduct will result in harm, the foreseeable severity of any harm that may ensue, and the burden of precautions to eliminate or reduce the risk of harm.[26]

---

[26] RESTATEMENT (THIRD) OF TORTS: LIABILITY FOR PHYSICAL AND EMOTIONAL HARM § 3 (2010).

While the Restatement does not require or even directly state the Hand formula, it was clearly influenced by it.[27]

But courts have not generally followed the Hand formula, and it has not generally been used in jury instructions.[28] Despite its helpfulness in teaching tort law and its prominence in classrooms, the Hand formula is very difficult or impossible to apply in the real world. For one thing, none of the symbols in the Hand formula admit of precise or even realistic valuation in normal cases; they are at most just guesses, especially when they apply to human injuries and loss of life. Judge Hand himself recognized this in later cases, writing that

> care is the only [factor] ever susceptible of quantitative estimate, and often that is not. The injuries are always a variable within limits, which do not admit of even approximate ascertainment; and, although probability might theoretically be estimated, if any statistics were available, they never are; and, besides, probability varies with the severity of the injuries. It follows that all such attempts are illusory; and, if serviceable at all, are so only to center attention upon which one of the factors may be determinative in any given situation. It assists us [in this particular case] to center on the factor of probability . . . .[29]

Similarly, it is often very hard to look backward in time and determine what a business or other actor would have thought were the expected costs or benefits from a precaution. The analysis is complicated further by the need to account for costs and benefits over time: how long would a precaution have lasted, and would its safety benefits need to be summed up over an indefinite time period? A general statement of community standards may, on the ground, be more reliable and match better with social morality and policy than a partial and imprecise attempt at quantification.

So what are juries actually instructed as to breach? Florida's standard general jury instruction is typical among the states:

> Negligence is the failure to use reasonable care, which is the care that a reasonably careful person would use under like circumstances. Negligence is doing something that a reasonably careful person would not do under like circumstances or failing to do something that a reasonably careful person would do under like circumstances.[30]

---

27 *See also id.* § 3 cmt. d.

28 *See* Richard W. Wright, *Hand, Posner, and the Myth of the "Hand Formula,"* 4. THEORETICAL INQ. L. 145 (2003).

29 Moisan v. Loftus, 178 F.2d 148, 149 (2d Cir. 1949).

30 FLA. STD. JURY INSTR. (CIV.) § 401.4 (2022).

Consistently with the discussion in this section, the book of standard jury instructions in that state disfavors more specific rules aimed at special topics like traffic or railroads. It notes in a comment: "Negligence is properly and completely defined as the failure to use that degree of care which a reasonable person would use under like circumstances."[31]

2.2.2 Variations from the Reasonable-Person Standard

There are a handful of more particular applications of, or departures from, the reasonable-person standard. They usually depend on particular features of the person whose behavior is being evaluated.

For example, children are not judged by a reasonable-person standard but instead by rules that take into account their status as children. Precisely how the law does this varies sharply, with no particular regularity or clear theory. Some children are so young that they can't be blamed for torts. Others are judged by what amounts to a "reasonable child" standard. Sometimes, children who take part in "adult activities" are judged by the general reasonable-person standard that applies to adults, but this rule is often misunderstood; the point of the rule is that in some adult activities, like driving a car on a highway, nobody can tell until it's too late that other participants (for example, the driver of another car) is a child, so everyone else's reasonable expectations require that the general reasonable-person standard applies. But in situations where children engage in "adult activities" but other parties can still clearly see that they're children, the rule tends not to apply.

Generally the reasonable-person standard tends to vary when defendants have significant physical disabilities (blindness, needing to use a wheelchair). For example, negligence law doesn't judge a blind person negatively for failing to see an oncoming bicycle. It tends to ignore less significant physical conditions—as well as *all* psychological conditions. The reasonable-person standard's disregard for psychological conditions probably rests on two historical types of reasons that have come to seem increasingly anachronistic. First, until relatively recently people tended to think of psychological conditions as somehow unreal and insubstantial, or at the very least hard to prove.[32] Second, people had little sympathy for those with psychological conditions, perhaps even blaming them somewhat for those conditions, so that those with mental illness "should pay for the damage they do, and that it is better that their wealth, if any, should

---

[31] *Id.* nn. 5–6.

[32] *See* RESTATEMENT (SECOND) OF TORTS § 283B cmt. b. (1965).

be used to compensate innocent victims than that it should remain in their hands"—or at least liability would encourage their guardians to make sure they didn't harm others.[33] If the trend of increased medicalization of mental illness continues, we might expect that rule to change. Note that as the rule stands, it essentially imposes a kind of strict liability on those with mental illnesses who have a reduced capacity to act with reasonable safety; people can't be blamed morally for things beyond their control, and if the law holds anyone responsible for such things it is effectively imposing a standard of strict liability rather than negligence.

In general, despite the otherwise universal and objective standard of the reasonable person, the law takes specific facts and circumstances into account. A driver facing a sudden emergency is judged against what reasonable people would do in such an emergency, not what reasonable people would do in general.[34] Special knowledge that actors have is always taken into account: if you have specific knowledge that a particular road is likely to be slippery when wet and ignore that knowledge, you are unreasonable for doing so even if the reasonable person would have no reason to know that the road is dangerous. The *Restatement (Third) of Torts* says that special *skills* are to be taken into account[35]—for example, a professional racecar driver is supposed to be held to a higher standard when driving a regular car on a public highway. That rule probably makes sense—after all, it is unreasonable to fail to use the skills one has—but actual US caselaw is unclear on the question. Particularly on public roads, maybe it is easier if the same standard applies to everyone. Also, do a professional racer's particular skills really translate to a better ability to handle a sedan safely at forty-five miles an hour on an arterial road in the suburbs?

Some cases, particularly older ones, impose a standard of "extraordinary care" or "utmost care" on parties who undertake particular activities, like running a transportation service or a hotel. The idea seems to have been that passengers and hotel guests put themselves at the mercy, under a contract, of their host or common carrier, so those parties have specially high duties. This notion has faded over time because the reasonable-person standard—that is, a unified general standard for breach—is flexible enough to include hotels and common carriers, just as it includes a wide variety of other situations. Negligence is always determined on an all-things-considered basis, in view of the available options, the time (or lack of

---

[33] *Id.*

[34] *See* RESTATEMENT (THIRD) OF TORTS: LIABILITY FOR PHYSICAL AND EMOTIONAL HARM § 9 (2010).

[35] *Id.* § 12; *see also* RESTATEMENT (SECOND) OF TORTS § 299 cmt. f (1965).

it) to think and react, and social expectations of the defendant and their role. So, for example, the New York high court wrote in 1998:

> the single, reasonable person standard is sufficiently flexible by itself to permit courts and juries fully to take into account the ultrahazardous nature of a tortfeasor's activity. Thus, we ruled in *Miner v. Long Is. Light. Co.* that applying the "common-law standard of due care" [i.e., ordinary or reasonable care] was sufficient to hold a utility liable for failing to exercise an elevated level of precaution commensurate with the foreseeable extreme danger of placing high voltage lines in a residential neighborhood. There is no empirical or policy basis why, in the case of common carriers, the reasonable care standard is not similarly sufficient to permit triers of fact to take into account all of the hazardous aspects of public transportation in deciding whether due care was exercised in a particular case.[36]

Courts have sometimes developed other similar, ultraspecific pockets of rules to help define breach, but none of them seem to encapsulate any important ideas beyond the reasonable-person standard. For example, as I mentioned briefly above, in emergencies the reasonable-person standard takes into account the existence of an emergency. Nonetheless, this notion still has a separate section in the *Restatement (Third) of Torts* (which reads "If an actor is confronted with an unexpected emergency requiring rapid response, this is a circumstance to be taken into account in determining whether the actor's resulting conduct is that of the reasonably careful person")[37] and is commonly taught as a separate topic. None of that seems necessary, however; it is like saying that the amount of traffic or nighttime visibility are factors to be taken into account in determining reasonableness, and those facts haven't needed special doctrines.

In a relatively recent case in Connecticut, *Kelly v. Stop & Shop, Inc.*,[38] the court approved of

> the so-called "mode of operation" rule, a rule of premises liability pursuant to which a business invitee who is injured by a dangerous condition on the premises may recover without proof that the business had actual or constructive notice of that condition if the business' chosen mode of

---

[36] Bethel v. N.Y.C. Transit Auth., 703 N.E.2d 1214, 1217 (N.Y. 1998) (internal citations omitted).

[37] RESTATEMENT (THIRD) OF TORTS: LIABILITY FOR PHYSICAL AND EMOTIONAL HARM § 9 (2010).

[38] 918 A.2d 249 (2007).

> operation creates a foreseeable risk that the condition regularly will occur and the business fails to take reasonable measures to discover and remove it.[39]

This too hardly needs a separate rule. It is hard, really, even to know what the rule is, as the passage above describes it. *Constructive notice* just means that someone should have known—that is, was unreasonable for not knowing—something. So the passage above seems to posit that the business (1) had no reason to know of a dangerous condition but (2) knew that the condition could arise and failed to take reasonable precautions against it. If the business chooses to create "a foreseeable risk that the condition regularly will occur and the business fails to take reasonable measures to discover and remove it," why is that not the same thing as saying they should have known about the condition? The precise situation that the court had in mind is that the business had no reason to know of a *specific* dangerous condition (in this case, a particular piece of lettuce on the floor near a salad bar) but knew in *general* that dangerous conditions were likely to arise and didn't respond appropriately to those conditions (by, say, putting down an appropriate mat). But what does drawing that distinction question add to the analysis of the supermarket's potential negligence? In other words, why even ask that question, rather than simply asking whether the supermarket's actions were reasonable or unreasonable? The reasonable-person standard is flexible enough not to require these extra doctrinal complications.

It may help to keep in mind the notion of unnecessary doctrinal complications when evaluating the doctrine of *res ipsa loquitur* in the next section.

2.2.3 *Res Ipsa Loquitur* ("The Thing Itself Speaks")

There is a famous but probably useless doctrine known as *res ipsa loquitur*—a Latin phrase often translated in English as "the thing speaks for itself," although a more literal and probably also more helpful translation is "the thing itself speaks." (If we were crafting the phrase natively in English, we might simply say "the circumstances speak for themselves.") The doctrine can seem complicated, with its own formal elements that plaintiffs need to prove, but conceptually it is very easy: sometimes we can tell from circumstances that a particular party has been unreasonable even if we don't know exactly *how*. In other words, plaintiffs can prove fault (again, breach, unreasonableness, "negligence," etc.) not by showing specifically what the defendant did wrong—what specific precaution

---

39 *Id.* at 252.

they failed to take, like not installing a guard on an electrical wire or hiring an attendant for their barge—but instead just from circumstantial evidence. As we will see, the law often allows that sort of escape hatch when it posits mechanical rules; for example, in section 3.5 on contract formation, we'll see that contracts are said to require offer and acceptance, but a rule has arisen under which they can also be proved without any particular showing of offer or acceptance. Similarly, though it may sound contradictory at first, a plaintiff can prove breach without a specific showing of breach.

The leading case in this area is one from nineteenth-century England, *Byrne v. Boadle*.[40] I think of it as the Donkey Kong case because it involves a barrel falling out of a window and injuring someone.[41] Nobody knew precisely how or why the barrel fell out of the window. There was clear enough evidence about where the barrel fell from, but there was no specific showing of any poor safety practice or a faulty or absent precaution on the part of the people in charge of those premises. Breach, as mentioned earlier (see section 2.2.1), can't ordinarily be inferred just from the occurrence of accident or an injury alone; sometimes nobody is at fault if, for example, a tree falls down or even if a car slides out of its lane in a storm.

Indeed, even in *Byrne*, unreasonableness was not the only logically or physically *possible* explanation for why a barrel could have fallen out of a window. Perhaps there was a significant earthquake in the north of England—but at least before fracking that was essentially unheard of, and more to the point none of the witnesses said there was an earthquake. Maybe an assassin (or someone looking to cause legal or business trouble for the warehouse owner) sneaked into the warehouse and threw the barrel onto a pedestrian below—but that is wholly implausible.[42] On the specific facts of the case, the story of the accident itself strongly suggests breach. In other words, "the thing itself speaks" or "the situation itself speaks": it says "breach."

We don't really need a doctrine to tell us the various ways that breach can be proved.[43] For example, in addition to a rule that tells

---

40 159 Eng. Rep. 299 (Ex. Ch. 1863).

41 *See* Wikipedia, *Donkey Kong*, https://en.wikipedia.org/wiki/Donkey_Kong.

42 *See* Stephen D. Sugarman, *Rethinking Tort Doctrine: Visions of a Restatement (Fourth) Of Torts*, 50 UCLA L. REV. 585, 601–02 (2002). I am significantly indebted to the late Professor Sugarman's exposition of and teaching on this issue; his particular views on *res ipsa*, features of duty, assumption of risk, and the application of negligence principles to the intentional torts have significantly influenced my own thinking and the discussion in this chapter. *See also* Robert L. Rabin, *Stephen Sugarman and the World of Responsibility for Injurious Conduct*, 109 CAL. L. REV. 369 (2021).

43 *See* Sugarman, *supra* note 42, at 601–02.

us that plaintiffs can use the story of the accident itself and other circumstantial evidence when they strongly suggest negligence, we might have hundreds of doctrines that would still never exhaust the various possibilities for proof: breach can be proved by video recordings, or by eyewitness testimony, or by a site inspection that shows poor safety practice, or by documents that kept a record of bad safety decisions, or in any number of other ways. All *res ipsa loquitur* adds to the background rules about breach is that breach can in some cases be proved circumstantially, just by noting that the accident happened and that there is no likely alternative explanation other than the defendant's fault. Negligence law would be fine if we didn't bother to say that; you could have figured it out from the general discussion of breach alone.

More importantly, it would be better if we didn't bother to lay out particular complicated "factors" or "elements" for *res ipsa* that make the doctrine more mechanical and harder to learn.[44] The *Restatement (Second) of Torts* laid out a multi-part test that many teachers still teach and many courts still follow:

> It may be inferred that harm suffered by the plaintiff is caused by negligence of the defendant when
>
> (a) the event is of a kind which ordinarily does not occur in the absence of negligence;
>
> (b) other responsible causes, including the conduct of the plaintiff and third persons, are sufficiently eliminated by the evidence; and
>
> (c) the indicated negligence is within the scope of the defendant's duty to the plaintiff.[45]

The intent of these factors is clear enough, and it is not as if the test is clearly *wrong*. But it is a meandering test that doesn't promote clarity in courts' reasoning. The normal way to prove breach, or anything else in a civil case, is by showing it was more likely than not. Considering what "ordinarily" happens under subsection (a) and then what has been "sufficiently eliminated by the evidence" under subsection (b) stands in the way of a simple determination about whether the defendant was, more likely than not, negligent given all the evidence. For example, is the test in subsection (a) really meant to eliminate from *res ipsa* an event of a kind that *can* ordinarily occur in the absence of negligence but that, in a particular case, was overwhelmingly likely to have been caused by the defendant's negligence? Indeed, why not just stop the statement of the rule after

---

44 *Cf. id.* at 619.

45 RESTATEMENT (SECOND) OF TORTS § 328D(1) (1965).

saying "It may be inferred that harm suffered by the plaintiff is caused by the negligence of the defendant"?

There is a further problem with *res ipsa*: sometimes it refers to a completely different doctrine, one that is not about the implication of breach from circumstantial evidence, background knowledge, and the like. Sometimes *res ipsa* refers to a relatively rare but potentially important practice by courts to shift the burden on the element of breach from the plaintiff to the defendant. As noted earlier, breach is an element of the plaintiff's case, which ordinarily means that the plaintiff has the responsibility to prove it. Burdens don't always matter that much in their details, but they have one clear implication: in the absence of any helpful evidence pointing in either direction—in other words, without any *reason* to think the defendant was or wasn't at fault—normally the plaintiff will lose because they can't prove that the defendant did anything wrong.

However, sometimes for policy reasons, usually related to the plaintiff's potential access to evidence, courts are willing to shift the burden.[46] This is relatively rare, and most courts tend to resist doing it, but it may be helpful to note that whether something is an element in a case or a defense is often an arbitrary or historical feature of the law. Alternatively, we could say it's entirely formalistic that listing something as an "element" of a case means the plaintiff has the burden to produce evidence about it and persuade the factfinder; maybe there are policy reasons suggesting that some element should really be the defendant's responsibility to *disprove*. For example, in some cases, all evidence may be under the control of the defendant. Or maybe there is a "conspiracy of silence" among a group of possible defendants, and the only way to learn the truth is to give each of them an incentive to give evidence by holding them liable if they don't. Whatever the policy rationale, cases where courts shift the burden are not properly considered *res ipsa* cases—the evidence doesn't itself speak and say "breach"; rather, courts simply make a policy choice to relax the burden for plaintiffs because there is otherwise too much risk that wrongful conduct will escape legal consequences. Steve Sugarman gives the following examples for these kinds of cases:

> Examples of this second sort of case might include those in which young children come home from day care settings with unexplained injuries, those of exploding soda bottles that the victim thinks occurred because of carelessness at the bottling plant, and the famous *Ybarra v. Spangard*[47] case, in which the plaintiff awoke from surgery with an injury that was almost surely caused by one of the

[46] Sugarman, *supra* note 42, at 602.

[47] 154 P.2d 687 (Cal. 1944).

> independent contractors involved in the surgery but in which the patient had no way of knowing which medical professional was responsible.[48]

Perhaps, as Sugarman also points out, these rationales are no longer persuasive in an era of widespread *civil discovery*, a set of procedural rules that give plaintiffs strong rights to demand evidence in the possession of defendants. But it may still be needed to break a conspiracy of silence. Most courts have not followed *Ybarra*,[49] but it still lays out an option for courts to choose in the interest of justice in unusual cases.

Compared to the *Restatement (Second) of Torts*, the *Restatement (Third)* significantly improves the *res ipsa loquitur* test, simply saying:

> The factfinder may infer that the defendant has been negligent when the accident causing the plaintiff's harm is a type of accident that ordinarily happens as a result of the negligence of a class of actors of which the defendant is the relevant member.[50]

This formulation gets rid of most of the unnecessary "factors" but still combines the burden-shifting cases with the genuine *res ipsa loquitur* cases where facts already speak for themselves. (That is what the "class of actors" language is doing; it would be clearer to speak directly of a burden shift as a policy choice.) As another way to put it, when the facts themselves say "breach," there is no reason for a shift in the burden to prove breach. The *Restatement (Third)* also retains language referring to a "*type* of accident that ordinarily happens as a result of the negligence" (emphasis added), rather than simply referring to the likelihood of the defendant's negligence in a particular case.

Some commentators have confused *res ipsa loquitur* with strict liability. But it should be easy to avoid that mistake. In the type of *res ipsa loquitur* case in which the facts prove negligence, strict liability simply doesn't come up. In the case of a burden shift, defendants still can avoid liability by showing that they were not at fault.[51] That is not true with strict liability, where behaving reasonably does allow the defendant to avoid liability (see sections 2.1 and 2.8).

---

48 Sugarman, *supra* note 42, at 602.

49 *See* FRANKLIN ET AL., *supra* note 15, at 109.

50 RESTATEMENT (THIRD) OF TORTS: LIABILITY FOR PHYSICAL AND EMOTIONAL HARM § 17 (2010).

51 *Cf.* RESTATEMENT (THIRD) OF TORTS § 17 cmt. a (2010).

2.2.4 Customs and Statutes

Violations of safety customs can be very persuasive evidence in tort law, but they are not themselves decisive. The same is true of *adherence* to widespread safety customs in an industry; maybe that is *evidence* that a defendant behaved reasonably while operating in that industry, but factfinders might still determine that an entire industry's customs are unreasonable. The objective standard of the reasonable person isn't the same thing as an inquiry about a "reasonable business planner in a particular industry"; perhaps a whole industry is unreasonably unsafe.[52]

There is one general exception to this rule: in professional malpractice, the law ordinarily defers to the custom of professionals. For example, the fact that doctors in fact behave a certain way (in, say, reading a diagnostic scan or responding to a patient's reports of particular symptoms) is ordinarily decisive on the question of a doctor's negligence. The difference may come partly from respect for professionals and the difficulty of judging their jobs from the outside—although that policy-based notion may be eroding as medicine has become more of a business and as patients (particularly in the United States, compared to prevailing practices in other countries) do more medical research on their own. It may relate in part to the notion that patients ordinarily purchase doctors' services in the United States, so the doctor-patient relationship often has a contractual component that implicates the patients' reasonable expectations—and doctors who behave like other doctors are meeting those expectations. The deference to professional standards in professional malpractice may also come from common sense: it is not helpful in a lawsuit against a doctor to ask how the regular, nonprofessional "reasonable person" would perform surgery, read a radiological scan, or deliver a baby. In any event, on one hand the standard is deferential to doctors' customs. On the other, it requires them to live up to the higher standard of professionals in order to avoid tort liability.

Even if customs are not decisive (outside cases of professional malpractice), they have some other, fuzzier roles to play in negligence cases. A custom can help convince a jury that a precaution is *possible*—for example, technologically and economically feasible. Customs may also create expectations in others, so that violating a custom can sometimes come very close to simply *being* negligence. For example, if a very strong custom among restaurants in a particular region is to identify potential food allergies in dishes (for example, on a menu or through a waiter), rather than expecting

---

52 *See* RESTATEMENT (THIRD) OF TORTS § 13 (2010).

customers to raise those allergies themselves, the custom itself changes what customers expect and thereby may be a very important factual part of a negligence case.

Violation of statutes work differently from violations of customs. Violation of a safety statute is said itself to *be* negligence formally; such a violation is often called *negligence per se*, or "negligence by itself." ("Negligence on its own" would be a more idiomatic translation.) In other words, the very act of violating a safety statute can amount to negligence, with no further proof needed for a plaintiff to show that a defendant breached the duty of reasonable care. It is easiest to think of negligence per se as a shortcut toward proving breach; plaintiffs may have been able to prove breach anyway, but negligence per se settles the question if it applies to a case.

The idea behind negligence per se is more complicated than it may seem at first. Violating a statute—say, speeding or running a stop sign—is legally wrong, but it is an infraction or criminal violation, not *necessarily* a matter relevant to tort law. Instead of the typical statute that addresses speeding or stop signs in a regulatory or criminal context, we could imagine a statute aimed directly at negligence lawsuits; that statute might read: "In any negligence lawsuit, someone who violates the speed limit must be treated as having acted unreasonably." But statutes do not normally say this. The rule of negligence per se is a rule of common law under which courts have *chosen* to apply technically unrelated statutes to negligence lawsuits. In other words, it is a common-law doctrine that draws tort policy from criminal or regulatory safety statutes. The doctrine rests on the recognition that when the legislature has prohibited some type of behavior, it is generally *also* unreasonable under tort law to engage in that behavior. Therefore, violation of the statute *is* or *amounts to* breach.

Because courts that apply the doctrine of negligence per se are not simply enforcing or interpreting criminal or regulatory statutes but instead using them as a source of policy, courts are not *bound* by those statutes when deciding tort cases. As a result, they do not always apply the doctrine rigidly. In a famous case, *Tedla v. Ellman*,[53] two pedestrians violated a statutory command about what side of the road to walk on: they were walking with traffic rather than against it. They did this because traffic was much lighter on that side of the road at the time of day when they were walking. They were pushing baby carriages filled with goods. There were no suitable sidewalks, and the median was made of soft grass. The pedestrians could have waited and walked at another time, but otherwise their

[53] 19 N.E.2d 987 (N.Y. 1939).

decision to walk on the "wrong" side of the road was made for safety-promoting reasons. The pedestrians were struck from behind by a car; one of them was killed and the other was injured. In the surviving pedestrian's lawsuit against the driver, the court refused to infer the pedestrians' negligence based on their statutory violation alone:

> We may assume reasonably that the Legislature directed pedestrians to keep to the left of the center of the road because that would cause them to face traffic approaching in that lane and would enable them to care for their own safety better than if the traffic approached them from the rear. We cannot assume reasonably that the Legislature intended that a statute enacted for the preservation of the life and limb of pedestrians must be observed when observance would subject them to more imminent danger.[54]

It may be worth adding, however, that as a matter of legal realism the court may have been motivated to reach this result because of the harshness of the old rule of *contributory negligence* (see section 2.7.1), under which plaintiffs who were even slightly negligent couldn't win a negligence case against a defendant even if the defendant had clearly acted unreasonably. Under the modern rule of *comparative negligence* (see again section 2.7.1), perhaps there would be no particular difficulty in saying that the driver of a car that unreasonably swerved and injured these pedestrians was 98% responsible for driving badly and the pedestrians were 2% responsible for putting themselves in a position where it was a little harder to see oncoming cars.

Even so, negligence per se—while it often makes sense as a way of importing standards of reasonableness from statutory commands—can sometimes have a harsh edge. Suppose that in *Tedla* the statute that told pedestrians which side of the road to walk on prescribed nothing but a $10 penalty for its violation. It is true that the statute provides a standard of conduct, but it may seem disproportionate to allow the statute to affect a tort lawsuit potentially worth orders of magnitude more than $10. The legislature may not have intended that result, although as the *Tedla* court points out, legislatures at least in theory could be well aware by now of negligence per se (and therefore of the effects of their statutes on tort cases).[55] But that theoretical opportunity for knowledge of tort law may be very different from practical or factual knowledge of tort law.

---

[54] *Id.* at 991.

[55] *Id.* at 990 ("The Legislature, when it enacted the statute, presumably knew that this court and the courts of other jurisdictions had established the general principle that omission by a plaintiff of a safeguard, prescribed by statute, against a

2.3 Negligence: Duty

Another foundational element in negligence lawsuits is called *duty*. The name is almost entirely unhelpful today and serves as a reminder that you can't learn legal concepts by paying too much attention to what their names suggest (see section 1.5.2).

The term, roughly speaking, comes from a time in English history when interactions with strangers were relatively rare. For example, several hundred years ago it was much less commonplace to behave dangerously in a way that could hurt a stranger: there were no highways with cars and other vehicles, no mass-produced products sold to the general public, no workplaces with thousands of employees, and not that many public places where people might run into each other or fall down. In that environment, though the history is complicated and disputed,[56] perhaps it made sense to legal thinkers to say that before there could be liability the plaintiff needed to show that the defendant owed a "duty" of some kind to the plaintiff. Often these duties followed the existence of particular relationships; the legal claim was effectively "you hurt me, and you shouldn't have done so because I was your apprentice" or "you undertook to transport me by carriage to Liverpool and caused me injury because of your carelessness." In other words, the legal responsibility was conditioned on a particular preexisting relationship between the parties, and the law didn't need to pay much attention to injuries outside of such relationships because strangers rarely hurt each other.

That sort of thinking has been entirely reversed today, at least with regard to physical injuries. In modern tort law, everyone owes everyone else a "duty" to behave with ordinary care—that is, not to "breach" the duty of reasonable or ordinary care, as discussed in the previous section. (The "breach" discussed in section 2.2 is a breach of that "duty" of reasonable care.) So, for example, the modern *Restatement (Third) of Torts* states the following very general, very simple rule: "An actor ordinarily has a duty to exercise reasonable care when the actor's conduct creates a risk of physical harm."[57] In other words, there is a general duty to be reasonable; if an actor's conduct creates a risk of physical harm and does in fact cause harm, there is ordinarily no "duty" question in the case.

---

recognized danger, constitutes negligence as matter of law which bars recovery for damages caused by incidence of the danger for which the safeguard was prescribed.").

56 *See* sources cited *supra* note 4.

57 RESTATEMENT (THIRD) OF TORTS: LIABILITY FOR PHYSICAL AND EMOTIONAL HARM § 7(1) (2010).

There are, however, several exceptions to the general principle that everyone owes duties to everyone else. These cases are not as frequent as students might think from their prominence in Torts courses, and they do not influence most modern tort cases. But there is still the possibility for an exception to apply. To quote the modern Restatement again:

> In exceptional cases, when an articulated countervailing principle or policy warrants denying or limiting liability in a particular class of cases, a court may decide that the defendant has no duty or that the ordinary duty of reasonable care requires modification.[58]

Because of the possibility of this kind of exception, disputes about duty still arise in modern tort cases. "Duty" remains as an element in the negligence cause of action, though it is not meaningfully an *element* because the plaintiff doesn't ordinarily need to *prove* anything. That is, duty is ordinarily a question of law to be decided by judges, so the burden of proof as to duty normally doesn't matter. Indeed, if anything, in practice duty normally comes up functionally as a *defense*: a plaintiff will ordinarily plead quickly in general terms that the defendant had a duty to exercise reasonable care, and if the defendant doesn't raise anything new about duty then duty is unlikely to be an issue in the case. If the defendant responds by introducing some argument about why they did *not* owe a duty, the court has a legal question to decide.

The word *duty* is not a useful word for this state of affairs. It incorrectly conveys to many students that the defendant has some *moral* duty, when the role of the "duty" element is very different: it is merely an opportunity to exclude an entire class of cases from the tort system, for reasons of (as the Restatement puts it) "principle or policy"—that is, some principle or policy that overrides the normal policies of tort law (deterrence of injuries, compensation of victims, etc.). Indeed, saying that a defendant "has no duty" to a plaintiff is tantamount to saying that even if the defendant *has* behaved immorally, wrongfully, unreasonably, and so on, the defendant is exempt from tort liability because of some overriding principle or policy. It may help to remember that "no duty," in this context, really just means "no tort duty"; in cases where courts say "no duty," the defendant may still have moral duties and could even have duties under other areas of law. As a simple example, modern US workers' compensation systems generally provide an exclusive insurance mechanism to handle workplace injuries; that is, if those systems apply to a particular injury, the worker must file a workers'

58 *Id.* § 7(2).

compensation claim to be compensated and cannot sue their employer for negligence. The employers therefore may be said to have "no duty"—that is, systematically they have no liability in negligence lawsuits. But they still face workplace regulations and must maintain workers' compensation insurance.

Overall, then, it would probably be clearer for negligence law to treat duty as a defense and to call it something else (perhaps "policy exemption to negligence liability"), but legal terminology usually takes a very long time to change. Still, many teachers make one small update in structuring this material, and I will follow that convention in this book: instead of talking just about "duty," it is much easier to speak of the types of cases that the law has exempted from liability as "no duty" cases. This emphasizes their exceptional nature—the idea that there is generally a duty of reasonable care, with small exceptional islands of "no duty."

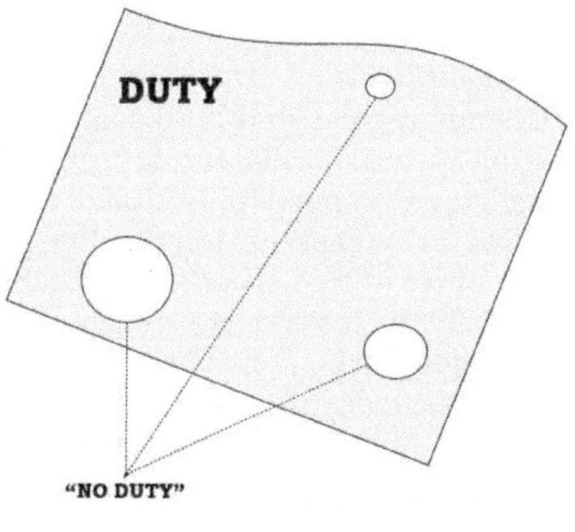

Figure 2.1: In modern negligence law, there is a general duty to behave reasonably, with exceptional cases of "no duty."

Understanding duty, then, simply requires understanding what kinds of principles or policies can override tort law's normal goals. Those principles and policies can come from a variety of sources.

As an initial matter, it should not be surprising that the goals associated with injury law—deterrence, compensation, and so on—may not always be the law's most important values. As discussed earlier (see section 2.2.1), the policy of the law is not to prioritize safety at the expense of all other things, or else we would avoid cars or limit their speed to four miles an hour. Similarly, the no-duty cases effectively permit people to act unsafely, without recourse in tort law, when some other type of goal or rationale displaces tort law's concern with safety or compensation.

In general, there are three types of no-duty cases.[59] In the first, the courts' reasons for avoiding tort liability are largely *administrative* or *institutional*. That is, they are concerned with the management of litigation. For example, in some cases the plaintiff's injury is too small to bother with the relatively expensive machinery of lawsuits. In others, courts are afraid of opening the so-called "floodgates of litigation" because there will be too many potential plaintiffs for the courts to manage effectively. Relatedly, courts might sometimes predict that they will not be able to distinguish honest claims of a particular type from fraudulent ones, so that the courts' involvement with that type of case won't promote the general goals of justice or policy. (Perhaps, as the 1980s movie *Wargames* put it in a different context, "The only winning move is not to play.") Another type of institutional or administrative reason for no-duty cases is that there is some better forum (or at least an alternative one) to resolve the dispute—like the workers' compensation system discussed earlier—so the courts decline to get involved.

In the second type of no-duty case, there is some clear principle or policy that *conflicts with and overrides* the usual goals of tort law. That is, a court has some reason simply to care less about imposing liability, compensating victims, or deterring injuries than achieving some other goal suggested by a particular kind of case. Those reasons may come from moral principles or from policy-related ones. For example, maybe the values of free speech and the First Amendment mean that some activity is beyond the reach of tort law. Maybe certain victims—like thieves who are injured on the premises they've broken into—are undeserving of compensation even if they are wronged by someone else's unreasonable conduct.

In these two types of cases, the courts are asking the same general question: "Do we want this class of cases to be part of the tort system in the first place?" If the answer is no, the plaintiff loses even if the defendant has acted unreasonably and caused harm. That is, the plaintiff fails on the "duty" element of their negligence claim.

Finally, there is a third type of no-duty case that is probably best understood as being in a class by itself (or *sui generis*, as lawyers sometimes pretentiously say): the historical common-law rule that there is "no duty to rescue" a stranger in peril (see section 2.3.2). That rule doesn't have a clear rationale in policy or principle. As we have already seen in passing in section 1.1, it has been severely criticized; its main justification is historical or conceptual, and like most rules

[59] *Cf.* Stephen D. Sugarman, *Why No Duty?*, 61 DEPAUL L. REV. 669 (2012) (arranging similar reasons into six categories instead).

that have little practical utility or relationship to morality, it has been eroding, although it is still a part of the law.

The next two subsections consider these no-duty rationales in turn.

2.3.1 "No Duty" for Reasons of Principle or Policy

The first two types of no-duty cases discussed in the previous section are relatively straightforward to understand: courts simply have an opportunity to decide, before imposing liability, that a group of cases should not be candidates for successful tort cases even when defendants have behaved wrongfully. Consider the administrative or institutional types of cases first. Some injuries, even if physical, are just too small for the court system to remedy. Suppose a driver on a local road plays their car stereo quite loudly, and this causes a small headache and a temporary ringing in the ears of another driver when the two are stopped together for twenty seconds at the same red light. Perhaps the first driver has behaved unreasonably, without regard to other people's wellbeing, and perhaps the injury, though temporary, is real. It is nonetheless hard to see a US court entertaining a negligence lawsuit on those facts alone.[60]

The same case is perhaps an example, too, of courts' skepticism of their own ability to differentiate legitimate claims from fraudulent claims—and of concerns about "floodgates of litigation." If everyone could sue anyone else and reach a jury by claiming that they had suffered a headache in response to other people's unreasonable transient noise, then there could be groundless cases—and a lot of them. The groundless cases could be hard to detect because anyone might suffer a headache but may not easily be able to prove it. Similarly, there is no easy to way to prove, in most cases, how loud anyone's car stereo had been. So cases in this pattern might resolve to little more than questions of which party the jury believes, and perhaps judges think that is not a reliable enough basis to allow a jury to decide anything. Moreover, if such cases could get to juries, they might lead to substantial settlements even for groundless claims because defendants often want to avoid the unpredictability of juries.

It's important not to overstate these points. Arguments about "floodgates of litigation" are not necessarily persuasive; it still takes time and effort, and ordinarily costs money, to file a lawsuit in the

---

[60] *But see On Noise, in* ESSAYS OF SCHOPENHAUER 28, 29 (Rudolf Dircks trans., W. Scott Publishing ed. 1903) ("This is why the most eminent intellects have always been strongly averse to any kind of disturbance, interruption and distraction, and above everything to that violent interruption which is caused by noise; other people do not take any particular notice of this sort of thing.").

first place, and there are rules against fraud, perjury, nuisance lawsuits, and the like. But at least in principle these concerns could motivate a judge to declare "no duty" in a class of cases. To be clear, this sort of rationale could conceivably apply even if the injuries involved are serious—but as the seriousness of the injury increases, so does the courts' recognition that a remedy is needed and therefore the likelihood that the court will decide that the case should be heard on its facts and that a jury should make a decision about reasonableness.

Sometimes a statute is the basis of an administrative or institutional no-duty rule because it creates a forum that serves as an alternative dispute-resolution system, taking cases out of court. As mentioned above, under modern systems of workers' compensation—covering injuries at work, whether negligently caused or not—an alternative claims system is an employee's exclusive remedy against an employer. Roughly speaking, the tradeoff for insurance coverage against *all* injuries (negligent or not) is that the employee relies exclusively on that insurance coverage and cannot sue an employer for taking insufficient precautions against workplace accidents. This is often not described as a no-duty rule but functions as one.

The notion that courts may be the wrong forum for some negligence lawsuit can overlap with the second type of no-duty case—those involving social values that override the tort system's goals. For example, a professional football player can't typically sue another player in court for an unreasonably forceful tackle; the penalty is within the game (e.g., a fifteen-yard penalty for "unnecessary roughness") or within the league (e.g., suspension for a more serious violation). That principle is not absolute; a football player who takes out a bat on the field and repeatedly hits another player could well be sued or face criminal liability. But some degree of "ordinary" violations is covered by the rules of the game and the sports league. Tort law abstains from imposing liability, even if a jury could find a player's actions unreasonable, for two closely related reasons: (1) the rules of the game and the league are the best (least costly, most accurate) way to deter and penalize bad behavior on the field, and (2) if tort law were to get involved, that could have a negative influence on the game, causing players to think twice and fear judgment from a general jury rather than specialists within the league. (Recall that adhering to custom is not normally an excuse for a defendant, though it may be a persuasive fact for the factfinder. See section 2.2.4.)

Again, these rationales may not be persuasive, and it's important not to overstate them. Football players could purchase insurance against negligence liability, so they would be somewhat insulated from any deterrence effects of tort law. And it would probably be uncommon anyway for players to sue each other even if the lawsuits could succeed; they would face social pressure from other players, from fans, and so on. Moreover, maybe extending tort liability earlier and more fully on football fields would have prevented some serious injuries that have ruined the lives of many football players.

Other social policies or moral propositions may influence patterns of no-duty cases. For example, suppose someone is injured in a violent act that they think was inspired by a violent movie. If a court blocks the resulting lawsuit on the grounds of the First Amendment rights of the moviemakers, that is conceptually a no-duty rationale for reasons of policy. When courts prevent a burglar from suing a homeowner when the burglar falls down on a negligently maintained staircase in the home they were burgling, that is a no-duty rationale for reasons of morality—and perhaps also policy because judges don't want to encourage or protect burglars.

As another general example, courts have avoided imposing liability on hosts of private gatherings—often called *social hosts*—when they serve alcohol that later causes car crashes, even if the victim of such a crash can prove that the social hosts were unreasonably unsafe because they served too much alcohol, continued to serve alcohol to guests they knew would soon be driving, and so on. When courts have imposed such liability, it has typically soon been reversed by statute. Our society appears simply not want to impose tort liability in such situations. This too is a no-duty rationale—not necessarily a persuasive one, but one apparently based on the policy of encouraging social interactions (with alcohol as a social lubricant and a conventional and widely valued part of private gatherings). The results would likely be different for other drugs, like marijuana, so the policy seems to depend specifically on the social role of alcohol in US society. As the modern Restatement puts it in a comment:

> In deciding whether to adopt a no-duty rule, courts often rely on general social norms of responsibility. For example, many courts have held that commercial establishments that serve alcoholic beverages have a duty to use reasonable care to avoid injury to others who might be injured by an intoxicated customer, but that social hosts do not have a similar duty to those who might be injured by their guests. Courts often justify this distinction by referring to commonly held social norms about responsibility. The rule [in the Restatement] does not endorse or reject this particular set of rules. It does support a court's deciding this

issue as a categorical matter under the rubric of duty, and a court's articulating general social norms of responsibility as the basis for this determination.[61]

Another type of policy-based rationale for a no-duty rule is that entertaining liability in a class of cases may provide what Steve Sugarman has called "perverse incentives."[62] For example, defendants have argued that they should not be liable for writing misleading letters of recommendation because such liability would cause defendants not to write letters of recommendation at all.[63] This argument by defendants is not typically persuasive, but if it were, it would serve as a no-duty rationale.

One last rationale to consider, although it is not usually a good one, combines the administrative and policy rationales in no-duty cases. It is the notion that in some circumstances there will be too many plaintiffs against a particular defendant—a concept closely linked to what has been called "crushing liability."[64] For example, in *Strauss v. Belle Realty Co.*,[65] a utility company had earlier been judged grossly negligent—which just means "really badly negligent"—for causing an extended power outage that affected New York City in 1977. Because there was no electricity, a tenant in an apartment building was injured in the common area of that building. The New York court refused to allow liability because the tenant was "not a customer of [the utility company] in a place where the accident occurred."[66] The court was particularly concerned about cabining the number of plaintiffs rather than facing what it regarded as open-ended liability that could be hard to manage:

> If liability could be found here, then in logic and fairness the same result must follow in many similar situations. For example, a tenant's guests and invitees, as well as persons making deliveries or repairing equipment in the building, are equally persons who must use the common areas, and for whom they are maintained. Customers of a store and occupants of an office building stand in much the same position with respect to [the utility company] as tenants of an apartment building. In all cases the numbers are to a certain extent limited and defined, and while identities may

---

61 *See* RESTATEMENT (THIRD) OF TORTS: LIABILITY FOR PHYSICAL AND EMOTIONAL HARM § 7 cmt. c. (2010).

62 Sugarman, *supra* note 59, at 678–83.

63 *See id.* at 682–83; Randi W. v. Muroc Joint Unified Sch. Dist., 929 P.2d 582, 585 (Cal. 1997).

64 Sugarman, *supra* note 59, at 687–88.

65 482 N.E.2d 34 (N.Y. 1985).

66 *Id.* at 35.

> change, so do those of apartment dwellers. While limiting recovery to customers in this instance can hardly be said to confer immunity from negligence on [the utility company], permitting recovery to those in plaintiff's circumstances would, in our view, violate the court's responsibility to define an orbit of duty that places controllable limits on liability.[67]

The court also noted that a utility company's liability in the event of a widespread outage "could obviously be 'enormous,' and has been described as '*sui generis*,' [i.e., in a class by itself] rather than strictly governed by tort or contract law principles."[68]

Steve Sugarman has described an attention to the enormous potential liability in this case as "somewhat dubious" because large utilities can readily absorb new costs and pass them onto customers, so it is unlikely that the extension of liability would threaten the provision of orderly utility services.[69] It is also hard to see how *Strauss*'s particular limit on classes of plaintiffs would be a helpful solution in the event liability were truly crushing or vast numbers of cases were brought; whatever finite number of injuries occurred in the power outage would just be reduced by some percentage based on whether the plaintiff happened to be the utility company's customer at the precise place where the power loss led to an injury.

The very notion of crushing liability or facing too many plaintiffs is itself suspect. For example, as a large utility company, the defendant in *Strauss* had trucks and utility poles all around the city. Those trucks could crash into anyone, and the utility poles could fall on anyone if negligently maintained. Is the number of plaintiffs or the potential liability from such activities greater—more unmanageable, more "crushing"—than from people who injure themselves on a badly lit flight of stairs because of a power outage? Still, a court's genuine and plausible concern that imposing liability in a particular type of case would lead a utility company to go out of business could, in principle, be a sound basis for a no-duty rule.

Strauss, and as it happens many other no-duty cases of this type, has at least a tinge of "no duty to rescue," the rule to be discussed in the next section. In particular, it is less common to see a concern that there will be too many plaintiffs or crushing liability when a defendant has *actively* harmed many separate people, as opposed to more *passively* allowing them to come to harm. (In *Strauss*, the defendant's negligence has features of both activity and passivity

---

67 *Id.* at 38 (citations omitted).

68 *Id.* at 36.

69 Sugarman, *supra* note 59, at 687.

because it promised to supply electricity and then failed to do so. This is part of what the quotation from the court above means in suggesting the liability depends on both contract and tort principles.) For example, it is hard to see the New York court using its particular rationale in *Strauss* if, instead of a power outage, the utility's gross negligence had caused utility poles to shoot out small bolts of lightning at thousands of pedestrians around the city.

Other cases where this kind of no-duty rationale may come up include those where a medical professional fails to detect a contagious disease or fails to warn a patient properly against spreading it. Courts show some tendency to limit the class of potential negligence plaintiffs to a manageable number. They have rarely articulated clear, persuasive rationales for doing so, however. There appears simply to be a fear of unmanageable amounts of litigation or crushing amounts of liability from downstream victims. But why not exhaust a doctor's insurance policy when such injuries do arise—which would presumably cause insurance companies to price medical-malpractice insurance policies to take into account risks to public health and also thereby encourage doctors to be more careful in managing risks to people other than their patients?

We will see other applications of no-duty rules later in this chapter (see for example section 2.6). Indeed, we will see them throughout the book, even beyond tort law, because rules in other legal subjects often act specifically as no-duty rules, even though they are not usually described that way. For example, the requirement for consideration in contract law functions as a no-duty rule: for reasons of administrability and policy, courts determine that even though it is morally wrong to break a promise, the law will not enforce certain promises.

2.3.2 "No Duty to Rescue"

A rule distinctive to the common law is that the general duty of reasonable care (see section 2.2) applies only to *action*, not *inaction*. It is commonly said, and taught in most or all Torts courses in the United States, that people have "no duty to rescue" other people in US law.

That no-duty rule extends to what is sometimes called *easy rescue*. If I walk past a lake and see a child drowning, I have no legal obligation under the general common law to try to save the child, even if the water is shallow and I know how to swim. I don't even have a legal obligation to throw the child a rope or to place a call to emergency services. (Difficult or dangerous rescue may well not even count as breach: it is not unreasonable for me to fail to jump into a lake to save someone if I don't know how to swim. That kind of heroism, putting one's own life in danger, is not expected even of reasonable people, and failing to live up to that standard is therefore not unreasonable.)

The upshot of the no-duty rule involving rescues, then, is that it exempts even *unreasonable* failures to rescue from legal liability. The word *duty* can be particularly confusing in cases like this. To say that there is "no duty to rescue" is not to say there is a moral justification for unreasonably failing to attempt an easy rescue by calling emergency services or throwing a life-preserver to a drowning child. That is, it is not meant to say that the such a failure is not blameworthy, immoral, unreasonable, at fault, etc. The failure to attempt an easy rescue *is* a violation of the reasonable-person standard. A no-duty rule simply means that courts won't let the victim recover damages for it.

There have been attempts to shoehorn the no-duty-to-rescue rule into the kinds of administrative justifications or policy-based rationales discussed in the previous section, but they generally seem to have the character of just-so stories—that is, of fables created by theorists to explain how things are rather than genuine explanations. For example, in many Torts courses, professors try to get across various ideas: we don't want to encourage "officious intermeddlers" to try to rescue others when rescue isn't needed; lots of people might fail to rescue, so there would be too many potential defendants and too much liability in general; we want to protect the virtue of heroism, so that if someone jumps in a lake we know they're a good person rather than just acting on the law's command to act reasonably. None of those is a persuasive explanation for a general no-duty-to-rescue rule; indeed, it is mystifying why the last of them would even count as a rationale for a modern legal rule.

The explanation for the rule's *origin* is probably historical. As we saw at the start of section 2.3, the early law tended not to impose duties in the first place among strangers, possibly because before industrialization accidents between strangers were rare. The no-duty-to-rescue rule seems to be a remnant of that older pattern in the common law. The rule's *persistence* is surprisingly hard to justify as a theoretical matter. Perhaps it depends on the social value of autonomy; if you're sitting at home, minding your own business, perhaps society should leave you alone and not allow people to sue you if you don't meddle in the affairs of your neighbors, even if you see something dangerous happen through your window. The difficulty with those explanations is that social *morality* is not in line with it. Social *practices* may be consistent with the rule—there have been many famous cases where large numbers of people witness terrible events and nonetheless do nothing to intervene, without even simply putting through an emergency phone call—and maybe there is something in human psychology that causes people to freeze in the face of events like these. But that all goes to breach, rather than duty—that is, to unreasonableness rather than whether we should craft a policy exemption for people who unreasonably fail to attempt even easy rescues—and it does not morally justify inaction or prevent social disapproval of inaction. That is, social morality will seriously condemn someone who laughs and relaxes while watching a child drown when saving the child was easy.

Moreover, the no-duty-to-rescue rule does not comport with instrumental views of law or morality—with *utilitarianism* or other *consequentialist* views. On those views, we care only about consequences, not about motivations or virtues. For example, a utilitarian judges something good based just on the happiness and pain that results. As a result, those views are committed to ignoring what is called the *act/omission distinction* in other moral theories. A utilitarian theorist or policymaker, in other words, would judge the person who laughs and does nothing while a child drowns quite harshly too—and would not, as a theoretical matter, support a rule that relies on a distinction between action and inaction. Consistently with morality and policy, most other legal systems have the opposite rule; that is, there is no legal immunity in those legal systems for failing to engage in an easy rescue of someone else's life. As we saw in section 1.1, the rule has received scathing criticism from legal commentators; the leading US tort-law treatise of the 1900s described cases under the no-duty-to-rescue rule as "revolting to any moral sense" and lists many law-review articles that have "denounced" the rule "with vigor."[70]

To the extent the rule persists, the most likely reason is probably that the rule simply doesn't matter much: the law doesn't need to encourage rescue of people in distress because exceedingly few people are injured because of a failure to rescue. Most people sadly know of someone who's been injured or killed in a car crash; few can name an acquaintance harmed by a failure of "easy rescue." If everyone had tragic stories of childhood friends who had drowned in lakes because no passersby were willing to try to save them, the law probably would have changed by now. Instead, situations requiring rescue by individual nonprofessional rescuers are rare in the first place, and when those situations arise in the real world the law's incentives are not particularly important: most people are moral and indeed eager to save others in danger. And most nonlawyers probably don't know about the rule anyway, so it's not as if the rule influences incentives in the real world. On this view, the no-duty-to-rescue rule persists

70 KEETON ET AL., *supra* ch. 1, note 8, § 56, at 376.

simply because it doesn't matter; there haven't been enough test cases where courts would have a chance to overturn it.

In fact, in the relatively small number of cases that have arisen under the no-duty-to-rescue rule, the rule has in fact significantly eroded over time, with many exceptions that have developed and have been inconsistently applied. That pattern of erosion and inconsistent exceptions, which we will see many times throughout this book, is one of the common law's frequent responses to rules that are broadly inconsistent with morality and policy.[71] The notion, put simply, is that while common-law courts have the power to overturn a bad rule, they often see themselves as constrained, or they wish to appear to continue to be acting under an old rule. Developing a small exception to a rule—affirming the existence of the rule but determining that a particular set of facts doesn't fall within it—draws little attention from the bar and the press, is not perceived as radical, and allows the judges to craft rules slowly and cautiously.

Though it is not often taught this way in Torts courses, that pattern is exactly what has happened with the no-duty-to-rescue rule. It is possible to learn the exceptions in isolation, but an easier way to understand both those exceptions and the overall doctrine is to recognize that the no-duty-to-rescue rule has been under significant doctrinal pressure over time.

The rule has ended up with many exceptions, not all of which even make sense or are easy to apply. We saw in section 1.1 that a historical exception was that limited categories of "special relationship" operated as carveouts from the general rule. The question of which relationships were "special" enough to be recognized as exceptions to the rule developed in arbitrary and piecemeal fashion. Hotel managers ended up with a duty to save their guests, common carriers to save their passengers, ship captains to save their crew, parents to save their children, and so on.[72] It would be possible to try to explain these specific categories with general principles—maybe these are the categories where those who need rescue would particularly expect it—but those explanations are makeshift and incomplete. As discussed in section 1.1, they never would have been sufficient, on their own, to predict that *Farwell v.*

---

[71] *See* EISENBERG, *supra* ch. 1, note 13, at 136–40; *cf. also* POUND, *supra* ch. 1, note 36, at 101–02 ("The strict law . . . conceives of application of law as involving nothing but a mechanical fitting of the case with the strait-jacket of rule or remedy. The inevitable adjustments and extendings and limitations, which an attempt to administer justice in this way must involve, are covered up by a fiction of interpretation in order to maintain the general security.").

[72] *See* KEETON ET AL., *supra* ch. 1, note 8, § 56, at 376–77; RESTATEMENT (SECOND) OF TORTS § 314A (1965) (also including the relationship between land possessors and public invitees onto the land).

Keaton[73] would extend it to some new category like "friends out causing trouble in town."

Another exception that we also saw in *Farwell*, in chapter 1, is that one who starts a rescue will be judged by a reasonableness standard in how they proceed with or abandon the rescue. This rule is often misunderstood to be blunter than it is; students often seem to remember the rule as "if you start a rescue, you need to complete it," but negligence law never requires more than reasonableness. The rule—the exception to the no-duty-to-rescue rule—is that if you start a rescue, the no-duty rule goes away and liability will be imposed on unreasonable conduct. The modern Restatement frames the duty that arises after someone starts a rescue to be specifically "a duty of reasonable care to refrain from putting the other in a *worse position* than existed before the actor took charge of the other."[74] A typical kind of unreasonable conduct associated with starting a rescue and then botching it, as in *Farwell*, is partially rescuing someone in a way that makes a later, more effective rescue by someone else less likely. This can happen if someone moves the person who needs rescue out of the sight of others or acts in such a way that others think there is no further need of rescue. Waving off other rescuers, for example, but then failing to do anything useful would probably be unreasonable.

It is possible to conceive this principle not as an exception to the no-duty rule in the first place but simply as liability for acting unreasonably (rather than failing to act). In other words, on this exception, people aren't liable for *omissions* but for an affirmative course of conduct that is unreasonable and causes harm. As it happens, the distinction between acts and omissions is often difficult to maintain clearly. For example, imagine a bicyclist is riding illegally on a sidewalk, sees a pedestrian, has the opportunity to swerve, but fails to swerve and plows into the pedestrian. The bicyclist could theoretically say "I didn't *do* anything to hit the pedestrian; I simply failed to swerve to avoid a collision, and that is just an omission." The law won't take that argument seriously or apply the no-duty-to-rescue rule to that situation, but it shows that the boundary between act and omission is not always sharply defined.

There are other exceptions to the no-duty-to-rescue rule. For example, one commonly stated rule is that someone who causes harm to a stranger, even innocently, needs to use reasonable efforts to rescue that stranger. Many formulations of this rule don't make

---

[73] 240 N.W.2d 217 (Mich. 1976).

[74] RESTATEMENT (THIRD) OF TORTS: LIABILITY FOR PHYSICAL AND EMOTIONAL HARM § 44 (2010) (emphasis added).

much sense. For example, as the *Restatement (Second) of Torts* tried to describe it:

> If the actor knows or has reason to know that by his conduct, whether tortious or innocent, he has caused such bodily harm to another as to make him helpless and in danger of further harm, the actor is under a duty to exercise reasonable care to prevent such further harm.[75]

But consider the case of someone driving innocently (that is, reasonably and not in violation of any statutes) through a suburban neighborhood in a bright red, very expensive sports car. A ten-year-old child is climbing a tree on the side of the road and is so impressed by the car that he stares at it and falls out of the tree. If we take the Restatement's principle seriously, the car driver might have a duty to rescue the child. Maybe that is indeed the right result if the no-duty-to-rescue rule is as problematic as it seems, but few lawyers would expect courts to apply this particular exception that way. It is probably meant instead as a narrower exception for people who innocently create and then unreasonably ignore a persistent risk—for example, a truck driver whose truck (through no fault of the driver's) loses a wheel, which the driver then leaves in the middle of the highway without bothering to try to remedy the situation.[76] Conceived that way, however, the exception isn't really an exception; the truck driver's overall (affirmative) course of conduct was negligent.

Most or all states have adopted statutes that require everyone, or at least some people in particular roles, to report dangers to children or crimes against children.[77] These statutes sometimes impose criminal penalties and sometimes impose civil ones. Some states have adopted statutes that criminalize failures to rescue more generally. It is hard to square these statutes with whatever policies are supposed to underlie the no-duty-to-rescue rule; the statutes presumably have arisen just because the no-duty-to-rescue rule is undesirable and the targeted cases—usually involving protection of particularly vulnerable groups, like children and the elderly—are those where more incentives to rescue others may be needed. For example, while there is probably no need for a legal rule encouraging people to jump into a lake to save a drowning child, there may well

---

75 RESTATEMENT (SECOND) OF TORTS § 322 (1965).

76 *Cf.* RESTATEMENT (THIRD) OF TORTS: LIABILITY FOR PHYSICAL AND EMOTIONAL HARM § 39 (2010) ("When an actor's prior conduct, even though not tortious, creates a continuing risk of physical harm of a type characteristic of the conduct, the actor has a duty to exercise reasonable care to prevent or minimize the harm.").

77 *E.g.*, CAL. PENAL CODE § 152.3 (West 2017); FLA. STAT. § 39.201 (2022).

be a need for more incentives to encourage reporting of child or elder abuse.

The end result is that there are so many exceptions that, though the no-duty-to-rescue rule is universally taught in the United States, it would unwise for a lawyer to advise a client to rely on it. In general, behaving reasonably is a much stronger safeguard against liability than trying to avoid acting at all, risking a lawsuit after an injury occurs, and then trying to defend against the lawsuit based on a rule that has eroded and that has unpredictable and inconsistent exceptions. For example, consider a university that has shut down its operations temporarily because of an oncoming major hurricane.[78] Students have been advised to abandon the dorms and to go home, because the dorms do not provide particularly good protection against hurricanes. But the university has not shut the dorms because some students have nowhere else to go. Suppose the university's classroom buildings are likely to provide greater shelter than dorms. Should the university shut off students' keycard access to the university's classroom buildings, as it usually would when classes are not being held, because of a vague concern about liability if anything were to happen to students while those buildings are unmonitored—and then tell students they are barred from the safer buildings because the university has "no duty to rescue" them? A good lawyer wouldn't want to bet on that path. It is not the safety-promoting choice and is probably not reasonable under the circumstances, and a court like *Farwell* could extend the "special relationship" categories to students who have enrolled at a university. A court could also treat the university's whole set of decisions as a course of active conduct that's unreasonable—it did, after all, take affirmative steps to shut off keycard access—rather than treat its decision not to open the buildings as simply an omission. A court could also decide that the university contributed to the students' risk by building and operating the dorms—conduct that, even though it reflects no unreasonableness on its own, is an innocent creation of risk that mandates rescue.

Considered as a planning problem for lawyers, this example suggests that it would be unwise to rely aggressively on the no-duty-to-rescue rule. Yet that rule is still taught, often uncritically, in many US classrooms. The exceptions are taught, of course, but they are sometimes taught discretely as if they are static, rather than in a way that suggests how much pressure the no-duty-to-rescue rule has been under overall. When rules are under pressure, they often eventually

---

78 I am indebted to Dean Erin O'Hara O'Connor for a version of this example, which could realistically arise as a decision for college deans at universities in Florida.

erode and are often overturned[79]—and wise or careful lawyers do not rely on them.

2.3.3 Distinguishing "No Duty" from "No Breach"

The key to understanding duty is to distinguish it from breach. Courts do not always preserve this distinction clearly or helpfully. In particular, they often make statements like "the defendant had no duty" imprecisely when they really mean "no jury could find that the defendant was at fault."[80] The easiest way to be sure that you're dealing with a case in which there's really "no duty" is to imagine a very obviously unreasonable defendant, who very clearly causes harm to a plaintiff, and then ask yourself "Would the plaintiff still lose against that defendant?" Another way to say this is that when there's "no duty," we don't even *ask* whether the defendant was unreasonable; we are just unconcerned with that question and don't care about it for the purposes of negligence law. Courts decide such cases against the plaintiff simply by saying, "This kind of tort case can't be brought."

For example, when tort doctrine prevents a burglar from recovering damages from the homeowner they were attempting to steal from, even if the homeowner was unreasonable in leaving a dangerous large dog to run freely in their unfenced front yard, the homeowner has behaved unreasonably but avoids liability because the rule that burglars can't sue homeowners in negligence overrides the unreasonable risk that the homeowner happened to create. The question of the homeowner's unreasonableness doesn't even arise, at least in a lawsuit by the burglar. If a batter in a professional baseball game sues the pitcher for not taking due care to avoid hitting the batter with a baseball, tort law doesn't entertain the question of whether the pitcher was careful enough under negligence law's reasonable-person standard. These two examples are clearly no-duty cases—where defendants are exempt from liability because of some principle or policy—rather than judicial determinations that the defendant hasn't done anything unreasonably unsafe.

Sometimes, however, courts blur the questions of duty and breach, and this blurring has created persistent confusion for many students and lawyers. This blurring is partly a matter of inconsistent terminology in the courts. Recall that courts have the power to determine most questions for themselves, without a jury, if they think that no reasonable jury could reach a particular result. For

---

79 *See* EISENBERG, *supra* ch. 1, note 13, at 136–40.

80 *See* Stephen D. Sugarman, *Misusing the "No Duty" Doctrine in Tort Decisions: Following the Restatement (Third) of Torts Would Yield Better Decisions*, 53 ALTA. L. REV. 913 (2016).

example, in section 2.2.1 we saw a case, *Baltimore & Ohio Railroad v. Goodman*,[81] in which Oliver Wendell Holmes, though he had apparently never driven a car, declared that certain behavior by drivers was necessarily unreasonable while they were crossing railroad tracks. In that case, Holmes was concerned only with breach; he was deciding that a driver's conduct was unreasonable. But that sort of statement often gets translated—as it does in the *Goodman* case for the headnotes on both Lexis and Westlaw, though not in those of the main books, or *reporters*, where the opinion was originally published—to language that involves "duty." So for example some people will describe *Goodman* by saying that drivers have a "duty" to stop at railroad tracks.[82]

That sort of description confuses the casual use of the word *duty* with the notion of duty as an element of the negligence cause of action. The confusion tends to be more serious in cases where a court determines that a party has *not* behaved unreasonably, because parties and often the courts themselves will often say "the defendant had no duty to do what the plaintiff asked" rather than say "the defendant did not *breach* the duty of ordinary care by failing to do what the defendant asked."[83]

For example, in *Harper v. Herman*,[84] the twenty-year-old plaintiff was one of a few guests on a private boat. The boat's owner took the boat to an area of a lake that he knew was "shallow enough for his guests to use the boat ladder to enter the water, but still deep enough so they could swim."[85] Then, without warning, the plaintiff dived off the boat, hit the bottom of the lake, and suffered an extremely serious and disabling injury. The Minnesota Supreme Court framed the legal question as follows:

> The sole issue on appeal is whether a boat owner who is a social host owes a duty of care to warn a guest on the boat that the water is too shallow for diving.[86]

In other words, the court essentially treats the case as a no-duty-to-rescue case. But the owner of the boat hadn't stayed home and avoided helping anyone; he was clearly engaged in an ongoing course

---

81 275 U.S. 66 (1927).

82 In his teaching, Professor Steve Sugarman called judicial determinations of breach "*Goodman* rules" because it is helpful to keep *Goodman* in mind as an example where a court lays down particular rules about what constitutes reasonable or unreasonable conduct.

83 *Cf.* Sugarman, *supra* note 80, at 923–24.

84 499 N.W.2d 472 (Minn. 1993). For further discussion of this case, see Sugarman, *supra* note 59, at 692.

85 499 N.W.2d at 473.

86 *Id.* at 474.

of activity that *could* have been negligent. For example, he could have piloted the boat to an area that he but nobody else knew was infested with sharks and then lowered the ladder, implicitly encouraging everyone to go swimming. More simply, he could just have managed the boat negligently so that it overturned. In other words, his actions on that day can be judged as reasonable or not. Those actions seem to have been reasonable because the plaintiff dived into the water without warning, so there was nothing for the boat owner reasonably to have done to prevent the injury—no reasonable precaution that was missed. To put it differently, it was not negligent for the boat owner to move the boat to an area where people might swim but not dive and then to fail to anticipate that a guest would quickly dive off the boat.

Had the facts in *Harper* played out in slow motion, it is easy to imagine a different result. If the plaintiff had asked the boat owner "Is this water safe for diving?" and the boat owner had given any indication that it was, or even had said "Why don't you try it and find out?" then the boat owner clearly would have been acting unreasonably. That is to say, the boat owner almost certainly was subject to duties in general to the plaintiff—and could have been liable for acting unreasonably. *Harper* simply reflects a judicial determination that the boat owner had not *breached* the duty of reasonable care, not that that duty didn't exist. Just as in *Goodman*, the court has determined whether a party's conduct has been reasonable or not; in *Goodman*, the answer was no, and in *Harper* the answer was yes, but the courts were making similar types of decisions. They were not, by contrast, exempting people from liability based on some policy or principle apart from the tort system—based on some separate policy goal other than safety and compensation or some special concern about the administration of cases. In other words, *Harper* is not a no-duty case at all, much less a no-duty-to-rescue case.[87]

Another way to help distinguish no-duty cases from no-breach cases is to ask whether a court is making a decision about a *class* of cases or the facts of an individual case. Duty cases typically involve general principles that apply to large groups of cases: no baseball player can sue other players because of ordinary injuries that happen on the field; no burglar can sue a homeowner they were trying to burgle; no victim who thinks that a movie caused someone to attack

87 *See* RESTATEMENT (THIRD) OF TORTS: LIABILITY FOR PHYSICAL AND EMOTIONAL HARM § 40 cmt. d (2010) ("When a court is persuaded that, under the particular circumstances involved in the case, no reasonable jury could conclude that the defendant acted unreasonably, the court should find the evidence of negligence insufficient as a matter of law. Such a resolution is preferable to employing a no-duty rule that is based on the particular facts of the case."); Sugarman, *supra* note 59.

them can sue the producer. Breach cases concern whether an individual injurer has behaved reasonably or not in their particular circumstances. In his teaching, Professor Sugarman described this distinction as the difference between "wholesale" (bulk) and "retail" (one-by-one) determinations: duty treats cases at the "wholesale" level, whereas breach treats them one by one.

In other words, in learning duty, it is very helpful to be skeptical that courts are really talking about duty when they use the term "duty." Often they are referring instead to a concept that is more sensibly analyzed as breach.

The Role of Foreseeability in Breach and Duty

The role of a potential injury's foreseeability has been one of the most needlessly confusing and inconsistently treated features of negligence law. As background, in many cases an injurer hurts someone but responds to a negligence lawsuit by arguing that, factually, they should not be liable because there was no way they could have known that the injury would occur. (*Harper* is essentially one such case.) Because they didn't know the injury was likely to occur, there was no precaution they should have taken against it.

For example, suppose a customer purchases a take-home sandwich from a cafe and serves it to their child, and the child has a severe allergic reaction to a tomato in the sandwich (and tomatoes are listed on the sandwich's packaging as being among the sandwich's ingredients). If the child files a negligence claim against the restaurant, the restaurant's factual argument may be something like, "We could not have foreseen that our customer would serve our sandwich to a child who was allergic to tomatoes, particularly when we listed tomatoes as an ingredient."

Some courts, more commonly in the past, may have had an instinct to treat such a case as a "no duty" case—of the administrative, institutional type (see section 2.3.1)—on the thought that a restaurant could face unpredictable liability if it could be liable to the whole world for selling a sandwich. But that is not a particularly useful analysis: the restaurant could obviously be liable to "the whole world" (that is, any plausible consumers of its food) if it had negligently included large amounts of arsenic in its sandwiches, and we generally in modern law wouldn't care that the injured party was not, themselves, the customer.[88]

The restaurant's real argument, properly conceived, is simply that it has done nothing wrong. It labeled the sandwich appropriately. There was nothing more it reasonably should have

---

88 *Cf.* MacPherson v. Buick Motor Co., 111 N.E. 1050 (N.Y. 1916).

done to prevent injury to the child who ended up eating it. The "unforeseeability" of that particular injury simply means, conceptually, that the *P* in the Hand formula, $B < PL$ (see section 2.2.1), was low—or to say it more plainly, that the likelihood of harms was so small that there was no reason for the restaurant to have taken more precautions. The restaurant *could* have taken more precautions: it could have stopped selling sandwiches, or made customers fill out a form certifying to whom they would serve the sandwich and requiring medical notes about those people's allergies. But none of those are reasonable precautions for the restaurant, given the likelihood of a tomato allergy and the responsibility of parties other than the restaurant to prevent it given a properly labeled sandwich. If the likelihood of harms were greater—if the cafe's use of a particular ingredient might cause airborne allergens to affect hundreds of passersby—there would be more it should have done to prevent the problem.

All that sort of analysis is simply an ordinary analysis of whether the restaurant acted unreasonably—breached the duty of ordinary care—or not. In other words, the foreseeability of potential physical injuries is one of the facts that matters when determining whether the restaurant behaved reasonably. The question is one of breach. Courts, however, have sometimes confusingly treated the foreseeability of injuries as if it is a feature of duty—and some courts have done this so prominently and so forcefully that the error has been persistent and has only recently been corrected. For example, in a famous California Supreme Court case, *Tarasoff v. Regents of the University of California*,[89] the court first laid out an analysis of duty that was consistent with the modern treatment of duty, very similarly to the way this book has described it so far:

> liability should be imposed "for injury occasioned to another by his want of ordinary care or skill" as expressed in section 1714 of the Civil Code. Thus, Justice Peters . . . stated: " 'whenever one person is by circumstances placed in such a position with regard to another . . . that if he did not use ordinary care and skill in his own conduct . . . he would cause danger of injury to the person or property of the other, a duty arises to use ordinary care and skill to avoid such danger.' "
>
> We depart from "this fundamental principle" only upon the "balancing of a number of considerations" . . . .[90]

---

[89] 551 P.2d 334 (Cal. 1976).

[90] *Id.* at 342.

The court then continued by listing a number of factors, concluding: "The most important of these considerations in establishing duty is foreseeability."[91] That kind of statement has led to widespread confusion. As discussed above, it would be much clearer to say that potential injurers have a general duty to everyone to use reasonable care; they simply do not *breach* that duty when they have no reason to know that an injury is likely to occur.

Modern courts have slowly come to the recognition that foreseeability is a part of the analysis of breach, not duty, as has the *Restatement (Third) of Torts*, which in a comment titled "the proper role for foreseeability" says:

> Foreseeable risk is an element in the determination of negligence [i.e., breach]. In order to determine whether appropriate care was exercised, the factfinder must assess the foreseeable risk at the time of the defendant's alleged negligence. The extent of foreseeable risk depends on the specific facts of the case and cannot be usefully assessed for a category of cases; small changes in the facts may make a dramatic change in how much risk is foreseeable. . . .
>
> A no-duty ruling represents a determination, a purely legal question, that no liability should be imposed on actors in a category of cases. Such a ruling should be explained and justified based on articulated policies or principles that justify exempting these actors from liability or modifying the ordinary duty of reasonable care. These reasons of policy and principle do not depend on the foreseeability of harm based on the specific facts of a case. They should be articulated directly without obscuring references to foreseeability.
>
> . . .
>
> Despite widespread use of foreseeability in no-duty determinations, this Restatement disapproves that practice and limits no-duty rulings to articulated policy or principle in order to facilitate more transparent explanations of the reasons for a no-duty ruling and to protect the traditional function of the jury as factfinder.[92]

Thoughtful modern courts have more or less apologized for their previous confusion in treating foreseeability as a component of duty rather than breach. For example, the Supreme Court of Nebraska, in

---

[91] *Id.*

[92] RESTATEMENT (THIRD) OF TORTS: LIABILITY FOR PHYSICAL AND EMOTIONAL HARM § 7 cmt. j (2010); *see also* Sugarman, supra note 80, at 926.

a 2010 opinion,[93] considered the negligence liability of a school district for failing to prevent an attack on one of its students and wrote:

> we reasoned that because the attack at issue in [an earlier] case was foreseeable, the defendant had a duty to protect against foreseeable acts of violence. Our reasoning was tautological. It is evident that the university had a landowner invitee duty to protect against *foreseeable* acts even had the attack in that case *not* been foreseeable. While we purported to be discussing duty, we were in fact assuming the conclusion we claimed to be proving, and we were actually evaluating the sufficiency of the evidence to sustain a conclusion that the university had breached its duty to take reasonable care.
>
> Our mistake was a common one. . . . Simply put, whether a duty exists is a *policy* decision, and a lack of foreseeable risk in a specific case may be a basis for a no-breach determination, but such a ruling is not a no-duty determination.[94]

While the Nebraska court's general reasoning is sound, there is a further point that has often gone unnoticed even in modern cases: many judicial opinions that purport to wrestle with the foreseeability of injuries aren't importantly about foreseeability at all, and courts are still distracted by earlier misuses of the notion of foreseeability as a component of the duty analysis in cases like *Tarasoff*. Even in the example of the breakfast cafe, foreseeability of an injury to a third party is not a significant feature of the case; the question is just whether the cafe took reasonable steps to prevent food allergies—for example, by labeling its food properly. In the Nebraska school case, the important question wasn't whether the particular attack on the student victim was foreseeable; the question should just have been whether the school district had adopted reasonable procedures under the circumstances to protect its students against attacks from third parties. The foreseeability of injuries is a part of that analysis but not necessarily an important one; for example, general best practices for schools, which could take into account the general safety of the communities in which they are located, are probably more useful than asking whether a third-party intrusion on the school grounds was "foreseeable."

In other words, it is right to say that that the question in the cafe hypothetical or the Nebraska case is breach, but it is probably

93 A.W. v. Lancaster Cty. Sch. Dist. 0001, 784 N.W.2d 907 (Neb. 2010).

94 *Id.* at 916.

wrong to treat them as if they raise important questions of foreseeability in the first place. The likelihood of harms is *conceptually* part of how breach may be determined, but it is ordinarily an implicit feature of the analysis that remains well in the background when reasonable actors determine how to act. To put that differently, foreseeability *could* matter in these cases: if there is a rash of foodborne illness or if schools in a particular area have frequently been the subject of intrusions by third parties, that makes injuries more foreseeable and will influence reasonable safety precautions in response. But that is often not the case, and foreseeability appears to arise as a question of fact in many cases only because of its earlier misplaced role in the analysis of duty.

2.3.4 Reduced Duties: The Case of Entrants onto Land

The *Restatement (Second) of Torts* has twenty-six separate sections on the liability of landowners and land possessors to people who enter their land. Seven of those sections, or about a quarter of them, concern liabilities to potential trespassers onto land. It is possible to memorize and recite these rules in the abstract, but learning the duties of land possessors benefits greatly from applying general principles and an attempt to see the bigger picture.

The classical rules, though they have varied in their details from state to state, imagined three different types of entrants onto land: invitees, licensees, and trespassers. The words themselves are terms of art and don't carry their ordinary meanings. An *invitee* is someone on the land pursuant to a *public* invitation (a visitor to a city park, a parent at a school for a parent/teacher night) or because of *business* dealings with the land possessor (like a courier delivering a message to a private office). A *licensee* is anyone who has permission to be on the land; the origin of the term is that, as with intellectual property, one can give a *license* to others to use property (and thus to enter land). A *trespasser* is someone with no permission to be on the land. Under the older rules, versions of which are still in force in many states, these categories had consequences for *duty* in negligence cases. The categories were expressly conceived as reducing or eliminating the duty of ordinary or reasonable care toward certain types of entrants onto land, sometimes barring liability completely and sometimes imposing a lower standard of care on landowners (that is, making breach harder to prove by requiring less of landowners than the reasonable-person standard).

The core of the classical rule was that landowners owed invitees the usual duty of reasonable care, owed licensees a lesser duty only to fix or warn about known conditions that were unsafe, and owed trespassers no duty at all. There were, however—as the number of the Restatement sections suggests—so many exceptions and qualifications to these rules that the exceptions came to overwhelm the rules.

The rules and their exceptions, at bottom, were probably just a long, slow, and ill-fated attempt by courts to mechanically state standards of conduct that might have worked in a particular time but were always under pressure because of changing social expectations, uses of land, residential and business patterns, and so on. We have seen this pattern before in the tension between the general reasonable-person standard and courts' occasional attempts to list specific behaviors that count as reasonable or unreasonable. In other words, the rules for land possessors were very similar to the Minnesota court in *Harper v. Herman* (see section 2.3.3): the real question they were trying to answer is whether particular conduct was reasonable or unreasonable (that is, *breach* or *not breach*), but the courts responded by laying out special standards of conduct for landowners and calling them "duties." For example, there is probably no policy, principle, administrative concern, or other no-duty consideration that suggests that a homeowner, having taken or failed to take the same precautions to keep their porch free from snow or their tiled bathroom free from slippery water, should face different levels of liability to a social guest (a licensee) as compared to someone at the house to install cable television (an invitee). The courts, in laying out these rules, were just trying to tell us what they thought constituted reasonable or unreasonable conduct: warning a friend about a bad stairwell, but not bothering to fix it, is okay; not posting a sign inside your house while you're away reading "Warning—this staircase is broken" is not unreasonable, because you had no reason to know that anyone would trespass and then hurt themselves on the stairs; and so on.

In any event, the area of law became very complicated—full of rules and exceptions, not all of which were consistent or principled. Some of the exceptions just stated the obvious: landowners should warn others of unsafe conditions, but they don't need to bother if the conditions are "open and obvious."[95] So you'd have to warn of a trapdoor but not bother to tell guests, "don't sit on that sculpture of a spike." But that is just what a reasonable-person standard would suggest. In other words, there don't need to be special rules for this type of warning, because the special rules simply echo the general duty of reasonable care.

---

[95] *Cf.* RESTATEMENT (SECOND) OF TORTS § 343A (1965) ("known or obvious").

Particularly with the older categorical no-duty rules toward trespassers, an important pattern in this area is one we have seen before: the erosion of rules that courts have opposed for reasons of morality and policy. If the no-duty-to-trespassers rule were taken seriously, it would suggest that completely callous conduct toward unexpected but not extremely wrongful entrants onto land—accidental trespassers, children, and so on—is exempt from tort liability. Therefore, exceptions arose to cover those kinds of entrants: even if there are no duties to trespassers, there are duties to child trespassers, duties not to engage in unsafe activities that harm known trespassers, and so on. Even with a lot of exceptions, a strict application of the categorical rules would cause significant outcomes in tort cases to turn on very little—on minor differences in the status of visitors determined by rules that the public probably knew very little about. And because of the complexity of the rules, it was difficult for most people to plan in view of them. So the whole area of law was filled with traps for the unwary.[96]

The erosion of the older rules with a number of complex and potentially inconsistent exceptions led, in this case, to direct overturning of the older rules in many states. The law of England and Wales adopted statutes in the mid-to-late 1900s that got rid of most of the effects of the older types of categories for entrants onto land.[97] In the United States, courts began to abandon the older rules, recognizing them as needlessly complicated and inconsistent with the general negligence (fault) principle and tort law's general goals of deterrence and compensation. Again, because the older categories of entrants onto land affected the *duties* of land possessors, what was at stake under those rules is whether a land possessor who *was* negligent—who *had* acted wrongfully, *without* due care for the safety of others—could escape liability for formal reasons. As the California Supreme Court wrote in 1968:

> A man's life or limb does not become less worthy of protection by the law nor a loss less worthy of compensation under the law because he has come upon the land of another without permission or with permission but without a business purpose. Reasonable people do not ordinarily vary their conduct depending upon such matters, and to focus upon the status of the injured party as a trespasser, licensee, or invitee in order to determine the question whether the landowner has a duty of care, is contrary to our

---

[96] *See* Hoffmann v. Young, 515 P.3d 635, 641 (Cal. 2022) ("Over time, various exceptions to these rules developed. Confusion arose surrounding the scope of these exceptions, as well as the definitions of invitee, licensee, and trespasser.").

[97] Occupiers' Liability Act, 1994, ch. 3 (Eng.); Occupiers' Liability Act, 1957, ch. 31 (Eng.).

> modern social mores and humanitarian values. The common law rules obscure rather than illuminate the proper considerations which should govern determination of the question of duty.
>
> It bears repetition that the basic policy of this state set forth by the Legislature in section 1714 of the Civil Code is that everyone is responsible for an injury caused to another by his want of ordinary care or skill in the management of his property. The factors which may in particular cases warrant departure from this fundamental principle do not warrant the wholesale immunities resulting from the common law classifications, and we are satisfied that continued adherence to the common law distinctions can only lead to injustice or, if we are to avoid injustice, further fictions with the resulting complexity and confusion. We decline to follow and perpetuate such rigid classifications.[98]

Many states have followed suit, and the doctrine has been dramatically simplified overall, with a trend toward using the general reasonable-person standard in more cases. The modern Restatement has only six sections on the topic, down from twenty-six in the older Restatement.

Some states have abandoned the formal distinctions between invitees and licensees but have maintained some distinction for trespassers. Behind that trend, there may be a genuine no-duty rationale—perhaps the only one in this area. Particularly when there are trespassers with bad criminal intent—the *Restatement (Third) of Torts* calls them "flagrant" trespassers, "in the sense of egregious or atrocious rather than in its alternative meaning of conspicuous"[99] and recognizes that it is not a sharply defined category—it seems intolerable to allow them to sue their potential victims and recover in negligence. For example, suppose someone tries to break into an art gallery to steal rare paintings and is injured by unreasonably unsafe conditions on that property. Under a normal reasonable-person standard, we might judge the manager of the gallery to be in breach of the duty of ordinary care. But to permit a thief to sue the gallery—the intended target of the crime—for simple carelessness violates most people's sense of justice, and it could also, at least in theory, encourage crime. The *Restatement (Third) of Torts* elaborates in a comment, explicitly treating these cases under a modern no-duty analysis:

---

98 Rowland v. Christian, 443 P.2d 561, 568 (Cal. 1968).

99 RESTATEMENT (THIRD) OF TORTS: LIABILITY FOR PHYSICAL AND EMOTIONAL HARM § 52 cmt. a (2010).

> The idea behind distinguishing particularly egregious trespassers for different treatment is that their presence on another's land is so antithetical to the rights of the land possessor to exclusive use and possession of the land that the land possessor should not be subject to liability for failing to exercise the ordinary duty of reasonable care otherwise owed to them as entrants on the land. That is, when a trespass is sufficiently offensive to the property rights of the land possessor it is unfair to subject the possessor to liability for mere negligence. This reflects a specific application of the [concept of no-duty rules] permitting a determination that, based on an articulated principle or policy, the ordinary duty of reasonable care should not apply. The policy justifying the lesser duty owed to flagrant trespassers is protection of the rights of private-property owners, which would be unfairly diminished if possessors were subject to liability to flagrant trespassers based on ordinary negligence.[100]

It may be helpful to consider whether the underlying policy is really "protection of the rights of private-property owners" or a sense that the thief should not benefit from the crime. Compensation for injuries is not normally seen as a benefit—just a reversal of an injury—but allowing a thief financial recovery from their intended victim seems somehow morally perverse. (And perhaps people don't conceive compensation correctly in cases like this, treating it imprecisely as if it were in fact a net benefit to the thief—perhaps because tort damages in the US can sometimes seem high.) Perhaps there is simply a desire in social morality to punish wrongdoers by denying them compensation. That said, people who are engaged in crimes do not lose their legal rights in general; for example, if a getaway car, twenty minutes after a robbery, is driving safely and is hit by another car that runs a red light, there isn't any no-duty rule that prevents the driver of the getaway car from suing the other car's negligent driver. We might conceive that injury as being able to happen to anyone, whereas a thief who cuts their hand on the artwork they're trying to steal shouldn't, in many people's view, receive any money that is so closely connected to the attempted theft.

The modern state of the law here, then, is much simpler than it used to be: reasonable care is often the standard for at least invitees, licensees, and trespassers who aren't "flagrant." Even for flagrant trespassers, the modern Restatement doesn't provide a complete no-duty exemption for land possessors; it instead requires land possessors "not to act in an intentional, willful, or wanton manner to

---

[100] *Id.*

cause physical harm" and also requires affirmative, reasonable efforts to rescue even flagrant trespassers who are "helpless."[101] That said, many states still maintain the older, more formal categories of entrants onto land.

2.3.5 Immunities

The law historically has recognized several *immunities* to tort liability. These have been conceived as defenses that defendants could establish to avoid liability. These include *sovereign immunity*, the notion (probably misguided)[102] that people shouldn't be able to sue governments unless the governments waive that immunity. Public officials like judges are often exempt from lawsuits related to their official functions—or, like police officers, they may receive *qualified immunity*, a controversial notion that is often regarded as theoretically bizarre by lawyers outside the United States. Doctrinal immunities also traditionally included a number of badly conceived and sharply outdated notions, such as the notion that spouses cannot sue each other and that children cannot sue parents; these immunities have largely fallen away, though there is still some controversy about exactly what children should be able to sue their parents for.

Tort doctrine has probably made a mistake by treating "immunities" under a separate category from "duties." If there are rationales for any immunities, they are going to be no-duty rationales (see section 2.3.1) and should be considered similarly. Many no-duty rationales, as we have seen, are not persuasive either, but at least when immunities are treated as no-duty rules they can be debated directly in terms of policy. Even just as a conceptual matter, it is needlessly cumbersome to maintain both the concept of duties and the concept of immunities.

2.4 Negligence: Causation in Fact

Duty and breach can seem tricky at first, but most students and commentators can eventually reach a pretty clean understanding of them. The third element of the negligence cause of action, *causation in fact*, is considerably messier, and it is sometimes hard to find clear principles in the cases. States do not all apply causation doctrine in the same way, and the exceptions that have developed are confusing and potentially inconsistent. Though this element is often just called *causation*, the terms *causation in fact* or *factual causation* commonly

---

[101] *Id.* § 52.

[102] *See* Ayala v. Phila. Bd. of Pub. Educ., 305 A.2d 877, 881 (Pa. 1973) ("[N]o reasons whatsoever exist for continuing to adhere to the doctrine of governmental immunity.").

arise to distinguish it from *proximate causation* or *legal causation*, which are traditional terms for what is now better called *scope of liability* (see section 2.5). The basic idea behind factual causation is that even negligent defendants (i.e., those in breach of the duty of ordinary care) are liable only if their negligence caused the plaintiff's harm.

Many negligence cases raise no special problems of causation. If the driver of a car negligently runs over a pedestrian's foot, and the pedestrian's foot wasn't broken before the incident and is determined to be broken right after it, there is no serious question about whether the driver's negligence caused the plaintiff's injury.

It may be helpful, though perhaps initially counterintuitive, to ask why tort law requires a showing of causation at all. It is possible to imagine a system that doesn't. For example, to start with, consider a very general government-administered claims system coupled with a regulatory system, roughly like New Zealand adopted to replace most of its tort system in the 1970s. Under such a system, plaintiffs who were injured could file a claim for compensation, regulations and criminal laws would serve the functions of deterrence and punishment, and tort law would have little role to play.

Perhaps even more exotically, it is at least possible to imagine a system where anyone who was injured could sue anyone who behaved badly; if strong wind causes a tree branch to fall on me, injuring my shoulder, I could file a claim against a bicyclist caught on camera across town illegally riding on a sidewalk, on the theory that the bicyclist *could have caused* a similar injury. Such a claim, after all, would provide some measure of both compensation and deterrence. A system that worked like this, however, could be hard or impossible to administer. Would there be a rush to sue every bicyclist who was caught on camera on a sidewalk, with a waiting list for injured parties to identify some wrongdoer they could sue? What if the amount needed for compensation didn't match the amount needed for appropriate deterrence? Such a system would also violate the intuitions of social morality that posit some *connection* or *relationship* between injurers and victims. So the tort system we actually have does generally—but not always—require some sort of connection.

Probably the most practical causation problem in negligence cases is simply factual uncertainty: we haven't yet learned enough about science, or there is not enough evidence about a particular case, to say definitely that the defendant's negligence caused the victim's harm. In this sort of case, the policy question is just what to do about scientific or factual uncertainty: does the plaintiff or the defendant bear that risk? Causation is an element of the plaintiff's claim, so perhaps just for formal reasons the plaintiff is ordinarily said, by default, to face the burden of proving causation.

That burden is often relaxed or shifted, however. Suppose a plaintiff is found dead at the bottom of a stairwell. Evidence shows that the stairwell was negligently maintained, but there is no specific evidence about whether the negligent maintenance caused the fall. After all, people can fall down even properly maintained staircases.[103] In the absence of any further evidence, what should the law do? One solution is to relax the plaintiff's burden because the defendant is clearly wrongful and the parties have a close enough relationship that it is at least plausible that the defendant's negligence *actually could have caused* the plaintiff's injury. In a less stylized, more complex case, *Zuchowicz v. United States*,[104] a doctor prescribed a ridiculously high overdose of a drug to a patient, who several months later developed complications that *could have been caused* by the overdose, though the link was uncertain. Part of the reason the causal link was uncertain is that there was little statistical evidence about the risks of such high overdoses because doctors were rarely so idiotic as to give overdoses in that amount. Under circumstances like that, it would be an unfortunate result if the plaintiff loses a negligence lawsuit simply because of lack of general evidence. In *Zuchowicz*, Judge Calabresi, a former dean of Yale Law School and a leading common-law judge, wrote an opinion that upheld the trial court's finding that there was causation. In some sense, what courts do with cases like this, where factual causation is uncertain, simply reflects a policy choice about which of the two parties should bear the costs or risks of uncertainty.

Note that the defendant's *negligence*—that is, their breach—needs to have caused the harm. The question is not whether the *defendant* or their general activities caused the harm. One way to think of this is to ask, hypothetically, how the defendant would have behaved if they had not been negligent and then to ask whether the plaintiff still would have suffered an injury. This hypothetical or *counterfactual* reasoning leads to the notion of what is commonly called *but-for causation*: but for (i.e., except for, or without) the defendant's negligence, would the plaintiff still have been injured? Other names for this concept include *sine qua non* ("without which not") causation.

It is surprisingly difficult to come up with general principles of causation that consistently explain US cases. But one way to conceive this area is that the rules about causation differ depending on whether there is sufficiently reliable statistical evidence about

103 *See* Kenneth S. Abraham, *Self-Proving Causation*, 99 VA. L. REV. 1811 (2013).

104 140 F.3d 381 (2d Cir. 1998) (Calabresi, J.).

causation or not. When there is sufficient statistical evidence for a factfinder to reach confidence in a particular figure of probability (e.g., 20% or 70%) that the defendant's negligence caused the plaintiff's harm, the law will tend to ask the factfinder to rely on that figure. The plaintiff's usual burden is to prove each element of the negligence cause of action (including causation) by a preponderance of the evidence, which for this purpose requires showing that causation was more likely than not. So if there is very reliable evidence that the likelihood that a particular defendant's negligence caused the plaintiff's injury was 55%, then the plaintiff has established causation against that defendant. If the reliable evidence instead shows that the probability is only 45%, then the plaintiff has failed to establish causation against the defendant.

That rule leads to a potentially harsh discontinuity where small differences in the statistical data can lead a plaintiff to win entirely or to lose entirely. That kind of harsh continuity is commonplace under classical common law, but it is often regarded as arbitrary and unhelpful today. One solution, proposed by a lot of legal scholars, would be for negligence law to adopt a more general principle of *proportional liability*—for example, making any defendant liable for 40% of the plaintiff's injury if we are 40% confident that they caused it—but the law has not adopted that position in the general case. As we'll see below, the law has perhaps taken some small steps toward that position in specific cases, but the general rule (under the view of the doctrine we are discussing) is still that if we are clear about the probability of a defendant's negligence having caused the plaintiff's harm, the plaintiff establishes causation if that probability is greater than 50%—that is, more likely than not.

The more difficult (and probably more typical) cases arise when there is *not* a particular settled quantitative probabilistic figure for factual causation, as in *Zuchowicz*. In those cases, courts look at factors like the plausibility of causation, whether the defendant's behavior significantly increased the risk of the plaintiff's injury, the degree of the defendant's fault, the plaintiff's access to evidence (as in the cases that shift the burden of proving breach; see section 2.2.3), and perhaps other factors that are hard to quantify. Maybe the goal is only to tie the defendant to the plaintiff in a manner sufficient to avoid the counterintuitive procedures discussed above where plaintiffs can sue any unrelated defendant as long as the defendant was negligent. This is why *could have caused* or *played a plausible part in the historical story of the plaintiff's injury* is sometimes enough, rather than an affirmative, confident, or specific finding of but-for causation.

That, such as it is, is perhaps the clearest way to describe the background rule of causation in tort law. Its messiness is illustrated by *Stubbs v. Rochester*.[105] A plaintiff contracted typhoid fever after the city had negligently maintained its water system. The court recognized that the plaintiff could have contracted typhoid fever from at least eight theoretical causes other than drinking the water, as well as from causes that experience and medical science had not yet determined. Statistical evidence tended to show, though inconclusively, that the city's negligence probably made a difference to the case rates of typhoid fever in general. As to the plaintiff's particular situation:

> The plaintiff was employed in the immediate locality where the water was contaminated. He drank the water daily. The consumption of contaminated water is a very frequent cause of typhoid fever. In the locality there were a large number of cases of typhoid fever and near to sixty individuals who drank the water and had suffered from typhoid fever in that neighborhood appeared as witnesses on behalf of plaintiff. The plaintiff gave evidence of his habits, his home surroundings and his method of living, and the medical testimony indicated that his illness was caused by drinking contaminated water.[106]

On these facts, taken as a whole, a jury was permitted to determine causation-in-fact; "a verdict rendered thereon for either party would rest not in conjecture but upon reasonable possibilities."[107]

On this view of the law, then, quantitative probability is used when it's available and reliable enough; when it's not, courts rely on a variety of open-ended factors about the plausibility of causation and potentially leave the matter to a jury. It is hard to pin down the background rule of causation much beyond that general statement. If the major policy question in this area is which party ought to bear the risk of uncertainty or lack of evidence, courts may address that question directly by paying attention to such factors as how wrongful the defendant was and whether the plaintiff's showing of evidence matches the evidence that could plausibly (or fairly) have been available to them.

Against that background rule, fuzzy as it may be, there are several particular exceptions in causation doctrine. These are probably not as important in the real world as Torts professors and bar exams make them out to be, but they are commonly discussed

---

105 124 N.E. 137 (N.Y. 1919).

106 *Id.* at 140.

107 *Id.*

and tested just because they encapsulate some specific material—and perhaps they are theoretically interesting. There are at least three significant types of exceptions to the general background rules of factual causation.

First, the notion of *lost chance* or *loss of a chance* has arisen in medical context. In a recurring kind of medical case, a plaintiff who is already more likely than not to die (or to have some other poor medical outcome, like the loss of a limb)—but who still has a chance to avoid that outcome—sees a doctor. The doctor's negligence reduces or eliminates that chance. If the plaintiff sues the doctor, under the rules we have just seen the doctor might be able to avoid liability entirely, even if their malpractice is clear, by arguing that the plaintiff was more likely than not to experience the outcome anyway—so the plaintiff cannot prove that the doctor's malpractice was the cause of any harm. Because of the unfairness of exempting that whole class of cases from liability and because statistics in medical situations tend to be more robust than elsewhere, the law has extended a kind of proportional liability to these cases: if a plaintiff had (say) a 30% chance of living and the doctor's negligence squandered that chance, the plaintiff's estate may recover 30% of the damages associated with the patient's death from the doctor. Without lost-chance liability, the plaintiff would lose because the doctor could successfully argue that the patient had a 70% chance of dying even without the doctor's negligence. Note that if a patient had (say) an 85% chance of living instead of a 30% chance of living, they wouldn't need to use the lost-chance doctrine; if the doctor's negligence took away their 85% chance of living and then they died, it is more likely than not that that the doctor's negligence caused their death.

Many courts have been keen not to present lost-chance liability as a simple application of proportional liability, saying instead that the "chance" is itself a kind of legally recognized property that the doctor's negligence took away. That sort of reasoning is artificial, however, and if taken seriously would lead to potential confusion. For example, suppose that a plaintiff's chance of a medical recovery is 30%, a doctor's negligence reduces it to 25%, but then the patient is lucky and recovers. The patient will probably not be able to recover 5% of the damages that they would have been able to receive had they died; the doctor's negligence in fact didn't end up causing any harm.

Courts have not adopted proportional liability in medical cases in general, however, so lost-chance cases are still doctrinally distinct. For example, if a plaintiff undergoes a medical operation, has a bad outcome, and proves that there was a 5% chance that the doctor's negligence caused that outcome, the plaintiff has failed to establish causation. That is not considered to be a lost-chance case, even if it could conceptually be framed as "the patient had a reduced chance of a successful operation." Normally, the lost-chance doctrine applies to a doctor's negligent failure to stop a disease process from progressing.

Second, based on cases like *Summers v. Tice*,[108] courts have sometimes relaxed the plaintiff's requirement to prove causation. In *Summers*, two defendants each negligently shot birdshot pellets from guns in the direction of the plaintiff. The plaintiff was hit at least twice, but one of the shots landed in his eye and caused a serious injury. There was no way to tell which defendant's gun had fired the particular shot that caused that serious injury. On formal principles of causation, the plaintiff can't show that either defendant was more likely than not to have been the cause of the serious injury, even though both were negligent. In other words, each is 50% likely, so the plaintiff just barely fails to establish that either of their negligence was more likely than not to have caused the harm. The court, however, imposed liability against both defendants under a principle that is sometimes called *alternative liability*. *Summers* involved just two defendants, but the principle can be extended to similar cases involving relatively small numbers of defendants. In cases with large numbers of defendants—for example, dozens of drug companies that negligently supply a dangerous drug to the public—courts have adopted a more general version of the *Summers* principle called *market-share liability*. The idea is that each defendant can be liable for having negligently contributed to the problem, even if specific causation between the defendant and the plaintiff can't be established. The defendant's negligence *could have caused* the plaintiff's harm, and that is enough—there is at least a close enough tie between the plaintiff and the defendant to avoid any concerns about unbounded liability or liability of defendants to wholly unrelated plaintiffs.

A slightly different way to interpret *Summers* is to see it as a shift in the burden of proving causation. Again, it is arbitrary and formalistic that the plaintiff is the one to bear the risk of uncertainty about causation; that background rule is not so much a policy choice as a logical deduction from an arbitrary axiom that plaintiffs need to establish *elements* of claims and defendants need to establish *defenses*. Interpreted in this way, perhaps *Summers* is not very different from *Zuchowicz*: it is just a more focused shift of the burden to prove causation, based on a more stylized situation: two or more defendants are wrongful, the plaintiff can establish breach against them, and the plaintiff can establish causation against the group but not against the individuals; in that case, the burden shifts to the defendants to exonerate themselves individually if they can. As we

108 199 P.2d 1 (Cal. 1948).

saw when discussing *res ipsa loquitur* (see section 2.2.3), shifting the burden of the elements of a negligence claim may be justified by reasons related to fairness and to access of evidence.

Third, sometimes two negligent defendants are each a sufficient cause to produce a plaintiff's injury. In an often-discussed but stylized fact pattern, two negligent hikers in a forest each fail to extinguish their campsite fires. The two fires spread and reach the plaintiff's house simultaneously, destroying the house. Neither hiker is strictly a *but-for cause* of the house's destruction: if not for the first hiker's individual negligence, the house still would have been destroyed by the second hiker's; if not for the second hiker's individual negligence, the house would have been destroyed by the first hiker's. But it seems absurd to say that both hikers should escape liability on that basis alone. The law's response is simply to abandon the but-for causation rule in this case and impose liability anyway.

It is commonly said that causation is a factual question. But this is not quite true. At least conceptually it requires some judgments to be made in constructing *counterfactuals*—that is, the hypothetical worlds in which defendants didn't behave negligently—and these judgments may depend on social norms and other factors. For example, in *Zuchowicz*, where doctors prescribed an overdose, it may seem natural to say that if the doctors hadn't been negligent, they would have prescribed the maximum dose that does not count as a negligent overdose. But that is something of an arbitrary determination. Defining a world "without negligence" is not sufficient to specify all the facts in a counterfactual universe, because we are just listing an absence of something—not specifying new hypothetical facts.[109]

Pressing on the notion of constructing counterfactuals can lead to surprisingly complicated, and little-discussed, questions. For example, suppose a car enthusiast replaces their car's headlights with special high-powered xenon headlights but then, just after twilight, negligently fails to turn those headlights on and crashes into a pedestrian. Suppose the crash could have been prevented by the driver's special xenon lights but not by ordinary headlights. The driver is (by hypothesis) negligent, but has their negligence caused harm to the pedestrian? Most common lawyers are inclined to find causation on these facts alone. But consider a slight variation: the driver installs the special xenon lights *in addition* to the car's regular headlamps, rather than *instead of* them, and as a result there are two on/off switches on the car's dashboard: one for the regular lights and

---

[109] *Cf.* David W. Robertson, *The Common Sense of Cause in Fact*, 75 TEX. L. REV. 1765 (1997).

one for the xenon lights. The driver negligently fails to turn either on. Has the driver's negligence still caused the crash? In this variation many lawyers are disinclined to find causation (because they think of the driver's negligence as simply failing to turn on the *ordinary* headlamps, which by hypothesis would not have made any difference), but is there any difference in morality or policy between the two variations, or is the difference in lawyers' intuitions entirely mechanical and formalistic? Surely we don't intend to give the driver an artificial incentive to install two sets of headlamps rather than just one.

2.5 Negligence: Scope of Liability (Proximate Causation)

A conceptually distinct element of the negligence cause of action is *scope of liability*, a newer name for a concept that has traditionally been called *proximate causation* or sometimes *legal causation*. The element doesn't really have anything to do with causation; it is just an opportunity to recognize that not all causes *matter*, and not all negligent causes are fair targets for liability. The principal motivation for the element is fairness—fair assignment of responsibility.

It is easy to recognize as an intuitive matter that not all causes of an event are important. It is probably accurate to say that a particular car crash would not have happened in Alabama in 2025 if the United States hadn't been founded in 1776 or if Henry Ford's grandparents had decided not to have any children. (No special causal or scientific knowledge is needed for that conclusion; the world would be different enough that the specific accident in question wouldn't have happened because the plaintiff and defendant probably would not exist, would certainly not have been in exactly the same places, and so on.) But when asked about the causes of a car crash, nobody has in mind causal factors like that. Similarly, when assigning praise or blame for an event, it is rare to search so far afield for a target.

In the typical scope-of-liability case, something very unusual has happened. Because the course of events was so unusual, their very weirdness also complicates our sense of praise and blame. If a golfer hits a ball into the air, and an eagle appears out of nowhere, snatches the ball, and drops it into the hole, nobody would praise the skill of the golfer for that outcome. Similarly, if the golfer is negligent in failing to yell "fore!" to give notice of a potentially dangerous golf ball, but then an eagle grabs the ball, flies in an unexpected direction far from the direction in which the golfer hit the ball, and then drops it on someone's head, nobody thinks the golfer is fairly responsible for that injury—even though the golfer was originally negligent. This is true even if the accident wouldn't have happened without the golfer's negligence: suppose shouting "fore!" would have scared off the eagle, even though that's not the reason golfers are supposed to shout it.

That specific notion—that someone was negligent and was *a* cause of an injury but not really to blame because an unusual sequence of events also caused the injury—is the clearest way of conceiving scope of liability in modern law. As the *Restatement (Third) of Torts* puts it, "An actor's liability is limited to those harms that result from the risks that made the actor's conduct tortious."[110] To apply that formulation to the example involving the golfer, the result that materialized is not one of the risks that led us to say the golfer's failure to warn people of his oncoming golf ball was unreasonable. It was unreasonable for a different reason (failing to warn people in the usual path of the golf ball).

One way to make the central modern scope-of-liability question more intuitive is to imagine a slightly different version of the golfer example: suppose the golfer knows nobody is in the path of his ball; perhaps he is golfing on his own private golf course or the area has very good visibility. As a result, he shouts no warning before hitting the ball. When he hits it, an eagle appears out of nowhere, snatches the ball, flies behind the golfer, and drops it on someone's head, causing injury. We would all agree that the golfer is not liable there simply because he has done nothing wrong: he acted reasonably rather than breaching any duty of care. The only difference between the two examples is that in the first, the golfer was negligent—but in a way that turned out to be irrelevant. Should the golfer's slight negligence in an irrelevant way matter to an effectively unrelated tort suit?

A famous case commonly known as the first *Wagon Mound* case,[111] arising in Australia and decided by the Privy Council in 1961, uses a slightly different comparison to present a similar intuition about fairness and the scope of liability. In that case, a ship had spilled some furnace oil in a harbor, which led through unusual events to a fire that damaged a wharf and other ships. The facts of the case are counterintuitive to many readers the first time they encounter it; one important factual feature of the case is that while furnace oil is meant to burn, it had a high "flash point"[112] and is not normally considered a fire risk if spilled into a harbor. The fire that

---

[110] RESTATEMENT (THIRD) OF TORTS: LIABILITY FOR PHYSICAL AND EMOTIONAL HARM § 29 (2010).

[111] Overseas Tankship (U.K.) Ltd. v. Morts Dock & Eng'g Co., 1961 App. Cas. 388 (P.C.) (appeal taken from N.S.W.).

[112] *Id.* at 391.

resulted apparently arose through very unusual circumstances, resulting from sparks that set alight floating cotton debris,[113] which then apparently acted much like a candle's wick, causing the furnace oil to burn unexpectedly. The owners of the ship that spilled the oil were negligent, but the typical consequences of that negligence would be pollution and inconvenience, as with oil spills in general, not fire. The question was whether they should be liable for the harms caused by the fire, just because they were negligent in leaking oil that would ordinarily have a different typical result. The court declined to impose liability.

In his opinion, Viscount Simonds elaborated a moral intuition associated with scope of liability in a helpful but dense passage, presenting a hypothetical, schematic example where *B* owes a duty to *A* and breaches it:

> to hold B liable for consequences however unforeseeable of a careless act, if, but only if, he is at the same time liable for some other damage however trivial, appears to be neither logical nor just. This becomes more clear if it is supposed that similar unforeseeable damage is suffered by A and C but other foreseeable damage, for which B is liable, by A only. A system of law which would hold B liable to A but not to C for the similar damage suffered by each of them could not easily be defended.[114]

In other words, if *B* has negligently caused the same unusual harm to two people in the same way, it would be unprincipled to say that *B* is liable only to one of them because *B* happened to harm that person in a different, unrelated way.

Another technique that might make scope of liability easier to analyze is to ask the following question: would the defendant's breach still have been a breach if the harm that occurred was the only type of harm that could have occurred? In this formulation, "type of harm" is an open-ended notion, subject to argument and framing, but asking that question is a way to get at the core question that the scope-of-liability element is asking. Indeed, on a more formal, economic view of breach like the Hand formula, we could conceptually ask whether $B < PL$ was true for the particular L that occurred. For example, in the case of the golfer, the failure to shout "fore" was so unlikely to reduce the potential harms from an eagle that it would not have been negligent to fail to shout it if that were the only harm on the table. To be clear, the golfer could have *actually* breached, but on this

---

113 *Id.* at 389.

114 *Id.* at 425–26.

hypothetical or counterfactual analysis their actions would not have been blameworthy if the eagle had been the only possible risk.

In any event, the notion of "the risks that made the actor's conduct tortious" is the modern view, as the *Restatement (Third) of Torts* indicates, but two alternative conceptions of scope of liability or proximate causation still arise in cases. An older view, which still occasionally echoes through the common law and is more commonly seen outside the United States, is the notion that liability extends to *direct* consequences but not *remote* ones. On this view, something like the distance in time and space between the negligence and the harm, or alternatively perhaps the number of conceptual "steps" between the negligence and the harm, is what matters. Past a certain (ill-defined) point, liability is cut off. Echoes of this notion arise in cases where liability is unavailable because a large amount of time has passed and responsibility for new harms seems to have drifted away from the original defendant. For example, if a car hits a pedestrian and breaks the pedestrian's leg, leading to an ongoing small limp, the pedestrian can recover damages against the driver that will include "pain and suffering" damages for the limp. But if twenty years after the car hits the pedestrian, the pedestrian is in an airplane crash and initially survives can't easily escape because of the limp, the original driver's responsibility seems to be have been cut off by that point.

One way to analyze a situation like this is to say that every harm has many causes, and some—the more recent, the nearer—tend to predominate. The problem with this test is that it lacks a clear motivation and is also hard to apply consistently. Writers that try to capture it tend to veer toward poetry rather than analysis. For example, Justice Andrews, writing a dissent in a famous case, *Palsgraf v. Long Island R.R.*,[115] gave this attempt:

> Any philosophical doctrine of causation does not help us. A boy throws a stone into a pond. The ripples spread. The water level rises. The history of that pond is altered to all eternity. It will be altered by other causes also. Yet it will be forever the resultant of all causes combined. Each one will have an influence. How great only omniscience can say. You may speak of a chain, or if you please, a net. An analogy is of little aid. Each cause brings about future events. Without each the future would not be the same. Each is proximate in the sense it is essential. But that is not what we mean by the word. Nor on the other hand do we mean sole cause. There is no such thing.

115 162 N.E. 99 (1928).

> Should analogy be thought helpful, however, I prefer that of a stream. The spring, starting on its journey, is joined by tributary after tributary. The river, reaching the ocean, comes from a hundred sources. No man may say whence any drop of water is derived. Yet for a time distinction may be possible. Into the clear creek, brown swamp water flows from the left. Later, from the right comes water stained by its clay bed. The three may remain for a space, sharply divided. But at last, inevitably no trace of separation remains. They are so commingled that all distinction is lost.[116]

Though this view does capture some intuitions about fairness, it has faded because—again—it lacks a clear principle and is difficult to apply.[117]

A third view, probably still dominant in US common law, particularly when courts apply the rule to relatively simple cases without reconsidering the doctrine, relies on *foreseeability*: harms that were foreseeable at the time of the negligence lead to liability; other harms don't. This test, too, is not clearly principled on its own: why does foreseeability matter and how foreseeable does something have to be? But perhaps fair enough results are reached simply by letting lawyers argue about how to analyze the harm and its foreseeability in front of a jury. And the notion of foreseeability seems to relate to the idea that scope-of-liability cases tend to involve injuries that come about in unusual ways. In any event, jury instructions tend not to be very clear on the matter; sometimes they mix elements of directness, foreseeability, and even factual causation. The *Restatement (Second) of Torts* was not especially helpful on this element; the *Restatement (Third)*, quoted earlier, reflects a substantial improvement in clarity.

Sometimes courts and commentators have attempted to add special rules or labels to the doctrine of scope of liability. For example, courts write about and law professors still sometimes teach the notion of *superseding cause*. But this is just a conclusory label and does very little analytical work. In the *Restatement (Second)*'s definition, a superseding cause simply "is an act of a third person or other force which by its intervention prevents the actor from being liable."[118] In other words, if something happens between negligence and harm, it is *called* a superseding cause if it places the harm outside the scope of liability of the negligence. That third parties or

---

[116] *Id.* at 103 (Andrews, J., dissenting).

[117] The "directness" view of proximate causation is often associated with *In re Polemis & Furness, Withy & Co*, [1921] 3 K.B. 560 (C.A.).

[118] RESTATEMENT (SECOND) OF TORTS § 440 (1965).

other forces intervene is not, however, as a general matter, a factor that is especially important in determining scope of liability—or even foreseeability. For example, suppose an apartment building's managers are negligent in maintaining its security system, and an apartment in that building is burgled as a result. If the building's managers were negligent in maintaining the security system, the risk of burglaries is exactly the sort of risk that made their conduct negligent. That a criminal intervened should not cut off the building's liability—although the criminal too, of course, is responsible, and if available as a defendant should pay some or all of the plaintiff's damages.

Regardless of the particular conception of scope of liability or proximate causation that courts adopt, there are a handful of rules in this area that can be seen as special judicial determinations about scope of liability. First, under the *eggshell-plaintiff rule*, all injuries that result from physical harm (including those exacerbated by preexisting medical conditions)[119] are within the defendant's scope of liability in causing a physical injury. Under this rule, or perhaps a similar but distinct rule, original injurers are liable for things that go wrong in treating the injury (including medical negligence, ambulance crashes, and so on).[120] Second, as Cardozo once put it, "[d]anger invites rescue."[121] That is, negligence that causes someone to need rescue is typically deemed, by judges, to include within its scope of liability any attempts at rescue, even if those attempts might not be specifically foreseeable. For example, someone who negligently causes someone to fall off a boat is liable to those who injure themselves trying to rescue the person who fell overboard.

One possible way to conceive scope of liability is that it is simply a judgment about the defendant's responsibility—and that harms outside a negligent defendant's scope of liability are simply those for which the defendant's negligence is only trivially responsible, so that under a comparative-responsibility analysis (see section 2.7.1) we round their responsibility down to 0%. In other words, to say that a harm falls outside a defendant's scope of liability is simply to say that their negligence is not an important enough cause of the harm for the law to take notice of it; the only important causes of the harm, on this view, are other defendants, innocent third parties, natural forces, background conditions, the plaintiff themselves, and so on. On this view, scope of liability does not depend on a distinctive type of qualitative judgment (a difference in kind) but rather on a familiar

---

119 RESTATEMENT (THIRD) OF TORTS: LIABILITY FOR PHYSICAL AND EMOTIONAL HARM § 31 (2010).

120 *See id.* § 35.

121 Wagner v. Int'l Ry., 133 N.E. 437, 437 (N.Y. 1921).

quantitative judgment: it is just like any determination that a defendant is 70% responsible or 2% responsible for a harm (see again section 2.7.1). When we say a harm falls outside a defendant's scope of liability, perhaps we are simply saying that a defendant's share of responsibility for the harm is so low that, for administrative reasons, it is best ignored.

2.6 "Pure" Emotional and Economic Harms

Up until this point, we have discussed only physical injuries. For example, the general duty of reasonable care that we have seen applies to protect potential victims against physical injuries. It also extends to property damage. Therefore, someone who drives a truck negligently on a bridge is liable for physical injuries and property damage they cause (to other cars, to the owner of the bridge, and so on).

But tort law does *not* typically impose liability on the driver for injuries that are "purely" emotional or economic. "Purely" here refers to economic or emotional harm that does not arise secondarily from a physical injury. For example, if a car negligently crashes into a pedestrian, and the pedestrian suffers (1) a broken leg, (2) $28,000 in medical bills, (3) $5,000 in lost wages, (4) pain and suffering from the broken leg; and (5) clinical depression requiring medical treatment, triggered by the accident and resulting pain, then all five types of these types of harms are recoverable. The first comes directly from the physical injury, the second and third are two different types of economic harm, and the fourth and fifth are two different types of emotional harm. All are recoverable in a negligence action, and we say there is a duty to prevent them all by exercising ordinary care. These are not "pure" emotional or economic harms because they arise within the scope of liability of a physical injury. One reason it is negligent to drive badly is that it causes physical injury; another reason is that the resulting physical injuries lead to medical bills, physical pain, and so on.

But if someone witnesses a car accident on television and experiences severe anxiety as a result, that is a purely emotional harm, and courts often say there is *no duty* to prevent it. As we will see, there are both no-duty (see section 2.3) and scope-of-liability (see section 2.5) rationales that operate to prevent recovery for pure emotional and economic harms.

2.6.1 Economic Harms

As an example of a purely economic injury, consider again a truck driver who has driven negligently on a bridge, and imagine that the resulting crash is so severe that the bridge needs to be closed for a few hours. Imagine that a restaurant on one side of the bridge can convincingly prove that it lost $4,300 in profits during the time that the bridge was closed.

Tort law treats that as a no-duty case: the driver has no duty to prevent that sort of injury and is not liable even though they were unreasonable and caused the harm. There is no clear consensus about the rationale for that rule. Possibly it serves to cut off endless, disproportionate damages; the driver of every car could be liable for untold economic damages every time they're negligent, so it may be a form of crushing liability that tort law avoids for that reason. (Compare section 3.6.2, which discusses disproportionate damages in contract law.)

Maybe there is some concern that it is too hard even to start to determine the overall social cost of the economic harms in most cases—which would also be a no-duty rationale. Physical injuries and property damage are clear losses to society, even if they are sometimes difficult to measure in specific amounts of dollars. But if a restaurant loses money when a bridge is shut down, its customers were likely getting their food somewhere else, redirecting their economic activity there and allowing some other business to profit.[122] There is indeed probably *some* loss to society, because if the restaurant lost business it means that there were customers who would have preferred to be eating there while the bridge was closed but were prevented from doing so. But there is no reliable way to value that loss to society, and certainly the restaurant's privately lost profits are not a reliable guide to that overall economic loss. Perhaps courts are inclined not to allow lost profits to be recovered as a result. In other words, there is some call for compensation, but the amount of compensation isn't likely to match the need for deterrence closely. And the compensation would be only for lost future profits, which, as we'll see in discussing contract law (see section 3.1.7), are perhaps not always so significant an injury.

There may also be scope-of-liability concerns about economic harms. Especially as to disproportionate and far-away harms, it seems unfair to say that negligent driving is necessarily responsible for all the economic losses it causes.[123] For example, consider a negligent driver who crashes into a utility pole, cutting off electricity to a few streets for an hour and causing a businessperson to miss a Zoom meeting.

In any event, there are very few cases where pure economic harm is recoverable. Most types of cases where pure economic harms

---

122 *Cf.* RICHARD POSNER, ECONOMIC ANALYSIS OF LAW § 6.7, at 213 (9th ed. 2014).

123 *Cf.* Rickards v. Sun Oil Co., 41 A.2d 267, 269 (N.J. 1945).

lead to tort liability overlap with contract law somewhat and involve failures in rendering professional services.[124]

2.6.2 Emotional Harms

Broadly speaking, pure emotional harms have followed a path that is somewhat opposite to that of physical harms. That is, with physical harm there is a general background duty, but there are some no-duty exceptions; with emotional harm the general rule is "no liability,"[125] but the caselaw has developed several particular exceptions under which liability is possible.

As background, note that emotional harm may still be considered purely emotional, and still does not lead to liability in the general case, even if it manifests physical consequences. For example, severe anxiety that leads to sleeplessness (a physical consequence) does not ordinarily lead to tort liability on that basis alone. That said, the law has never been consistent in determining where emotional harms end and physical harms begin. According to a comment in the *Restatement (Second) of Torts*,

> long continued nausea or headaches may amount to physical illness, which is bodily harm; and even long continued mental disturbance, as for example in the case of repeated hysterical attacks, or mental aberration, may be classified by the courts as illness, notwithstanding their mental character. This becomes a medical or psychiatric problem, rather than one of law.[126]

Some potential no-duty rationales (see section 2.3.1) that have been at least broadly suggested by cases in this area include: (1) a recognition that minor emotional harms are very common, and courts fear that allowing recovery for them would encourage excessive litigation—and perhaps also lead to uncertain or crushing liability; (2) a concern about notice to potential defendants; for example, usually negligent drivers will know they have been in a physical crash, but they might not know if their negligent driving has caused severe anxiety to someone on the side of the road; (3) a concern that because emotional injuries may be easy to feign, our judicial system might be unable to differentiate deserving cases of emotional harm from fraudulent ones; (4) a lingering sense among judges, probably

---

124 *See* RESTATEMENT (THIRD) OF TORTS: LIABILITY FOR ECONOMIC HARM ch. 1 (2020).

125 *See* RESTATEMENT (SECOND) OF TORTS § 436A (1965) ("If the actor's conduct is negligent as creating an unreasonable risk of causing either bodily harm or emotional disturbance to another, and it results in such emotional disturbance alone, without bodily harm or other compensable damage, the actor is not liable for such emotional disturbance.").

126 *Id.* cmt. c.

misplaced and arising from an older sort of "stiff upper lip" mentality, that even serious emotional harms are unworthy in general of legal remediation.[127] As usual with no-duty rationales, it is not clear if any of them are persuasive.

Courts have also articulated scope-of-liability or proximate-causation concerns (see section 2.5) about recovery for pure emotional harm, also on a kind of "stiff-upper-lip" theory. Their thinking, which is increasingly out of date and perhaps even alien to some modern readers, has been that severe emotional harms from nonphysical injuries are unusual and that a significant part of their responsibility lies with victims. For example, as the New Jersey Supreme Court wrote in 1900, the exclusion of pure-emotional-harm cases

> rests upon the principle that a person is legally responsible only for the *natural* and proximate results of his negligent act. Physical suffering is not the probable or natural consequences of fright, in the case of a person of ordinary physical and mental vigor; and in the general conduct of business, and the ordinary affairs of life, although we are bound to anticipate and guard against consequences, which may be injurious to persons who are liable to be effected thereby, we have a right, in doing so, to assume, in the absence of knowledge to the contrary, that such persons are of average strength both of body and of mind.[128]

Though outdated, this sort of thinking perhaps explains why purely emotional harm that then manifests a physical injury does not ordinarily lead to liability in the general case. For example, if an office worker sees someone outside their window driving negligently, and it disturbs them so deeply that they experience severe anxiety that eventually leads to high blood pressure and heart problems, the law's refusal to impose liability is perhaps best explained by saying that such an injury is outside the scope of a driver's liability when they drove negligently. Emotional harms like that do not lead to liability even if they are severe, produce physical results, and have clear evidence in their favor.

---

127 *E.g.*, Mitchell v. Rochester Ry., 45 N.E. 354, 354–55 (N.Y. 1896) ("If the right of recovery in this class of cases should be once established, it would naturally result in a flood of litigation in cases where the injury complained of may be easily feigned without detection, and where the damages must rest upon mere conjecture or speculation. The difficulty which often exists in cases of alleged physical injury, in determining whether they exist, and if so, whether they were caused by the negligent act of the defendant, would not only be greatly increased, but a wide field would be opened for fictitious or speculative claims. To establish such a doctrine would be contrary to principles of public policy.").

128 Ward v. W. Jersey & S.R.R., 47 A. 561, 562 (N.J. 1900).

The easiest way to understand tort law's evolving approach to purely emotional harms is to recognize that the law has developed, from various lines of cases, a handful of arbitrary, specific, and often unprincipled categories where it will allow plaintiffs to recover for emotional harms. Some of the categories would be almost laughably specific, except that they tend to be very sad or very macabre. Outside the particular categories where emotional harm is recoverable, there remains a background rule that there is no liability. The particular categories themselves are probably not directly justified by morality or policy, but in general they collect classes of cases where emotional harm is likely to be very serious, easily understood, and unlikely to be feigned, so that they broadly address the potential rationales that underlie the general no-duty rule. And because the harms in these categories are easy to understand and would overwhelm even the "stiff upper lip" people, they tend to address the scope-of-liability concerns as well.

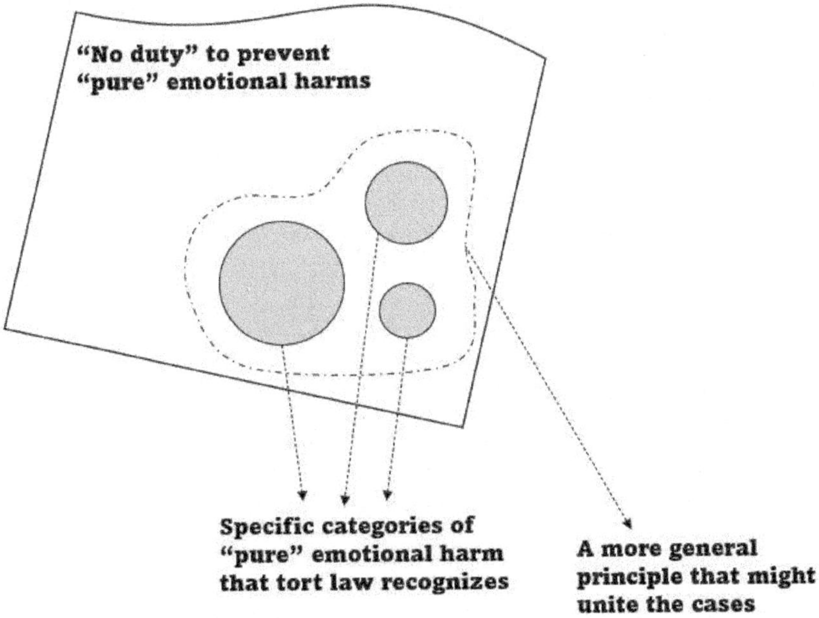

Figure 2.2: Tort law still provides remedies for "pure" emotional harms only in particular, often arbitrary categories. But the law may be moving toward a more general principle.

The specific categories where recovery for pure emotional harm has been available include the following:

- *Near misses, fear of imminent harm, or being in the "zone of danger"*: The plaintiff was nearly injured physically under circumstances in which they *could* have been injured physically but weren't. Historically, this category tended to require the victim suffer a physical impact of some kind (even a very slight one) from the defendant's negligence before imposing liability, but the vast majority of courts have abandoned that requirement as unjustified.

- *Watching a close relative be injured*: This category has typically required that the plaintiff be nearby in space and time to the injury and that the relative be a close one.[129] The defendant's liability to plaintiffs in this category is sometimes described as "derivative" of their liability to the person who was physically injured,[130] leading some sources to say that the negligence of the physically injured victim should be "imputed" to the emotionally injured victim (for the purposes of comparative responsibility; see section 2.7.1).[131] There is little support in actual caselaw for such a rule, though, and it is unclear why it should apply to this particular category of emotional harms but not to the others.
- *Mutilation of corpses*: Included in a chapter of the *Restatement (Second) of Torts* entitled "Miscellaneous Rules" is a rule that those who wrongfully mutilate a corpse are liable to "a member of the family of the deceased who is entitled to the disposition of the body."[132] The liability here is based on the subjective value of the body to the relatives, so the rule rests on an emotional harm.
- *Miscommunicating death*: Some states permit "recovery for emotional harm resulting from negligent transmission . . . of a message announcing death."[133]

Also, several kinds of *intentionally* wrongful acts may enable recovery for pure emotional harms (see also section 2.9). For example, *assault* (which in tort law means putting someone in imminent fear

---

[129] Dillon v. Legg, 441 P.2d 912 (Cal. 1968); *see also* RESTATEMENT (THIRD) OF TORTS: LIABILITY FOR PHYSICAL AND EMOTIONAL HARM § 48 (2012).

[130] *E.g.*, RESTATEMENT (THIRD) OF TORTS: LIABILITY FOR PHYSICAL AND EMOTIONAL HARM § 48 cmt. b. (2013).

[131] *E.g.*, RESTATEMENT (THIRD) OF TORTS: APPORTIONMENT OF LIABILITY § 6 cmt. f (2000) ("In a claim solely for emotional distress caused by physical injury to another person, the negligence of the person who suffers the physical injury is imputed to the plaintiff.").

[132] RESTATEMENT (SECOND) OF TORTS § 868 (1979).

[133] Johnson v. State, 334 N.E.2d 590, 592 (N.Y. 1975).

of battery)[134] and *intentional infliction of emotional distress*—a tort sometimes called *outrage* and which covers only extreme and outrageous conduct that goes well beyond what is socially acceptable—allow plaintiffs to recover for emotional harms without any physical injury.

Often, even when emotional harm falls into these various categories, it needs to reach some level of seriousness (as opposed to, say, transient distraction) for the law to permit a plaintiff to recover for it. The tendency to require some level of seriousness is probably related to the no-duty and scope-of-liability rationales discussed above.

It would probably be better to seek to unite these special categories rather than to keep them separate and disorganized. Again, the categories have a lot in common if viewed at the appropriate level of generality: they address concerns about seriousness (duty), difficulty of distinguishing good cases from bad ones (duty), and fair assignment of responsibility (scope of liability). Instead, the existing categories reflect a piecemeal, potentially inconsistent erosion of the older categorical rule that pure emotional harms do not lead to liability. As is often the case with erosion of older categorical rules, the erosion happens because courts don't see that rule as consistent with social morality or social policy. That explains the slow but steady expansion of liability for pure emotional harms.

The *Restatement (Third) of Torts* throws up its hands and, after listing the category that includes imminent harm, says simply, that "conduct [that] occurs in the course of specified categories of activities, undertakings, or relationships in which negligent conduct is especially likely to cause serious emotional harm" leads to liability if it does in fact cause serious emotional harm.[135] That general description, however, is consistent with the analysis above: when conduct is particularly likely to cause emotional harm and does so, it arguably addresses the general no-duty and scope-of-liability concerns. Ideally the courts and Restatements could eventually unify the categories under a general principle like that, suggesting that the law develop in response to principles rather than focusing on mutilated corpses, mistaken telegrams, or "zones of danger."

2.7 Negligence: Defenses

The two most conceptually significant possible defenses to the negligence cause of action are (1) that the plaintiff's own negligence was responsible, at least in part, for their injury, and (2) that the

[134] *See* RESTATEMENT (SECOND) OF TORTS § 21 (1965).

[135] RESTATEMENT (THIRD) OF TORTS: LIABILITY FOR PHYSICAL AND EMOTIONAL HARM § 47 (2012).

plaintiff *assumed the risk* of injury. The first of these has evolved from an extremely strict rule called *contributory negligence*, under which a plaintiff who was even slightly at fault could recover nothing from negligent defendants even if the plaintiff could prove every element of their prima facie case, to a more proportionate rule called *comparative negligence* under which the plaintiff's negligence reduces but does not eliminate their recovery. *Assumption of risk* is a classical defense but probably adds nothing to the doctrine, has not been consistently applied, and ought to be eliminated as a conceptual feature of the negligence cause of action.

2.7.1 Comparative Responsibility

In the *Goodman* case (see section 2.2.1),[136] where the driver of a car was hit by a train while crossing railroad tracks, the question for the Supreme Court was really the plaintiff's own negligence, not the negligence of the railroad. There had been a trial about whether the railroad should have posted better signals at the grade crossing (the place where a railroad crosses a road), and the jury found that it had not.[137] It also found that the plaintiff was not negligent; both issues had been submitted for trial.

Holmes didn't overturn the decision about the railroad's negligence; he overturned only the jury's decision about the plaintiff's own negligence. The plaintiff's negligence mattered because of a classical defense known as *contributory negligence*, in which a plaintiff loses their entire negligence claim if their own negligence contributed in any way to their harm. Even slight negligence by the plaintiff meant they couldn't recover.

That extremely harsh rule, which arose when the common law tended to prefer yes-or-no decisions over apportionment of damages, eroded in nearly all states in the mid-to-late 1900s. Only a handful of states preserve it. The modern rule that replaced it is called *comparative negligence*, under which a plaintiff's negligence, at least when it is small, reduces but doesn't eliminate the plaintiff's recovery against the defendant. The simple idea is that the jury or other factfinder uses some combination of (1) the degree of each party's fault and (2) an assessment of the importance of the causal role of that fault to determine how *responsible* each party is for the harms that the plaintiff suffered. Then, each party pays its share of the harms. So, for example, if the factfinder determines that the plaintiff was 20% responsible for their injury, the defendant was 80% responsible, and the plaintiff's harms amount to $100,000 in damages, the plaintiff can recover only $80,000, not the full $100,000,

---

136 Baltimore & O.R.R. v. Goodman, 275 U.S. 66 (1927).

137 Baltimore & O.R.R. v. Goodman, 10 F.2d 58, 59 (6th Cir. 1926).

from the defendant. Under the classical rule of contributory negligence, the plaintiff could recover nothing in this scenario.

The procedure just described is sometimes called *pure comparative negligence*. In contrast to that general approach, some states adopt what is called a *modified* approach, where a plaintiff can't recover anything if their share of responsibility is greater than (or in some states equal to) the defendant's. In other words, under *modified comparative negligence*, the old rule of contributory negligence still applies if the plaintiff's share of responsibility is great enough. Modern courts and legislatures have tended to regard either pure or modified comparative negligence as superior to contributory negligence because they allow fairer *apportionment* of harms rather than a general all-or-nothing result. Modified comparative negligence, however, still has potentially harsh discontinuities: under those rules a plaintiff who is 45% responsible for an accident can recover 55% of their damages, but a plaintiff who is 55% responsible can recover nothing.

Because of contributory negligence's harshness, there was a widespread sense that juries would work around it by finding that a plaintiff was not negligent when their negligence was small. Several inconsistent doctrinal exceptions also arose under the rule. Admiralty law, probably because it dealt with complex accidents involving multiple parties' fault before the rest of the law did (for example, before the rise of automobiles), the developed its own earlier principles of comparative negligence. In fact, when Learned Hand laid out the Hand formula, he was actually applying it to judge a *plaintiff's* negligence in an admiralty case, and Judge Hand's conclusion was that he could not "excuse . . . the bargee's failure to care for the barge, and . . . this prevents full recovery."[138]

The principle of comparative negligence generalizes beyond just single defendants; it also allows the factfinder to allocate responsibility among the plaintiff and multiple defendants. For example, in a complex car crash involving the plaintiff and three defendants, *A*, *B*, and *C*, a jury could conclude that the plaintiff is 20% responsible, *A* is 30% responsible, *B* is 40% responsible, and *C* is 10% responsible. If the plaintiff's total damages from the harm would be $100,000, the plaintiff could recover $80,000 from the three defendants combined, and if they were all solvent and all parties to the case, the end result should be that *A* pays $30,000 of that $80,000, *B* pays $40,000, and *C* pays $10,000, all in proportion to their responsibility. This generalization of comparative negligence is called *comparative responsibility*.

---

[138] United States v. Carroll Towing Co., 159 F.2d 169, 172 (2d Cir. 1947).

If some of the defendants are insolvent, a question arises as to whether the plaintiff or the other defendants bear the cost of that insolvency; in other words, does the plaintiff recover less or do the remaining defendants have to pay more than their shares of responsibility would otherwise have required? These rules are much easier than they may appear at first, in part because their terminology is confusing. Under a rule that is called *joint-and-several liability*—it is best simply to treat the phrase as an opaque term of art—the plaintiff is permitted to recover fully from any defendant and to shift the responsibility for allocating that harm any further to the defendants, perhaps in further proceedings (for what the law calls *contribution* among the defendants) that the plaintiff may not even be a part of. It does not permit the plaintiff to recover twice (from two separate defendants), only to pick which defendant should pay and make any further reallocation among defendants their problem rather than the plaintiff's. Joint-and-several liability is the background classical rule of the common law and allows the plaintiff to recover fully even if one of the responsible defendants is insolvent. The rule has been replaced in many states with a rule called *several liability*—again, it is best just to treat it as an opaque term of art—under which each defendant's liability is limited to their share. So, for example, in a case with multiple defendants where the plaintiff is not at all responsible for the harms, a defendant who is 40% responsible may personally have to pay 100% of the plaintiff's damages under a rule of joint-and-several liability but will not be responsible for more than 40% of the plaintiff's damages under a rule of several liability.

In general, this analysis applies to harms that the law considers to be *indivisible*, as might for example result from a complex car crash in which the plaintiff suffers a head injury. If harms are *divisible*—one car runs over the plaintiff's right foot and another runs over their left foot, and the medical bills and other costs of each of those two injuries can be measured separately—then responsibility simply tracks causation. That is, the first driver will be responsible for the injury to the right foot; the second will be responsible for the injury to the left foot.

2.7.2 Assumption of Risk

The classical defense of assumption of risk serves as an excellent lesson in evaluating tort doctrine and determining whether it is structured sensibly.[139] The question to ask about assumption of risk is whether it even adds anything to tort law.

---

[139] *See* Stephen D. Sugarman, *Assumption of Risk*, 31 VAL. U. L. REV. 833 (1997).

The famous case of *Murphy v. Steeplechase Amusement Co.*[140] illustrates the point nicely. The plaintiff was injured on at an attraction or "ride" at what was once the famous Steeplechase amusement park on Coney Island in Brooklyn. The attraction was apparently a high-speed people mover or treadmill. As Cardozo described it:

> It is a moving belt, running upward on an inclined plane, on which passengers sit or stand. Many of them are unable to keep their feet because of the movement of the belt, and are thrown backward or aside. The belt runs in a groove, with padded walls on either side to a height of four feet, and with padded flooring beyond the walls at the same angle as the belt. An electric motor, driven by current furnished by the Brooklyn Edison Company, supplies the needed power. . . .[141]
>
> . . . . Something more was here, as every one understood, than the slowly-moving escalator that is common in shops and public places. A fall was foreseen as one of the risks of the adventure. There would have been no point to the whole thing, no adventure about it, if the risk had not been there. The very name, above the gate, "the Flopper," was warning to the timid.

The plaintiff stood in line watching the attraction and then stepped onto it, at which point he said he experienced a "sudden jerk" and fell down, breaking his kneecap. When he sued the amusement park, their defense was that he "assumed the risk" of that injury: he had seen the ride and voluntarily chosen to get on it.

That argument may seem clear enough, but an important question is whether it is even needed. Did the amusement park do anything wrong in the first place? That is, did they breach their duty of reasonable care? Cardozo's opinion suggests there was nothing out of order on the ride—no bad maintenance, no interruption of the electricity, no lack of appropriate padding at the edge of the treadmill. Was the whole activity unreasonably unsafe? We might think so today: a ride with people falling on top of each other on a high-speed inclined treadmill may not fit with today's understanding of reasonable safety at an amusement park. But Cardozo's analysis of the ride suggests it was well within what was understood to be normal risks at the time. And out of a quarter of a million visitors, there had been some minor injuries but never a broken bone

---

140 166 N.E. 173 (1929) (Cardozo, J.).

141 *Id.* at 173–74.

before.[142] "One might as well," Cardozo concluded, "say that a skating rink should be abandoned because skaters sometimes fall."[143]

To be clear, there is certainly some threshold of unsafety past which, even in Cardozo's day, an amusement-park attraction could be negligent simply for existing and being open to the public. If the ride had not be the Flopper but the Exploder ("Can you survive standing too close to fireworks?")—or, more starkly, Russian Roulette for prizes—clearly the amusement park would be at fault, unreasonable, wrongful, and so on. But Cardozo's opinion makes clear that he has decided substantively from the bench, as in cases like *Harper*, that the defendant has done nothing unreasonable.

In other words, this is simply a no-breach case. The Flopper was more dangerous than walking around or sitting on a carousel, but it was not unreasonably unsafe. To be sure, it might have been unreasonably unsafe to impose the ride on to people who weren't expecting it. As Cardozo wrote:

> The antics of the clown are not the paces of the cloistered cleric. The rough and boisterous joke, the horseplay of the crowd, evokes its own guffaws, but they are not the pleasures of tranquillity. The plaintiff was not seeking a retreat for meditation. Visitors were tumbling about the belt to the merriment of onlookers when he made his choice to join them. He took the chance of a like fate, with whatever damage to his body might ensue from such a fall. The timorous may stay at home.[144]

Suppose that some "cloistered clerics"—that is, monks in an abbey—had decided to play a practical joke on a colleague by setting up a ride like the Flopper at the edge of a dark hallway. The unfortunate colleague enters the hall, steps unknowingly on the Flopper, and breaks his knee. In that case, the boisterous monks have behaved unreasonably—they have subjected their colleague to an unreasonably unsafe risk. So it may seem that voluntarily choosing to come to a risk is an important feature of these cases.

The reasonable-person standard, however, is flexible enough to accommodate the background circumstances (an amusement park vs. a normally quiet and safe abbey), the fact that visitors can see the rides before they choose to get on them, and so on. The question is just one of reasonableness. In other words, it is not unreasonable to set up the Flopper in the way that the Steeplechase park did (though it would be unreasonable to surprise someone with it in a dark

---

142 *See id.* at 175.

143 *Id.*

144 *Id.* at 174.

hallway). As a result, assumption of risk is redundant in *Murphy*; there is no need for a defense because the plaintiff's prima facie case fails on the element of breach.

As Steve Sugarman has pointed out,[145] just as assumption of risk in *Murphy* seems just to mean "no breach," it sometimes stands in for other parts of the negligence claim as well. For example, if athletes can't recover for injuries during a game caused by ordinary negligence, that may seem like (and is sometimes described as) a consequence of assumption of risk, but the no-liability result is based on policy, not specifically the result of voluntarily encountering a risk. So it is simply a no-duty rule.

The doctrine is also problematic because it suggests a principle that is not sound—that engaging in a known risky activity prevents a plaintiff from recovering. On the contrary, people who voluntarily encounter a risk can of course still be successful in negligence lawsuits, as the plaintiff in *Murphy* might have been if there were indeed something unreasonably unsafe about the Flopper. As perhaps a clearer example, automobile drivers well know that there is a risk that other cars might negligently hit them on the road, but nobody thinks there is an assumption-of-risk defense that covers all drivers on public roads. In other words, that the plaintiff voluntarily encountered a risk isn't *really* a defense to their negligence claim.

When plaintiffs voluntarily choose to subject themselves to risks that they knew or should know are unreasonable, that is simply comparative negligence—and the result should be an apportionment of damages between the negligent plaintiff and the negligent defendant, rather than foreclosing any recovery for the plaintiff. Many courts have moved away from assumption of risk on that basis, recognizing that it is inconsistent with comparative negligence. To put that differently, in a world with contributory negligence, the kind of assumption-of-risk doctrine that amounts to plaintiff negligence (sometimes called *secondary assumption of risk*) would do no harm, because plaintiff negligence would torpedo the plaintiff's negligence claim anyway. But in a world with comparative negligence, it is inconsistent to say that a plaintiff who unreasonably approaches a risk thereby exonerates a defendant completely. The proper modern approach is simply comparative negligence and apportionment based on relative responsibility.

Professors still often teach assumption of risk, but it is much easier to reduce it to other elements of the negligence claim. Incidentally, the discussion in this section has been of what some courts call *implied* assumption of risk; *express* assumption of risk is

---

145 *See generally* Sugarman, *supra* note 139.

simply a contract that waives liability—for example, a form that a ski slope gives customers that says that the ski slope is not liable for injuries. Courts are skeptical of such agreements, and their enforcement is inconsistent among the states. They may be treated as contracts that are void as against public policy (see section 3.2).

2.8 Strict Liability

As discussed briefly in section 2.1, a significant policy choice in tort law is whether it is in fact necessary for the plaintiff to prove breach. Sometimes, the law does not require that: it holds defendants liable even if they haven't done anything wrong. This is called *strict liability* and raises many complicated policy questions for the law. Strict liability is ordinarily treated as a separate claim available to plaintiffs—apart from negligence claims—but conceptually it is very much like negligence except for the plaintiff's need to prove breach. In other words, conceptually we can envision the strict-liability cause of action as having elements similar to those of the negligence cause of action, except that the requirement to prove breach is dropped.

2.8.1 A Policy Comparison Between Strict Liability and Negligence

To get across the important features of the policy debate, which has been influenced by the law-and-economics movement, it will be helpful to consider a simple economic analysis of a schematic example (as law-and-economics writers often do). This will also help us review the Hand formula and see several kinds of assumptions the law-and-economics movement tends to make when analyzing rules in the common law.

Imagine that a business faces a choice about whether to spend $800 on a particular type of safety precaution every month. The business expects to cause, on average, $1,200/month in harms to others if it doesn't take the $800/month precaution or $200/month in harms to others if it does take the precaution. So the $800 precaution saves $1,000 in harms. It would therefore be unreasonable and unjustified, under the Hand formula (see section 2.2.1), for the business to fail to take the precaution. In other words, from society's perspective—when considering all costs of accidents and of precautions—the world is better off if the precaution is taken. Therefore, a rule that encourages this outcome is more efficient than one that doesn't. The "cost of harms" may seem like an artificial or even objectionable notion if the harms are injuries to people, so for the purposes of this example it will be fine to imagine the potential harms as minor property damage.

Given this scenario, we might analyze the specific *incentives* the law will give to a hypothetical rational business owner.[146] Usually when legal economists consider the law's incentives for private parties, they analyze those incentives from the perspective of a hypothetical party who is extremely rational, fully selfish, and entirely amoral; this is an artificial, incorrect set of assumptions that often leads legal economists down the wrong path, but the economists do this because their models require it. We can adopt these assumptions for the purposes of this example, even though we wouldn't make assumptions like that in the rest of this book, just to understand the law-and-economics models in this area.

Suppose, then, the rule that the law imposes is one of strict liability. Under this rule, the business will pay for all the harms it causes to others—in other words, $1,200 if it fails to adopt the $800 precaution and $200 otherwise. Because it faces this cost structure, a business facing strict liability will adopt the $800 precaution—which is just what we wanted it to do. To be sure, as with all or nearly all economic models, there are other incorrect assumptions baked into the analysis: for example, the abstract discussion assumes victims will notice and sue for all harms that occur, which plainly isn't true in the real world.[147] But in a schematic example, as a rational, self-interested actor, the business owner will prefer to pay $800 to reduce the business's expected costs by more than $800. That is the result of the law's incentives under a strict-liability rule. To spell that out, if the business fails to take the $800 precaution, it will incur $1,200 in legal liability to others. If it does take the $800 precaution, its total costs will be $800 (for the precaution) plus $200 in legal liability to others, or $1,000 in total. The business would prefer the option that lowers its total cost, so it will take the precaution.

It may seem like a strict-liability rule is the legal rule that would give the business the greatest incentive to take the $800 precaution. But as it turns out, that is an illusion. Strict liability does give the business owner an incentive to take the socially optimal result—the use of the $800 precaution—but so do other rules as well.

Consider a negligence rule. As we noted above, because the precaution is worthwhile, we're imagining that the law treats the $800 precaution as reasonable and the failure to take it as unreasonable. If the owner fails to take the $800 precaution, the

---

[146] *See* ROBERT COOTER & THOMAS ULEN, LAW AND ECONOMICS 9 (6th ed. 2012) ("Economics conceives of laws as incentives for changing behavior (implicit prices) and as instruments for policy objectives (efficiency and distribution).").

[147] *See* William L.F. Felstiner et al., *The Emergence and Transformation of Disputes: Naming, Blaming, Claiming . . .*, 15 LAW & SOC'Y REV. 631 (1980).

owner will be judged (and we're assuming, artificially, that this judgment will be perfectly reliable in court) to be negligent and made to pay for harms that result. So the business owner will want to pay for the $800 precaution. If the business fails to take the $800 precaution, it will incur $1,200 in legal liability, as above. If the business does take the precaution, its total cost will be $800: it will pay for the harm but then avoid legal liability to its victims, because it has acted reasonably, and under a negligence rule the victims will not be able to prove breach.

A negligence rule, then, happens to give the same incentives as a strict-liability rule for the business owner to take precautions. This result generalizes too: it should be easy to work out that if the precaution were *not* worthwhile—socially optimal—the fully rational, fully selfish business owner would not have an incentive to take it under either a strict-liability rule or a negligence rule.

It may be counterintuitive that the incentives are the same between the two rules. This is perhaps one of the reasons that the law adopts both strict-liability rules and negligence rules in different areas. Though we should be cautious in generalizing too much from simple, schematic economic models, if one of the rules were in fact clearly more efficient than the other, we would at least expect there to be some systematic pressure in favor of that rule; unless it were very immoral, for example, or there were some strong policy other than overall social efficiency at stake, courts would favor the more efficient rule. But as the theoretical example suggests, one rule is not clearly more efficient than the other, at least in theory. Indeed, other types of instrumental analyses are similarly ambivalent when they compare strict liability with negligence. For example, as economists have pointed out, there will tend to be more lawsuits under a rule of strict liability (because more plaintiffs will have legal rights against the business owner—we've effectively removed an element from the negligence cause of action, meaning more victims will be able to establish prima facie claims), but those lawsuits will tend to be less expensive (because the parties to the lawsuits won't need to dispute breach).[148]

Note that while the *incentives* are the same between the two rules, not all other consequences are the same. As we saw above, the business pays more under a rule of strict liability than under a rule of negligence when it takes the precaution: under strict liability it still pays for the harm it causes, whereas under negligence it escapes liability to victims as long as it acts reasonably. Because of this, lawyers and economists say that rule of strict liability will force the

---

148 *See, e.g.*, COOTER & ULEN, *supra* note 146, at 223–24.

owner to *internalize* the costs of the harms that the business causes to others. A rule of negligence, by contrast, will let the owner *externalize* those costs onto others as long as it acts reasonably.

One further step of analysis is worth considering and comes up in many Torts courses in the United States, though less commonly in court cases. Suppose, hypothetically, the business owner faced a rule of *no liability*—rather than strict liability or negligence. For example, imagine the business owner is protected by a hypothetical no-duty rule that applies to the particular scenario in our example. If that is the law, it may seem like a fully rational, fully selfish business owner will not take an $800 precaution just to prevent harms to other people. But that may not be true. If the potential victims are aware of the $1,000 in harms that the business may cause them if the precaution isn't taken, and if they can organize successfully and bargain with the business owner, they would be willing to pay the business owner up to $1,000 to encourage the business owner to take the $800 precaution. The business would presumably not accept such a "bribe" unless it's $800 or more, because otherwise it would not cover the cost of the precaution. So between $800 and $1,000, the parties—the business owner and its potential victims—have a potential deal to make. If they can make this deal, the business owner will still take the precaution. This conclusion is called the *Coase theorem* after Ronald Coase, an early member of the law-and-economics movement who analyzed this kind of situation in 1960.[149] To restate the Coase theorem's conclusion as it applies to this formal example, it is that as long as there aren't significant enough impediments to bargaining between an injurer and its potential victims, the legal rule—strict liability, negligence, or no liability—doesn't have any effect on the precautions taken against injuries. All legal rules produce the same incentive. The rules matter only if the parties can't successfully bargain with each other.

In any event, the law adopts all three possibilities in different scenarios. The typical rule in US tort law is a negligence rule. Occasionally, as we have seen (see section 2.3), the law adopts a no-duty rule instead. And as we will see in the rest of this section, US tort law occasionally adopts focused rules of strict liability. In other words, in some specific situations, typically for reasons of policy or principle—just as in no-duty cases—the common law has determined that unreasonableness is not an element of the claim against some defendants.

There is no single justification, or even a consistent set of them, that explains why strict liability has arisen in the particular cases

149 R.H. Coase, *The Problem of Social Cost*, 3 J.L. & ECON. 1 (1960).

where it has arisen (which will be discussed in the next several sections). Instead, different courts and commentators have justified strict liability with different rationales. One is *cost internalization*, as suggested earlier: activities should pay their way. If the business in our earlier example sells soda, it is an appealing idea that the business face the costs associated with its operations; it can then pass these costs onto customers by raising the price of soda. This new, slightly higher price will more accurately reflect soda's true overall cost to society than a price that allows the soda manufacturer to externalize that cost. An idea closely related to cost internalization is *enterprise liability*, or the principle that a large business or group of them is an effective mechanism to absorb and spread risk. Strict liability also more readily ensures compensation for people who are harmed; an injured victim, facing uncovered medical bills and lost wages, needs compensation even if the person who injured them was not negligent.

Strict liability is hard to generalize, however. If it is tied only to causation—a notion sometimes called *absolute liability*—it is hard to put into practice because a single accident will have uncountably many factual causes: if a car hits a pedestrian, the car accident would not have occurred but for the driver's decisions to drive, the pedestrian's decision to walk, both parties' parents' decisions (or otherwise) to have children, the car manufacturer's creation of the car, the city's determination to put a road in a particular place, a company's construction of the road, and so on. Negligence—that is, a focus on wrongful conduct—allows courts to identify a limited set of these causes based on blame rather than causation alone. There are other, fairly complex economic arguments in favor and against negligence rules and strict liability rules in tort law,[150] and commentators have suggested many types of theoretical justifications for different forms of strict liability.[151]

2.8.2 Respondeat Superior

Probably the most important example of strict liability is *respondeat superior* ("the higher-up should answer"—that is, the employer should answer for the torts of its employees). Under this doctrine, employers are liable ("vicariously") for the torts of their employees within the scope of their employee. We already saw an example of the development of respondeat superior doctrine in the book's introduction (see section 1.5.2).

---

[150] *See* Shawn J. Bayern, *The Limits of Formal Economics in Tort Law: The Puzzle of Negligence*, 75 BROOK. L. REV. 707 (2010).

[151] *E.g.*, George P. Fletcher, *Fairness and Utility in Tort Theory*, 85 HARV. L. REV. 537 (1972).

Respondeat superior functions as a hybrid between negligence and strict liability: normally, a plaintiff needs to show that an employee was negligent—but once the plaintiff does that, they may recover against an employer as a matter of strict liability. In other words, the employer is responsible even if it has done nothing wrong, but only if the employee has done something wrong. If the employer *has* acted unreasonably—negligently failed to conduct appropriate background checks on its employees, negligently supervised its employees, kept someone on staff when it had a reason to know that person was unreasonably dangerous—it may be liable for the employee's torts *both* under direct negligence (for its own fault) *and* in respondeat superior.

Respondeat superior is a settled part of the common law, although perhaps surprisingly there is no consensus on its justifications. If strict employer liability is the right principle (perhaps on a theory of enterprise liability or cost internalization), why doesn't the law hold the employer liable even when its employees were acting reasonably? If negligence is the right principle, why isn't the employer liable only when it is at fault? Sometimes it's argued that respondeat superior is necessary because negligence liability is operationally unsuitable to fully judge employers' management of employees—given the complexity of large organizations and the difficulty of understanding them from outside—but it is hard to see why management of employees is harder to judge than many other types of conduct that the negligence standard applies to. (And employers are commonly sued directly for negligence or other wrongful activity, without any evident systematic problem in those lawsuits.) Sometimes the justification is tied to employees' control over—and their benefit from having—employees. Probably the most realistic reason that respondeat superior developed and remained important is that tort law would be substantially reduced without it: most individual employees don't have enough money to make a lawsuit worthwhile. And execution of a judgment for damages against individuals, as compared to companies, tends to be difficult and unreliable.[152] So perhaps it has simply been an important practical bulwark, even if not an entirely principled one, against the potential for widespread and uncompensated injuries.

As an aside, though it doesn't normally come up in Torts courses, under US business law partners in general partnerships (though not the owners or controllers of most other forms of legal organization) are effectively liable for each other's torts that occur in the course of

---

[152] For further reading on the justifications (or lack of them) for respondeat superior, see Gary T. Schwartz, *The Hidden and Fundamental Issue of Employer Vicarious Liability*, 69 S. CAL. L. REV. 1739 (1996).

the business. This liability has a very similar result to respondeat superior, except without the employment relationship and without some of the potential justifications of respondeat superior. That rule too has remained, though it is easy to avoid by setting up a business form other than the general partnership, like a corporation or a limited liability company (LLC). (It is very easy and typically very inexpensive to set up new legal organizations in US states.)

The two main legal questions that arise in respondeat superior cases are (1) whether the injurer was an employee and (2) if so, whether a tort occurred while the employee was within the scope of their employment. There are no simple answers to these questions, and different lawyers, professors, and courts have different views on them.

Probably the best way to answer the first question—is someone an employee?—is simply to ask whether the putative employer had control over the way that the putative employee did their job. When someone is not an employee—often the alternative is called an *independent contractor*, though that is not usually a formal legal term—they typically have freedom in how they go about completing their work, whereas an employer has a right to control the conditions of work to a great degree. The distinction between employees and independent contractors is one of degree more than one of kind. Another factor that may be relevant is simply convention: if someone shows up to an office building owned or rented by a single large company, and they work there from 9:00 to 5:00 alongside workers of the same company, they are probably an employee of that company. As an example of how convention can matter, professors are employees of their universities even though principles of academic freedom give the universities comparatively little control over the details of professors' work. Note that the labeling in the parties' contract and the tax treatment of the employer's payments don't dictate for tort law whether someone is an employee or not. Note also that employees, for the purposes of respondeat superior, may be unpaid; indeed they may even be casual volunteers.[153]

The *Restatement (Second) of Agency* listed no fewer than ten separate factors that could bear on whether someone is an employee or not.[154] These factors are quite specific and by now seem dated, oriented at a world where labor was structured differently from the way it is structured today. By contrast, the *Restatement (Third) of Agency* adopts a view similar to the one I described above, though it focuses only on whether the employer can "control the manner and

---

153 *E.g.*, Heims v. Hanke, 93 N.W.2d 455 (Wis. 1958).

154 RESTATEMENT (SECOND) OF AGENCY § 220(2) (1956) (using the antiquated terms "master" and "servant" instead of *employer* and *employee*).

means of the agent's performance" and does not list what I've called "convention" as a separate justification.[155] How the Restatement's rule would address professors, for example, is technically unclear—although professors are almost certainly employees for the purposes of respondeat superior.

The second question, *scope of employment*, has also been subject to significant confusion. This area was covered by the doctrine and cases we saw in section 1.5.2. A few further observations may be helpful here. First, scope of employment may depend on whether the tort that occurred was a characteristic risk of the employment or not.[156] Second, intentional torts can be included within scope of employment, even though many lawyers who don't specialize in tort law seem to think otherwise. Third, though courts and commentators tend not to recognize this principle overtly, scope of employment is somewhat "sticky": once an employee is acting within it, it takes a kind of escape velocity (to draw an analogy to physics) or activation energy (to draw one to chemistry) for them to move out of it, and vice versa.[157] (Commutes to and from home are not within the scope of employment, for example.) Fourth, some cases say, as we saw in section 1.5.2, that for employees to be within their scope of employment, they need to be motivated, at least in some tiny part, by the interests of their employer at the time the tort occurred. As we also saw in section 1.5.2, however, that principle has not been consistently applied and has led to significant confusion, and many cases simply ignore it; it would be better if courts stopped applying that principle.

Note that respondeat superior is not ordinarily a *benefit* of employment or a no-duty rule for employees. Though they rarely do so, plaintiffs can still choose to sue the individual employees who have negligently harmed them, rather than suing the employers; "I was just doing my job" is not ordinarily a defense to a tort suit. Indeed, if an employer is liable on a respondeat superior claim, it can normally seek *indemnification* from the employee—that is, it can require the employee to reimburse it for its liability—on the theory that the employee is at fault and the employer is innocent. This rarely happens because employees usually don't have enough personal assets or insurance to make a lawsuit worthwhile, and perhaps it would look bad for companies to do it in most cases. But it is

---

155 RESTATEMENT (THIRD) OF AGENCY § 7.07(3) (2006).

156 *See, e.g.*, Ira S. Bushey & Sons, Inc. v. United States, 398 F.2d 167 (2d Cir. 1968) (Friendly, J.).

157 *Cf.* Fiocco v. Carver, 137 N.E. 309, 311 (N.Y. 1922) (Cardozo, J.) ("The field of duty once forsaken, is not to be re-entered by acts evincing a divided loyalty and thus continuing the offense."); SHAWN J. BAYERN, CLOSELY HELD ORGANIZATIONS 63 (2d ed. 2020).

permitted by the underlying legal rules. An exception to this general pattern is for employees of the federal government[158] and volunteers to nonprofits or governments;[159] statutes provide no-duty rules that limit or eliminate liability of those individuals while acting within the scope of their employment.

2.8.3 Products Liability

The theory of enterprise liability (see section 2.8.1) may be particularly relevant to mass-marketed consumer products. Injuries from products—badly made cars, glass packaging that shatters too easily, and (in a famous case) exploding soda bottles[160]—can easily be internalized into the products' costs; those who mass-manufacture products tend to be large enough to absorb and spread the costs of the injuries that their products cause. Products-liability law has also been influenced by the contractual situation of products—they are purchased by consumers who may have particular expectations about how the products are supposed to function—even though under modern products-liability law, those who manufacture and resell defective products can be strictly liable to third parties who never bought the products. Another related potential justification for strict liability in this area is that consumer products are commonly mass marketed, so people interact with them as if they are the same as identically branded items and generally safe when sold to the public.[161]

It is commonly said that modern products liability is an area of strict liability, but that is only partly true. Modern law has developed three categories for product liability,[162] and only one of them is clearly and consistently strict. That category is known as *manufacturing defects*. A manufacturing defect occurs when a product turns out less safe than it was intended to turn out. For example, a jar of peanuts has a shard of glass in it, or a car has an incorrectly welded part that causes a crash. Often, but not always, manufacturing defects are unique, idiosyncratic results of the mass-manufacturing process. For example, even if all reasonable precautions are taken, one in a million products from a particular assembly line might not work correctly. Under modern law, the manufacturer—and in general downstream sellers like retailers—are strictly liable for manufacturing defects. This is true strict

---

[158] 28 U.S.C. §§ 2671–2680; *see* RESTATEMENT (THIRD) OF AGENCY § 7.01 (2006).

[159] 42 U.S.C. § 14503; *see* RESTATEMENT OF CHARITABLE NONPROFIT ORGANIZATIONS § 2.09(a) (2021).

[160] Escola v. Coca-Cola Bottling Co., 150 P.2d 436 (Cal. 1944).

[161] *See* Sugarman, *supra* note 42, at 608.

[162] *See* RESTATEMENT (THIRD) OF TORTS: PRODUCTS LIABILITY § 2 (1998).

liability; the cases are clear that manufacturers and retailers can be liable even if they've taken all reasonable precautions.

The second category is for *design defects*—where a whole line of products was designed badly. Note that "badly" is something of a value judgment, and at least one test that courts have used and that the Restatement has adopted comes very close to saying that products with design defects are simply those that were negligently designed. For example, the Restatement defines design defects as occurring

> when the foreseeable risks of harm posed by the product could have been reduced or avoided by the adoption of a reasonable alternative design by the seller or other distributor, or a predecessor in the commercial chain of distribution, and the omission of the alternative design renders the product not reasonably safe.[163]

In other words, a product has a defective design when some precaution should have been taken to adopt another "reasonable" design. That is just a negligence standard—not one of strict liability—because it depends on unreasonableness.[164] To be sure, even under this test the law imposes some strict liability. First, retailers and other intermediaries can be liable for selling a product that has a design defect even if they have done nothing wrong themselves. (That type of liability is not universal, however; often if a manufacturer is available as a defendant and is solvent, victims injured by a product are required to sue the manufacturer instead of retailers.) Second, the law's focus is on the product, not on proving fault on the part of some particular employee or other decision maker at the manufacturer. Still, under this rule for analyzing design defects, the law comes very close to saying that there is strict liability for doing something negligent—which isn't really strict liability.

An alternative legal test for design defects is called the *consumer-expectations test* and would simply ask whether a product departed from the reasonable safety expectations of consumers. If so, it is defective on that basis. That test, depending on how courts apply it, could come closer to strict liability for design defects.

The third category is for *warning defects*, or insufficient warnings. The Restatement just asks for "reasonable instructions or warnings,"[165] which again reflects a negligence rule rather than a strict-liability rule. For example, if a knife is sharper than it looks—perhaps it looks like a butter knife but is extremely sharp—the

---

163 *Id.* § 2(b).

164 *See* Sugarman, *supra* note 42, at 589.

165 RESTATEMENT (THIRD) OF TORTS: PRODUCTS LIABILITY § 2(c) (1998).

warnings that accompany it could be defective by failing to point out the sharpness.

The separation between the last two of these categories—design defects and warning defects—arises largely for historical reasons, and there is little principled basis for it. For example, under the Restatement's negligence-like tests, there is no reason to inquire about the boundary between "design" and "warning." A simpler approach that would unify the two categories is to treat things that are sold as a combination of physical features, marketing, warnings, circumstances, background knowledge, software, etc. Under all the circumstances, is the product appropriately safe? If so, it's not defective; if not, it's defective. Indeed, there is no way to know in the abstract, without at least some of that more general kind of analysis, whether a "product" is defective. Consider an unlabeled vat of white paint. If marketed as baby formula, it is clearly inappropriately unsafe. If it is very dangerous to inhale but is included in a shipment of paints to be used indoors, it could be defective on that basis unless it includes appropriate warnings. But it is not defective because of what it is; it is defective because of the context that the manufacturer or intermediary resellers have put it into. If the law's attention is to be focused on the product's safety rather than the conduct or decisions of the actors who made and distributed it, the question should simply be whether the product, all told, is inappropriately unsafe or not. That can be judged by asking about reasonable alternative designs or about consumer expectations, but under either approach there is little reason to have separate rules for "designs" and for "warnings."

2.8.4 Other Areas of Strict Liability

Some states have focused strict-liability rules, often in statutes, that extend strict liability to particular narrow areas. For example, under Florida's statutes:

> The owner of any dog that bites any person while such person is on or in a public place, or lawfully on or in a private place, including the property of the owner of the dog, is liable for damages suffered by persons bitten, regardless of the former viciousness of the dog or the owners' knowledge of such viciousness.[166]

The common law has developed some rules that are similarly specific. For example, people who choose to own "wild animals" are considered strictly liable even if they take reasonable precautions in

166 FLA. STAT. § 767.04 (2022).

handling and confining the animals.[167] Maybe keeping wild animals in areas where they could harm other people is itself unreasonable, though, so it is not clear how much of a difference this category makes unless courts refrain for artificial reasons from judging as negligent a land possessor's background decision to keep a dangerous undomesticated animal as a pet.

Perhaps wild animals are just a special instance of a more general category of liability that the common law has developed: liability for *abnormally dangerous* activities.[168] (Certainly another category of strict liability that applies to animals—specifically, for keeping *abnormally dangerous animals*, which is to say those that are not "wild" but individually have unusually dangerous tendencies[169]—is just a specific instance of this more general category.) The category of abnormally dangerous activities has not been consistently applied. Its core seems to be that doing something dangerous and unusual (at least in a particular locale) leads to strict liability. The canonical example is destroying a building with dynamite. If a demolition company is judged to be faultless, having taken all reasonable precautions, they will avoid liability for hurting third parties while destroying a building with a wrecking ball or jackhammers (because the background rule of negligence applies to those activities) but face strict liability for harms they cause if they use dynamite.

There has never been a clear rationale for that rule. One possible justification may come from the economic analysis of law, which would favor strict liability when the injurer is the only party who can take precautions against harms. Most situations involve what economists call *bilateral precaution*, or at least the potential for both the injurer and the victim to take precautions. But maybe cases of abnormally dangerous activities are those where there is no meaningful opportunity for the victim to take precautions because the activity is so unusual that victims can't have foreseen it. Still, is dynamite really different from jackhammers when it comes to potential victim precaution?

Cases in this category do not come up frequently, but they reflect a more general puzzle in tort law: why does the law sometimes, but not always, choose strict liability? Is there anything that unifies the various separate categories where the law imposes strict liability, from respondeat superior to abnormally dangerous activities, so that we can see where the law is heading and why? Are the categories

---

167 RESTATEMENT (THIRD) OF TORTS: LIABILITY FOR PHYSICAL AND EMOTIONAL HARM § 22 (2010).

168 *See id.* § 20.

169 *See id.* § 23.

sound in view of morality and policy in the first place? The major moral motivations for these categories, apart from the general need for compensation when victims are injured, may have to do with reasonable social expectations, at least with respect to products liability and abnormally dangerous activities.[170] In other words, in those categories, someone has caused something *unusual* to happen, and maybe focusing on the unusual is a sufficient basis for imposing and also limiting strict liability (because, again, strict liability for simply causing harms could never really be applied in the general case, given the large number of causes of every event). But an explanation along those lines wouldn't explain respondeat superior.

2.9 A Simple View of the Rest of Tort Law: Harmonizing the Intentional Torts

This chapter has focused on negligence and strict liability, which typically concern accidental harms. For several reasons, it does not cover intentional torts in detail.

As Steve Sugarman has put it, "there are simply too many separate 'torts.' "[171] This is particularly true of what are called the *intentional torts*: battery, assault, false imprisonment, defamation, and so on. For all those torts, the defendant has normally behaved wrongfully—that is, at least unreasonably—so they have breached a duty of care. The narrow individual torts can be subject to no-liability exceptions on policy grounds—for example, the possibility of *defamation* liability (for speaking falsely about others and causing reputational harm) is sharply limited in the United States because of the First Amendment—which are simply no-duty rationales. Causation and scope of liability work similarly between negligence and the other torts, or at least vary according to relatively straightforward principles. In the end, what we have learned in this chapter so far can very easily be applied to all the various narrow intentional torts; the same framework, with the same conceptual elements, governs—even if the doctrinal law would list different, more technical elements for each of the separate torts.

For example, because of this kind of correspondence, Sugarman has made "a bold proposal: eliminate the intentional tort of battery and merge cases of both the negligent and intentional imposition of physical harm into a single new tort."[172] As background, there remains a separate cause of action for *battery*—an intentional physical contact (e.g., touching or punching someone) that is harmful

---

[170] *See* Sugarman, *supra* note 42, at 608.

[171] Sugarman, *supra* note 42, at 591.

[172] Stephen D. Sugarman, *Restating the Tort of Battery*, 10 J. TORT L. (2018), https://doi.org/10.1515/jtl-2017-0020, at 1.

or offensive. Battery has its own defenses, like *consent*, which can be *implied* even when it doesn't exist—for example, in circumstances where it's not unreasonable to touch someone. Taken as a whole, in view of both its elements and its defenses, committing a battery is at least *unreasonable*. For example, if I tap an acquaintance gently on the shoulder in a public place to get their attention, that is not a battery—but we could also simply say I have done nothing wrong, not acted unreasonably, and so on. If I punch the acquaintance in the nose for no reason, I have acted unreasonably. On that view, it is not clear what battery adds conceptually to tort law; it doesn't add a new standard of conduct, for example.

Battery law is probably not going away anytime soon. But it is arguably easier to analyze in view of the general principles we've already studied—duty, breach, causation, and scope of liability—than to study separately. For that reason, many Torts courses—and probably an increasing number of them—spend the vast majority of their time focused on negligence and strict liability. As discussed at the start of the chapter, the negligence claim is of much more practical importance anyway.

Just for quick reference, the most significant intentional torts involving individuals are battery,[173] assault (putting someone in apprehension of an immediately forthcoming battery),[174] false imprisonment (detaining someone),[175] and intentional infliction of emotional distress (see section 2.6.2).[176] There are also torts more closely associated with property law, like trespass,[177] private nuisance,[178] and conversion (see section 4.6).[179]

2.10 Conclusion

The substantive elements and defenses of the negligence cause of action—duty, breach, causation, scope of liability, comparative negligence, and assumption of risk—can serve as a template for considering legal claims in general. They can helps us identify and organize the questions that are relevant to liability under the common law:

- *Breach* is an opportunity to determine whether the defendant's behavior was wrongful (unreasonable, at fault, etc.) or not. Ordinarily behavior needs to be

---

173 *See* RESTATEMENT (SECOND) OF TORTS § 13 (1965).

174 *See id.* § 21.

175 *See id.* § 35.

176 See *id.* § 46.

177 *See id.* §§ 158, 217.

178 *See id.* § 822.

179 *See id.* §§ 222A, 223.

wrongful to trigger liability in tort law, though in a handful of cases the element of breach is functionally waived. We say that a principle of *strict liability* applies to those cases.

- *Duty* is an opportunity to rule out an entire class of cases from the legal system, usually because of some specific policy or other value, or because judges think that the legal system can't easily administer some cases or that they aren't worth the resources of the court system.
- *Causation* ties plaintiffs to defendants, usually but not always through a specific imaginative but largely factual question: if the defendant had behaved differently, would the plaintiff still have been injured? In many cases, causation is obvious, but often there are problems proving it. In some of those cases, we relax or shift the plaintiff's burden to prove it, possibly because it was arbitrary that the plaintiff should be asked to prove it anyway. The policy of causation is, in many respects, the policy of risk management and assignment as between plaintiffs and defendants.
- *Scope of liability*, still more commonly called *proximate causation*, is an opportunity to deny liability on grounds of fairness, responsibility, or perhaps some other intuition that the plaintiff's injury isn't why we have declared the defendant's conduct to be wrongful. Older conceptions of this element tie it to a *direct* link between the defendant's negligence and the harm or to whether the harm was *foreseeable* at the moment the defendant was negligent.

If the plaintiff passes all those barriers, they have established a prime facie case. But they may still lose if the defendant establishes defenses. Putting aside *assumption of risk*, which probably adds nothing to the doctrine, the main defense in a negligence cause of action is *comparative negligence*: the plaintiff should not be able to recover fully if their own wrongfulness contributed to their harm.

That template, and its specific structure and terminology, arises from the elements and defenses in the negligence cause of action. But we can apply it to tort law more generally, and doing that makes other torts easier to understand and can help to simplify and clarify the doctrine. As we will see in the next chapters, a similar framework can help us understand other legal subjects as well. For example, in contract law, the rules of *consideration* act much like no-duty rules.

And while we don't normally speak of the difference between strict liability and negligence when discussing issues outside tort law, we may find the same struggle between those concepts in other areas of the law.

Chapter 3

CONTRACT LAW

Contents

Contract law is the law of enforceable promises.[1] A person who makes a promise is called a *promisor*, and a person who receives a promise is called a *promisee*. Often parties to a contract are both promisors and promisees, but when lawyers discuss breach of contract they use the term *promisor* to refer to the person who hasn't kept their word and the term *promisee* for the person who didn't receive what they were promised.

An important general theme that becomes apparent in the study of contract law is the significant historical change in the subject—between an apparently orderly[2] but overly formalistic *classical* version of contract law and a more adaptive *modern* contract law.[3] Because of that change, the chapter demonstrates some processes of long-term change in common law: the inconsistent application, erosion, and replacement of rules; the distinctly lawyerly practice of reaching a shared recognition of how to get around certain existing rules that are widely understood, even by judges, to be undesirable; and the development of helpful but incomplete statutes.

---

1 As the Restatement puts it, "A contract is a promise or a set of promises for the breach of which the law gives a remedy, or the performance of which the law in some way recognizes as a duty." RESTATEMENT (SECOND) OF CONTRACTS § 1 (1981).

2 "Despite appearances, coherence and uniformity [in classical contract law] were often more apparent than real, even within the covers of contract treatises. . . . [C]racks in the edifice were already very apparent." WARREN SWAIN, THE LAW OF CONTRACT 1670–1870, at 201 (2015).

3 In part because of the degree of historical change, the term *classical* is widely used by commentators across common-law systems to refer to the older and more formalistic contract law.

3.1 What Promises to Enforce? The Doctrine of Consideration

A major question in contract law is what promises to enforce. Just as no tort system in the world compensates victims for every physical injury—or even every physical injury caused by wrongful action—no legal system in the world enforces all promises. Instead, legal systems struggle with that question.

In the common law of contracts, the surprisingly rich and intricate doctrine of *consideration* answers this question. The doctrine is not of great operational significance itself—for example, most practicing lawyers don't deal with it on a routine basis, although it can be helpful for them to be aware of it in the background—but it is an extremely useful topic for showing the common law in action and for learning parallels between the subjects of the common law.

For one thing, consideration functions very much like no-duty rules do in tort law: it gives courts an opportunity to declare that some cases are best not heard by the legal system, for reasons of policy or principle, even if the defendant is at fault. Consideration isn't usually taught in this way—and sometimes it's presented in an extremely formalistic and technical fashion—but when courts hold that there's "no consideration," they're making a decision very similar to the one they make when they say "no duty" in negligence cases. That is, in saying that there's "no consideration," a judge is determining that a type of contract dispute is not one for the legal system to address, usually because an injury is too small, the case will be too difficult to hear or decide correctly, or the judge has identified a policy that's more important than remedying a broken promise in an individual case. Those are all classic no-duty rationales (see section 2.3.1).

Consideration caselaw also happens to be filled with examples of precedents that have eroded, purported rules that aren't really rules, complex policies, and interactions between policy and morality. It therefore serves as an excellent lesson about the kind of material that sophisticated common lawyers need to learn.

3.1.1 Promises and Social Morality

In modern law, consideration—despite the doctrinal mess—mainly serves a simple function: it distinguishes between promises to give a gift (*gift promises*)[4] from promises that are made as part of

---

[4] In opinions and commentary, *gift promise* and *donative promise* mean the same thing. *Gratuitous promise* is a formal term from classical contract law that many professors still use. It is not a particularly helpful term, however; it simply refers to any contract without consideration. In that term, "gratuitous" means "free" as in

a bargain (*bargain promises*). The general rule is that bargain promises are enforceable generally and gift promises are enforceable only when relied upon (or in a handful of other cases). That is more or less the current state of affairs in US contract law, but a lot of complexity and history underlies that simple statement.

As background, people make promises for various reasons. The most common reason is probably, as discussed in the next section, to induce other people to provide something of value (or to make their own promise). Another is like Odysseus in Homer's *Odyssey*—the example usually used to demonstrate this idea. Odysseus has been told of the legend of the Sirens, birdlike creatures with an alluring song that causes sailors to want to continue listening to the song rather than do anything else. (In that respect, Sirens operate a lot like social media.) To survive while sailing near the Sirens, sailors would plug up their ears with wax. But Odysseus, being the selfish captain he was—he eventually lost literally all his sailors!—wanted to hear the song himself. He also wanted not to die. So he told his sailors to plug up their own ears but to tie him to the mast of the ship and refuse any orders he later gave to release him. What he has done is to try to indicate to others, at an earlier time, that his preferences at that time should override his later preferences:

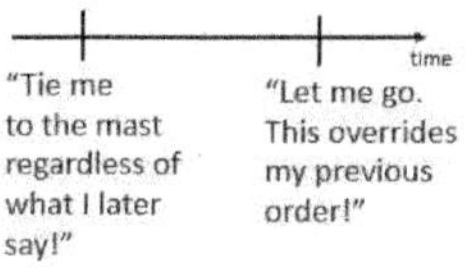

Figure 3.1

The same sort of motivation may underlie some promises. For example, someone might make a large pledge to a nonprofit today because it will discourage them from changing their mind in the future. Or someone might agree to complete a paid project because they know that the contract will motivate them to work in the future, despite what they regard as their own occasional tendency toward laziness.

Promises often don't use the word "promise." There are ordinarily no magic words in contract law, and a promise is normally anything reasonably understood to provide an assurance of one's future behavior. Saying firmly that you will do something can be

"freely made," but in that sense the term *gratuitous* is inaccurate because many contracts that classical law treated as lacking consideration are in fact not made freely but instead made for particular business purposes.

enough to constitute a legally binding promise; indeed, when people negotiate small deals, they often don't use the explicit language of promises but simply say things like, "I'll fix that door for $300" or "I'll give you $50 for that hat."

A clear feature of social morality is that it's wrong to break a promise. It's not *necessarily* or *absolutely* wrong; for example, it's not wrong to break a promise extracted at gunpoint or a promise to take someone to dinner but then suddenly be unable to do so because of a medical emergency. But people agree that promises should generally be kept and that breaking them is wrong. That sort of "wrong" is like breach in negligence cases; there is a judgment in social morality that someone has behaved in a way they shouldn't have behaved. It's wrong (in general) to break a gift promise and it's wrong to break a bargain promise; on that front, as a matter of social morality, the two types of promises are similar.

3.1.2 Bargain Promises

Breaking a bargain promise, however, gives the law a more significant reason to hear a case and to provide a remedy. In particular, legal enforcement of bargain promises provides important support for systems of trade and for a market economy.

The idea behind bargain promises' value is simple enough: making a commitment that others can rely on enables some exchanges that are difficult otherwise. For example, I may not want to pay a builder until they complete their work, but the builder may not want to begin work without an assurance of payment. If we exchange promises (of their work for my payment) and we think those promises will be carried out, we're more likely to enter a deal. Legal enforcement makes it more likely that each promise will be carried out, so it increases the likelihood of a deal.

It is important not to overstate the law's role in enabling commerce through bargain promises. Legal enforcement of promises is just one way for parties to a bargain to reach confidence that each other's promises will be followed. Contract law is a very important tool, but Contracts professors sometimes talk as if it is the *only* tool. In practice, people ordinarily follow through on their promises—including bargain promises—even when there is no meaningful threat of legal enforcement because the case is too small, the proof is too difficult, or the parties are otherwise unwilling to sue. In those cases, the internalized moral force of making a promise, the parties' reputational concerns, and other informal pressures are usually enough to discourage promisors from breaking their promises (and for promisees to reach confidence that promises won't be broken). Law supports those moral, reputational, and other social forces in general, however, and in borderline cases makes it more likely that commerce will be concluded successfully. For those reasons, bargain promises have the full weight of the market economy behind them, and courts and commentators consider it important to enforce bargain promises. Moreover, while breaking any promise is immoral, breaking a bargain promise may be particularly wrongful because it involves taking advantage of someone else and unilaterally rewriting or canceling a deal that both parties once thought was appropriate.

Enforcing bargains is also consistent with a broader notion that people are usually in a good position to figure out how to order their own basic affairs. At least in the kinds of societies we live in, we imagine that letting people allocate their money among particular groceries, and between groceries and mobile phones and other goods and services, is likely to promote their happiness more than the dictation of those choices by other parties. Enforcing bargains lets people bind themselves and, as a result, lets them make trades that might otherwise be difficult for them to make. These principles are not absolute, and there are doctrines for duress,[5] misrepresentation,[6] incapacity,[7] unconscionability (see section 3.2),[8] and public policy[9] that limit their application, but in general bargains have many reasons to be enforced.[10]

As a result, the general pattern in modern common law is that bargain promises are enforceable just on the basis that they're bargains. For historical reasons, however, legal doctrine is considerably more complex than the simple rule that bargain promises are enforceable. To put that differently, if we were starting from scratch, we could perhaps simply declare that promises in a commercial setting or promises that involve an economic bargain are enforceable. The law is moving toward but hasn't yet reached that point, instead getting there slowly and inconsistently. The resulting complexity is unfortunate but serves as an important lesson about how common law changes and about the difference between what courts say and what they do (see section 1.5.1). Much of consideration law that's "on the books" is very different from the way courts apply the doctrine, so learning simple statements of black-letter rules is likely to be particularly unhelpful in this area.

---

5 RESTATEMENT (SECOND) OF CONTRACTS §§ 174–176 (1981).

6 *Id.* §§ 159–173.

7 *Id.* §§ 12–16.

8 *Id.* § 208.

9 *Id.* §§ 178–199.

10 For background on the policies behind the enforcement (and occasional nonenforcement) of bargain promises, see Melvin Aron Eisenberg, *The Bargain Principle and Its Limits*, 95 HARV. L. REV. 741 (1982).

3.1.3 How Does the Law Distinguish Bargain Promises from Gift Promises?

Again, if our goal is simply to enforce bargain promises, contract doctrine could just ask whether the promise in any particular case is part of a bargain or made for reasons related to market transactions. But the doctrine developed differently, and the main black-letter rule is that promises are not enforceable unless each was given for *consideration*.

Under the common law, a party gives consideration when they give something up, no matter how small, as the price to get something in return from the other party. The most-taught case that expresses the modern view is *Hamer v. Sidway*.[11] An uncle promised his nephew a large amount of money "if [the nephew] would refrain from drinking liquor, using tobacco, swearing, and playing cards or billiards for money until he should become 21 years of age."[12] The court treats the nephew's adherence to these terms as consideration—that is, enough to constitute a bargain and therefore to enforce the uncle's return promise. To be clear, in reality the uncle's promise is largely a gift; nobody thinks the uncle would make the same offer to everyone in the city in an effort to purchase puritanical behaviors in bulk, and there's not even particular evidence in the case that the uncle is trying to do anything other than help his nephew. But because the situation contains even the tiniest bit of a bargain—"I will pay you if you don't do something that you could have done"—the "deal" is enforceable. That is still the rule in modern law, and it reflects a policy that it's better to err on the side of enforcing an interaction that's mostly a gift than to fail to enforce a bargain. After all, breaking even a gift promise is still wrong, and the reasons for enforcing bargain promises are so strong that they're not worth risking in borderline cases.

Hamer is often taught because it dispels an older confusion in consideration law that bargains must involve "benefits" or "detriments" on both sides. Courts, treatises, and study guides still sometimes use terminology like that, but it's more confusing than helpful. In *Hamer*, the uncle's estate argues that the nephew didn't give anything up—provided no consideration—because as a factual matter refraining from alcohol, tobacco, swearing, and gambling only *helped* the nephew by instilling good habits. That argument comes up only because of the confusing terminology of "benefits" and "detriments." As the *Hamer* court puts it, "It is sufficient that [the nephew] restricted his lawful freedom of action within certain

---

11 27 N.E. 256 (N.Y. 1891).

12 *Id.* at 256.

prescribed limits upon the faith of his uncle's agreement, and now having fully performed the conditions imposed, it is of no moment whether such performance actually proved a benefit to the promisor," adding that the uncle was "benefited in a legal sense," by definition, simply because the nephew met the terms of the deal.[13] In other words, the notions of benefit and detriment aren't in fact relevant; all that matters is that each side gives something up—no matter how small—by doing something they didn't have to do, refraining from something they could have done, or making a promise that restricts the scope of their freedom in some way.

3.1.4 The Illusory Doctrine of Illusory Promises

It's easy to see how an act or omission, even if small, can count as consideration. Promises can be a little more complicated because they concern future possibilities. Consider a promise like "If I win more than a million dollars in the lottery, I agree to invest in your company." That promise still restricts the scope of the promisor's freedom—and therefore can count as consideration—because, even though it's unlikely they'll win the lottery, they've made a commitment about what they'll do in that case. In other words, even though in practice it probably won't make a difference to the promisor's life, it causes them to give up a small bit of (probabilistic) moral freedom. Economically, the right to that potential million dollars has at least some value, even if small.

What about a promise like "If I buy this house, I promise I'll lease it to you for a year"?[14] That promise raises the additional complication that the promisor can *choose* not to buy the house, so it may seem as if the promisor can choose to avoid any obligation under the promise—and therefore that the promise doesn't restrict the promisor's freedom in any way. But that view is mistaken. Before making the promise, the promisor was free to buy the house and lease it to anyone else (or not lease it at all), but after making the promise, the promisor is no longer morally free to take those combinations of actions. If the promisor buys the house, the promisor is bound to lease it to the promisee. As a result, that promise, too, can count as consideration.

Sometimes, however, a promise appears to restrict the scope of the promisor's freedom but doesn't. It has the form, but not the function, of a promise. "If I feel like buying your house on Friday, I

---

[13] *Id.* at 257.

[14] *Cf.* Scott v. Moragues Lumber Co., 80 So. 394 (Ala. 1918). *Scott* is in many Contracts casebooks but contains an atypical and mostly unhelpful analysis because the promisor in *Scott* argues, poorly, that their *own* promise is illusory. Normally, as discussed in the text, a promisor tries to show that their own (real) promise is unenforceable because they received only an illusory promise in exchange for it.

will buy your house on that day." Maybe, very abstractly, the promisor could emotionally "feel like" buying the house on Friday and yet refuse to do so, but concretely there is no way for the promisor to violate that promise. Though the statement is made in the form of a promise, it isn't really a promise, and it doesn't morally bind the purported promisor in any way. For that reason, it's called an *illusory promise.* The dependence on the promisor's "feelings" could be removed to make the example even clearer: "If I decide on Friday at noon to buy your house, I will buy your house on Friday at noon."

Why does any of this matter? It doesn't under most legal systems, and truly illusory promises are rare and generally appear only in theory. The problem is that many real contract cases—routine deals that would be unremarkable to most businesspeople and most legal systems—trigger a technical, formalistic objection in the common law that has threatened to derail their enforceability. That objection is sometimes called the *illusory-promise rule* or the rule of *mutuality of obligation* (under which "both parties need to be bound under a contract or neither is bound"). It arises when one party argues that they shouldn't be legally bound because, technically, they received only an illusory promise from the other party (and the illusory promise doesn't count as consideration because it doesn't restrict the promisor's freedom).

The best example of that kind of case is *Wood v. Lucy, Lady Duff-Gordon.*[15] The defendant, known as Lucile, was an English socialite and fashion designer who, among other things, had survived the sinking of the *Titanic.* She hired Otis Wood, a prominent American marketing agent, under a contract that made Wood her exclusive licensing agent for certain purposes. Wood, as Justice Cardozo explained,

> was to have the exclusive right, subject always to [Lucile's] approval, to place her indorsements on the designs of others. He was also to have the exclusive right to place her own designs on sale, or to license others to market them. In return, she was to have one-half of "all profits and revenues" derived from any contracts he might make.[16]

This type of "exclusive" agency is commonplace because it encourages investment by agents and avoids potential disputes. For example, the seller of a house might agree to appoint a particular real-estate agent as an exclusive agent for four months and to promise the real-estate agent 6% of the value of any sale made in that period—rather than only those sales that the agent obtained through

[15] 118 N.E. 214 (N.Y. 1917).

[16] *Id.*

their own effort. That way, the agent will be motivated to sell the house without fearing that others are trying to do the same, and the parties don't have to worry about disputes over whether it was "really" the agent or the homeowner who identified a particular buyer.[17]

Anyway, Lucile breaches the contract in *Wood* by making a licensing deal herself and keeping the money—thus violating her promise that Wood was to have the exclusive right to make such deals. Wood sues. Lucile's response isn't "I didn't break my promise" but "it's okay for me to break my promise because you gave me nothing in return." To put it more precisely, Lucile's argument is that Wood's obligations under the contract do not count as consideration because the sum total of his promises in the contract are illusory: Wood, according to Lucile, hasn't in fact promised to do anything. For example, under the contract, he could make or not make licensing deals as he saw fit; he was not required to commit any specific amount of his time or resources to Lucile's account.

To be clear, Lucile's defense is purely a legal one, not a moral one. She is still wrong for breaking a promise. Her legal position is (in kind, if not in degree) much like that of a defendant in a tort suit who says "Yes, I could have thrown a life-preserver to that drowning child, but I didn't have any legal obligation to do so" (see section 2.3.2). That is often a weak position, and just as in the cases in which the "no duty for easy rescue" rule has been restricted, the illusory-promise rule has been sharply eroded. In fact, the illusory-promise rule is probably among the least favored black-letter doctrines in the common law. As one court has put it: "It is presumed that when parties make an agreement they intend it to be effectual, not nugatory. A contract will be construed in favor of mutuality. The modern decisional tendency is against lending the aid of courts to defeat contracts on technical grounds of want of mutuality."[18] Another agrees, in more vivid language: "As a contract defense, the mutuality doctrine has become a faltering rampart to which a litigant retreats at his own peril. . . . [T]he 'mutuality' doctrine crumbles of its own weight."[19]

The reason for this is simple. Consideration doctrine—which looks for both of the parties to have restricted some of their freedom as part of a bargain—often accurately identifies bargain promises,

---

[17] Judge Posner, in *Beanstalk Group, Inc. v. AM General Corp.*, 283 F.3d 856 (7th Cir. 2002), appears to neglect or reject these advantages of exclusive agency.

[18] Texas Gas Utilities Company v. Barrett, 460 S.W.2d 409, 412 (Tex. 1970) (internal citations omitted).

[19] Helle v. Landmark, Inc., 15 Ohio App. 3d 1, 12 (Ohio Ct. App. 1984) (citing *Corbin on Contracts*).

but it is sometimes a crude or imprecise way to do so. Lucile's defense amounts to little more than an argument that her promise to Wood was a gift promise—that, because she received no specific promise from Wood in return for her own promise, she is in the same position as an aunt promising to pay her nephew's college tuition and then changing her mind. But that is clearly inaccurate. Her contract with Wood is a licensing deal made at arm's length so that both parties can make money. If the goal of consideration doctrine is to separate contracts like that from personal gift promises that don't have the force of a market economy behind them, it fails dramatically if courts take the illusory-promise rule too seriously.

Lucile's argument is so bad that it's surprising it ever works at all. In *Wood* itself, it did persuade the intermediate appellate court in New York, but Cardozo declined to take Lucile's invitation to treat her promises to Wood as effectively gift promises. The way Cardozo does this is perhaps a little dishonest: in order to find that Wood has given consideration, he treats the contract as including an implied agreement by Wood to exercise "reasonable efforts" to market Lucile's name and make licensing deals. This isn't a terrible or unrealistic term to imply, and it happens to be broadly consistent with the Uniform Commercial Code's modern approach.[20] But it's important to see that the "implication" is needed only because the formalistic version of the classical consideration doctrine treats Lucile's promise as unenforceable unless Wood gave her something in return—even if the contract is clearly commercial. In other words, Cardozo is implying an obligation for Wood only because he needs to. He's working around a problematic doctrine because he doesn't feel as if he's in a position to overrule it fully. In doing so, he develops a new rule—exclusive agents implicitly promise to use reasonable efforts—but that rule doesn't have freestanding merit on moral or policy grounds; it exists mainly to erode the illusory-promise rule.[21]

To understand more fully how the illusory-promise rule has eroded, it will be helpful to see in more detail why Lucile's promise in *Wood* was, in fact, part of a bargain. Suppose Wood didn't in fact make any specific promises to Lucile and was forthright about his unwillingness to do so. "I'm quite busy," we might imagine him saying. "Lots of people want my services. My work speaks for itself, and most of my clients have become considerably richer. I can't make any specific promises to you, because I don't know in advance who

---

[20] *Cf.* U.C.C. § 2–306(2) ("A lawful agreement by either the seller or the buyer for exclusive dealing in the kind of goods concerned imposes unless otherwise agreed an obligation by the seller to use best efforts to supply the goods and by the buyer to use best efforts to promote their sale.").

[21] *See* Melvin Aron Eisenberg, *Probability and Chance in Contract Law*, 45 UCLA L. REV. 1005, 1026 (1998).

will want to license your name, but I think you'll be happy to have me scouting licensing opportunities for you." Lucile is of course free to walk away from such a deal; maybe she wants an agent who is more accountable or responsive to her particular wishes. But it's not crazy to think she'd sign on, because what she values is the *opportunity* Wood provides, not the specific promises that Wood has or hasn't made to her. Clearly, her motivation is commercial; even if Wood makes no promise to her, she's not giving him a gift but trying to increase the likelihood that she optimizes the value of her brand through licensing deals. In other words, Wood could have given her specific promises—"I'll spend 20% of my working time on your contract"—and his efforts would have been more valuable, and perhaps more costly, if he had done so. But that was not the deal the parties reached.[22]

Accordingly, Lucile has made a bargain with Wood, even if Wood hasn't made any specific promises about using "reasonable efforts" or any efforts at all. And as a bargain, it has all the usual reasons to be enforced. The law could recognize the particular bargain between the parties directly—or at least see that Lucile's motivation is commercial (and self-interested) rather than donative (intending to bestow a benefit on Wood)—and that is exactly what leading Contracts professor Mel Eisenberg has proposed[23] and what some courts have adopted.[24] In other words, Lucile's bargain is not for a promise but for an increased probability of valuable commerce—for Wood's attention, for being in his list of trademarks to license, for a chance that he would produce significant value using his connections. One of classical law's failures was not to pay enough attention to probability.

Though a bit unfair to Cardozo, we might say that he gets around the formal need for consideration in *Wood* just by making it up—by finding consideration that isn't there. Courts have developed many other strategies to get around the illusory-promise rule. One is simply to lean heavily in favor of consideration—to find the smallest possible consideration in a contract and say that that is enough.[25] For example, courts might find that even if a party can choose not to have any obligations under a contract, they were bound very briefly before they gave notice to cancel the contract.[26] Or courts might find some procedural or conventional or implied obligation that one of the

---

22 *See id.* at 1026–27.

23 *See id.*

24 *See, e.g.*, Harris v. Time, 191 Cal. App. 3d 449 (1987).

25 *E.g.*, Miami Coca-Cola Bottling Co. v. Orange Crush Co., 296 Fed. 693 (5th Cir. 1924).

26 *E.g.*, Gurfein v. Werbelovsky, 118 A. 32 (Conn. 1922).

parties had.[27] But probably the most honest approach is to recognize the structure of the underlying bargain and find consideration by following that structure. For example, in *Wood*, a court could simply say that what Wood "gave up" was some of his attention and time—an act rather than a promise. In other words, if Lucile is not specifically looking for a promise in her dealings with Wood, there's no reason to limit our search for consideration to Wood's *promises*. Contracting parties can easily trade a promise for an action or a course of conduct, and that is probably just what's happening in *Wood*. A chance at valuable future commerce can be an important part of a deal; for example, perhaps Wood's reputation and the upside possibilities of working with him were worth more to Lucile than specific promises by a competing marketing agent of lesser repute.

For that reason, as Mel Eisenberg has put it, perhaps "the illusory promise rule is not so much wrong as irrelevant."[28] In other words, maybe the rule doesn't need to be fully overruled; it can just be avoided. Indeed, maybe that's the only reason the rule still exists at all.

That leaves the doctrine on this topic in an interesting position, but one that is very instructive. There is a black-letter rule of law (an illusory promise is not consideration). It is based on an old formal axiom that formal consideration is needed to enforce a promise—that each party needs to give something up, even if small, for there to be a bargain. The rule can be found in many cases and other sources, like the Restatement.[29] But the rule is unlikely to be followed, at least by any knowledgeable court that is paying attention. The state of the law on the subject is captured best by the evocative quotes from courts given above: "The modern decisional tendency is against lending the aid of courts to defeat contracts on technical grounds of want of mutuality"[30] and "the mutuality doctrine has become a faltering rampart to which a litigant retreats at his own peril."[31] *That*, not the black-letter rule, is the law.

Note all the learning it takes to understand the state of the law on this topic: (1) the classical, formal principle of consideration (each party must give something up, even if small); (2) the application of that principle to produce a particular result (the law does not enforce even some fair, productive commercial deals that are in fact bargains); (3) the fact that that result is an undesirable one (because it gets in the way of fair, productive deals); that is, the rule is both

---

27 *E.g.*, Md. Supreme Corp. v. Blake Co., 369 A.2d 1017 (Md. 1977).

28 Eisenberg, *supra* note 21, at 1015.

29 RESTATEMENT (SECOND) OF CONTRACTS §§ 76–77 (1981).

30 *Barrett*, 460 S.W.2d at 412.

31 *Helle*, 15 Ohio App. 3d at 12.

unfair to litigating parties and gets in the way of productive contracts in the future; (4) the courts' tendency, because they reject the useless result of the classical formalistic rule, to avoid it, often by going out of their way to find consideration or even making it up. A common lawyer practicing in this field needs to understand all those steps in order to understand the law in this area. Stopping at the black-letter rule would cause the lawyer to make an entirely incorrect prediction.

There are other lessons that the rule of illusory promises (or, to say the same thing, mutuality of obligation) can teach us. Maybe the most important is that common-law rules can't easily be evaluated as good or bad in the abstract. When many people first encounter the rule of mutuality—"both parties need to be bound or neither is bound"—it sounds fair enough at that abstract level. But that proposition doesn't survive contact with real scenarios. Again, in *Wood*, there is no reason for Wood to be bound to do anything; the terms of the deal between the parties are probably that he provided value simply by taking Lucile on as a client in exchange for her commitment to make Wood her exclusive agent. There is no reason for both parties to be bound as a precondition for contract liability. To put that differently, the contract between Lucile and Wood is not unfair just because the parties are not equally bound. Contracts *could* be unfair because of that disparity, but this one isn't. Maybe in some early cases the illusory-promise doctrine gave courts a blunt tool to strike down contracts that today we would call unconscionable because they were so severely and substantively one-sided, but that problem is better addressed by a doctrine of unconscionability (see section 3.2).

Another lesson is that the common law is not monolithic or fully consistent, and it doesn't need to be. I said earlier that knowledgeable courts that are paying attention would probably not apply the illusory-promise rule. Not all courts are knowledgeable about contract law, however, and not all are paying attention closely to the progress of the law. Perhaps a law clerk (a recent law-school graduate working for the judge) learned a formalistic rule in law school and supplies it to the judge, whose practice area before they became a judge was criminal law or taxation. Some courts have more formalistic or classical tendencies. Some perhaps use the illusory-promise rule as a way to strike down a contract that they could strike down for other reasons, but they are motivated to avoid basing their decisions on those reasons because doing so would require implying terms that the courts aren't sure about into contracts. Whatever the reason, courts still occasionally apply the illusory-promise rule,[32] so

[32] *E.g.*, Office Pavilion S. Fla., Inc. v. ASAL Prods., Inc., 849 So. 2d 367 (Fla. Dist. Ct. App. 2003).

lawyers can't ignore it entirely. It is still a tool in a litigator's toolbox, even if it's a "faltering rampart."

A final lesson—an important but subtle one—is that the very inconsistency in the doctrine of illusory promises is a powerful indication that the rule is an undesirable one. Judges would not be motivated to create inconsistent or fictional exceptions, like reading in a duty to use best efforts when the parties probably didn't intend that duty, if the rule were sound. As with the complexity in the duties of landowners in negligence law (see section 2.3.4) or the erosion of the no-duty-to-rescue rule (see section 2.3.2), the complexity here—the fact that the current rule on the ground can't be simply stated but has to be described as a "faltering rampart"—itself gives us a reason to look more closely and more skeptically at the rule.

3.1.5 The Legal-Duty (or Preexisting-Duty) Rule

The legal-duty rule is similar to the illusory-promise rule in that it derives from a "logical" application of classical consideration doctrine but produces an undesirable result. The rule is simply that a promise to perform a preexisting legal duty is not consideration. The rule has three main applications. First, a promisor might promise not to do something that is prohibited by criminal law: "I promise not to burn down your shop if you'll pay me $1,000 a month." Second, a promisee might try to claim a reward for doing something that the law already obligated them to do: the victim of a crime might post a $50,000 reward, and then a police officer might solve the crime and try to claim it. Third, the parties to a contract might agree to modify it in such a way that only one side gives something up: "I know I agreed to finish this construction job for $20,000, but I now see that you're in a rush and nobody else is around to do it, so I refuse to complete the work unless you pay me $30,000 instead"—and the other side agrees because they don't have any reasonable choice.

The three particular examples I've just given are three cases where a promise *should not* be enforced. The apparent usefulness of the legal-duty is one of the great coincidences of classical contract law. In other words, the legal-duty rule, which is based simply on classical consideration doctrine—a promise to do something that was already legally required gives up no new moral freedom and is therefore not consideration under classical law—appears to achieve three useful policy goals cleanly at once. This apparent usefulness, however, is an illusion—and, again, just a coincidence.

Consider the first application of the legal-duty rule—promises not to break the criminal law. First of all, cases where parties negotiate about one side's adherence to the criminal law *are* bargains and have some of the normal policies of bargains behind them. The problem with a contract like "I'll pay you $1,000 a month if you don't burn down my shop" isn't that one of the parties is making a gift promise; it's that the contract constitutes extortion and is made under duress. Such a contract can and should be prevented simply on the ground of duress, a contract doctrine that provides a defense when one side threatened a crime (or made some other wrongful threat).

Not all contracts where one party promises not to break the law are products of duress, however. Consider a variation of *Hamer* in which the nephew is suffering from an addiction to meth and the uncle says, out of concern for his nephew and perhaps the family's reputation, "If you agree to check yourself into a clinic and don't use any meth for a year, I'll give you $100,000." The nephew agrees. That would be an uncontroversially enforceable bargain because the nephew doesn't have any obligation to check himself into a legal clinic. But suppose the uncle is slightly less forceful and simply says, "If you agree not to use any meth for a year, I'll give you $100,000," and the nephew agrees. There, the nephew is promising to do only something that he was already legally obligated to do—assuming he's in a society that knows about methamphetamine and has criminalized it, as opposed to the real case, which took place more than a hundred years ago. Suppose the nephew complies with his promise and doesn't use meth for a year, maybe because he was motivated to check himself into a clinic in order to cure his addiction and claim the $100,000. Is there any reason not to enforce the uncle's promise? First, the uncle would be morally wrongful to break the promise; it is, after all, a promise, regardless of whether the uncle received consideration for it. Second, the uncle is trying to extract something from the nephew (his compliance with the law) as a price; the parties are indeed bargaining. Third, the result of the bargain is useful to society: less crime. There is no duress; the uncle is initiating the transaction and isn't under any unreasonable pressure himself. Finally—and this is a lesson that creativity is often useful against formalistic reasoning—even on formalistic grounds, the nephew *has* in fact given something up in making his promise, even though the law already required him not to use meth. Before the nephew made the promise, if he used meth his only legal risk was that he'd be prosecuted criminally. After the nephew makes the promise, he additionally risks, at least formally, a lawsuit from his uncle for breach of contract.[33] So the uncle's promise should be treated as being made for consideration—that is, as part of a genuine bargain—and should be enforced.

---

[33] *Cf.* RESTATEMENT (SECOND) OF CONTRACTS § 73 cmt. b. (1981) ("If the legal duty is not owed to the promisor, there is consideration . . . .").

Consider the second application of the legal-duty rule: bribes to public officials. Those are simply illegal and can be struck down on that basis alone. Paying a police officer so that they'll pay special attention to your case is not consistent with how we want the police force to be run. Moreover, bribing a public official to do something to help you that's *not* within their job description is still wrongful, even though there would be consideration for such a deal: "If you let me cut this line at the DMV, I'll pay you $100" is not a deal that lacks consideration, but it's just as wrongful as the DMV officer insisting, "I won't process your application for a driver's license unless you privately pay me $100." Though it may appear relevant at first, consideration is not in fact helpful in these cases. It serves at best a coincidental, haphazard role. The problem is bribery, not gift promises.

As for the third application—contract modifications—the problem with the legal-duty rule is that it assumes contract modifications are problematic.[34] The example I gave above—a contractor who extracts an extra $10,000 after making a contract just because they can get away with it—is a case of a bad modification that also happens to lack formal consideration. The reason it is problematic is that it is the result of economic duress; the other party has no reasonable choice but to pay the extra fee that the contractor demands.[35] But a modification that lacks formal consideration could just as easily *not* be the product of duress. For example, suppose an employee has a one-year contract to work for $85,000 a year. The cost of living has increased recently, and the employer notices that the employee is experiencing some difficulty paying their bills. The employee asks for a small salary increase to $90,000, and the employer agrees, thinking that the employee will be more productive if they don't have to spend so much time figuring out how to pay bills. The parties draw up and sign a new employment contract with no new terms and the same end date as the original contract. The employer has received no consideration: formally the employee hasn't agreed to anything new but is receiving a raise. There is no duress. The employer has promised to pay the extra money; it would be wrong to break that promise. (Note that the employer did not have to agree; there is no general duty in the common law to accede to a requested modification, to negotiate toward one, or even to entertain the idea.) There appears to be no policy reason the new contract

---

[34] *See* Melvin Aron Eisenberg, *The Emergence of Dynamic Contract Law*, 88 CAL. L. REV. 1743, 1763–67 (2000) (adding that "there is nothing to show that an extremely high proportion of modifications are made under duress, or even that modifications are commonly made under duress").

[35] *Cf.* Lingenfelder v. Wainwright Brewery Co., 15 S.W. 844 (Mo. 1890).

should not be enforced. The only barrier is the classical rule of consideration.

In other words, in many cases of contract modification—to which both sides have agreed—the modifications have morality in their favor and have the usual policy of enforcing bargains in their favor as well. But cases of contract modification can be substantively tricky because of the need to resolve a tension between two contracts between the same parties that may contradict each other. Just like the case of Odysseus mentioned earlier (see section 3.1.1), the parties have given conflicting instructions (to each other and to the courts) at two different times:

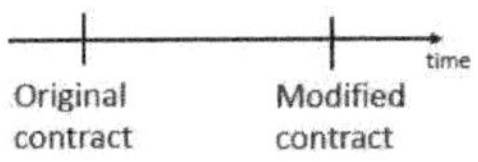

Figure 3.2

In Odysseus's case, it seems clear that his earlier instruction ("tie me to the mast") is a better order to follow than his later one ("let me jump off the ship to my death just to be closer to the Sirens") because we know that at the later time Odysseus's judgment is compromised. But we have no reason in the general case to think that the parties' judgment was compromised when they both chose to modify their contract. That is, there is no systematic reason to think that the parties were more trustworthy, capable, or wise when they made their original contract than when they modified it. And indeed there are some reasons to think that, if anything, the parties' judgment later in time is likely to be better: after all, over time people learn new information, and even if that weren't true, their later judgment is closer to the present day (and courts' deliberations) than the original contract is. The only significant reason to be skeptical of modified contracts is the possibility for economic duress by one of the parties, which is perhaps more likely when parties already have an ongoing relationship (on which one may have depended) than when they don't.[36]

In real-world disputes, contract modifications can pose difficult problems. The factors that seem to matter to courts in determining whether a modification should be enforced instead of the original contract are (1) whether the party who requested the modification was acting in good faith, rather than only in an attempt to extract more money from the other party for a selfish purpose, (2) how much pressure the other party was under in agreeing to the modification,

---

36 *See* Eisenberg, *supra* note 34, at 1763–67.

and (3) how much circumstances have changed since the original contract was made.[37] If, on the timeline in Figure 3.2, the parties have learned nothing new and circumstances have stayed entirely the same, there is at least an initial question about why a modification is worthwhile.

The Restatement's test for whether a contract modification is enforceable starts with the first factor, implicitly incorporates the second, but promotes the third factor perhaps a little more than it should: "A promise modifying a duty under a contract not fully performed on either side is binding . . . if the modification is fair and equitable in view of circumstances not anticipated by the parties when the contract was made . . . ."[38] This is not a wholly problematic test, but perhaps *external* circumstances haven't changed and the parties simply have realized that their original contract isn't quite right. We could treat that recognition among the parties alone as "circumstances not anticipated by the parties when the contract was made," but it would probably be better to *consider* but not *require* changed circumstances. The Restatement gives this illustration:

> *A* is employed by *B* as a designer of coats at $90 a week for a year beginning November 1 under a written contract executed September 1. *A* is offered $115 a week by another employer and so informs *B*. *A* and *B* then agree that *A* will be paid $100 a week and in October execute a new written contract to that effect, simultaneously tearing up the prior contract. The new contract is binding.[39]

Suppose, however, that *A* has not in fact gotten a new offer but the employer simply recognizes that $90 a week was perhaps too sharp a deal—perhaps not in line with salaries offered to *B*'s other employees—and voluntarily offers a raise. There, there are no changed circumstances, but there is also no bad faith and no pressure, so the modification should be enforced.[40] Note that, in classical terms, there is no consideration for the modification, but the employer's new promise of a higher wage is made in a commercial context. It is generous but not a gift. It is motivated by fairness but not love. Even in the Restatement's illustration, there is no classical consideration, but there is no reason of fairness or policy not to

---

[37] *Cf. id.* (emphasizing the first two of these factors).

[38] RESTATEMENT (SECOND) OF CONTRACTS § 89 (1981).

[39] *Id.* § 89 cmt. b illus. 3.

[40] Moreover, as I believe Mel Eisenberg points out in his teaching, employees get new offers all the time, so is an offer from another employer really, in the Restatement's terms, an event "not anticipated by the parties when the contract was made"?

enforce the modification; it is, after all, what both of the parties have voluntarily agreed to.

In cases of contract modification the legal-duty rule would strike down many modifications that are entirely unproblematic.[41] Moreover, because it is a blunt instrument, it is not a particularly effective tool against promises extracted under duress. Take a case that is sometimes promoted as an example of the effectiveness of the legal-duty rule, *Lingenfelder v. Wainwright*.[42] An architect agrees to draw up plans and oversee the construction of a brewery. Disappointed and perhaps surprised that the brewery decides not to purchase refrigeration services from a refrigeration company he happens to run, the architect refuses to work unless he is paid more. Facing delays and not having a good alternative, the brewery agrees to pay the architect more. The architect completes the promised work and demands the higher payment from the brewery, but the brewery agrees only to pay the original amount. The architect sues and loses.

The result is correct: the architect has tried to use the position that the contract puts him in just to extract more money from the brewery than he was able to negotiate originally. But the legal-duty rule, being just a rule of consideration, would be insufficient to stop the architect from doing this if he were more sophisticated in negotiating the modification that he demanded. If the architect were aware of contract law, there are many things the architect could do to extract the extra payment he seeks without running afoul of the legal-duty rule. First, he could simply demand a present payment. A payment that is actually made does not require consideration; consideration is needed only to enforce *contracts*, and binding transfers of property can occur without any consideration at all. To put that differently, consideration is just a doctrine of contract law; it doesn't prevent parties from transferring property (*cf.* section 4.4). Moreover, even if the brewery does not yet have the money that the architect wants, or what the architect wants is a promised stream of payments in the future, the parties can arrange future payments by presently granting the architect an interest in a company, like a corporation or an LLC. Second, the architect could in fact promise to do something he didn't have any obligation to do, thereby giving up some of his freedom in a way that constitutes consideration. For example, the architect could say "I will agree to revise my plans for the bathroom, adding special tiles on the wall, if you pay me an additional $50,000," when the work to revise such plans costs much less. As we will see later, this runs the risk of being merely *nominal* consideration (see section 3.1.7), but well-advised parties in a

---

41 *See* Eisenberg, *supra* note 34, at 1763–67.

42 15 S.W. 844 (Mo. 1890).

situation like *Lingenfelder* can probably get a court to err on the side of enforcing such a modification.

The legal-duty rule, then, strikes down some good modifications and is insufficient to stop some bad ones extracted under duress. We still need a doctrine of duress (or perhaps rules that develop specifically to evaluate the fairness of contract modifications) in order to determine whether a contract modification should be enforced.

The overall result is that in all three major types of case to which it applies—threats to commit crimes, bribery, and modifications—the legal-duty rule is either superfluous, ineffective, or wrong. Because of its poor fit with parties' functional business goals and fairness—and despite its apparent applicability to many cases, which again is just a coincidence—the legal-duty rule has been sharply eroded in modern law. Like the illusory-promise rule, it at least sometimes still lurks in the background, but courts and legislatures have gone even further in overruling or limiting the force of the legal-duty rule than they have done for the illusory-promise rule, possibly just because contract modifications are so commonplace and so important. Lawmakers have done this in several ways.

First, the Uniform Commercial Code (UCC), in its article that applies to contracts for the sale of goods, has simply repealed the rule: "An agreement modifying a contract within this Article [i.e., for the sale of goods] needs no consideration to be binding."[43] It is not as if the legal-duty rule is more appropriate to contracts for services, real-estate, or intangible items than it is for goods; it is just that the relevant article of the UCC happens to apply to contracts for the sale of goods. So, for example, if the architect in *Lingenfelder* had, instead of architectural services in the past, been supplying flooring or appliances today, the legal-duty rule would not apply to the case—and instead courts would need to focus on the substantive merits of the modification itself if they were to strike it down.

Second, recognizing that modifications may be fair and useful even when they formally lack consideration, many modern courts have simply chosen affirmatively and directly to overrule or disregard the legal-duty rule.[44] One court that did so referred to the "modern trend away from a rigid application of the preexisting duty rule."[45]

Third, as this chapter later discusses (see section 3.1.7), contracts that have been relied upon can be enforced even without consideration. In other words, the legal-duty rule treats a promise as

[43] U.C.C. § 2–209.

[44] *E.g.*, Angel v. Murray, 322 A.2d 630 (R.I. 1974).

[45] *Id.* at 636.

if it as gift promise, and gift promises have other ways they can be enforced. This again shows the brittleness of the legal-duty rule and its inability to police contract modifications effectively.

Fourth, there is a significant amount of flexibility in classical doctrine that would allow courts to find a modification enforceable even if it lacks consideration. One possibility comes from the doctrine of "waiver," which allows one party under some circumstances to substantively change the terms of a contract in the other party's favor. For example, in *Clark v. West*,[46] a professor of corporate law was writing a book for the corporate predecessor of West Academic—the publisher of this very book!—under a contract that would pay him more if he would "totally abstain from the use of intoxicating liquors" while writing the book. (West Academic no longer includes such a condition in its contracts.) The publisher agreed not to insist upon that condition—that is, it agreed to pay the author the higher rate even if he drank a little. Such a "waiver" is often enforceable without consideration, though the caselaw on the topic is elaborate and inconsistent.[47]

There is also some confusion in the doctrine about the difference between a contract modification and "mutual rescission" followed by a deal that purports to be an entirely new contract.[48] That is, perhaps even under the logic of classical consideration, parties who have an agreement can go through the following steps, each of which has consideration, to produce a result that if completed in a single step would appear to lack consideration: (1) the parties agree to release each other from their old contract; this step has consideration on both sides because neither party had an obligation to release the other from their contractual duties; (2) the parties then sign a new contract; this step has consideration because, having been freed from their contractual obligations, the parties had no obligation to work with each other again. Of course, there is little substantive difference between modifying a contract and executing the two steps above at the same time, but courts may treat the latter differently—at least if a modification is substantively unproblematic—because of their opposition to the legal-duty rule. The murkiness of the doctrines of waiver and mutual rescission suggest that they are occasionally used inconsistently to erode the legal-duty rule and are not based on independent principles.

In short, if the role of consideration doctrine is to make sure bargain promises are enforced (separating them from gift promises;

---

46 86 N.E. 1 (N.Y. 1908).

47 *See* RESTATEMENT (SECOND) OF CONTRACTS § 84 (1981).

48 *See, e.g.*, 2 CORBIN ON CONTRACTS § 7.15 (2022); Watkins & Son v. Carrig, 21 A.2d 591 (N.H. 1941); Schwartzreich v. Bauman-Basch, Inc., 231 N.Y. 196 (1921).

see section 3.1.7), the policies behind the doctrine are largely inapplicable to modifications of commercial contracts. That is, modifications to commercial contracts are not normally made out of affection or love; they are made as part of a commercial relationship. They should ordinarily be enforced, unless the modifications themselves are extracted unfairly—which is not something that a binary rule about the presence or absence of consideration is sensitive enough to detect.

3.1.6 The Legal-Duty Rule and Doctrinal Change

As the last subsection described briefly, the legal-duty rule has sometimes been affirmatively overruled, not just quietly eroded. An old case that, in its time, resisted that development provides a useful lesson on "certainty" in the common law.

The case is *Foakes v. Beer*, an English case from the 1880s.[49] Despite its age, *Foakes* is a helpful example to demonstrate how arguments against doctrinal change are sometimes groundless, because it exhibits very clearly (1) an undesirable precedent, and (2) a decision that rests almost entirely on a hollow appeal to the certainty of doctrinal stability. When examined carefully, it serves as a demonstration of the importance of context-sensitive analyses of certainty in legal reasoning. Cases like *Foakes*—a recurring pattern in contract cases—present a situation in which doctrinal stability is almost entirely irrelevant because it can lead to no fair or useful reliance or planning.

The facts of *Foakes* were relatively straightforward. After Julia Beer had received a judgment of a little more than £2090 against John Weston Foakes, the two parties entered into an agreement that modified the schedule and terms on which Dr. Foakes would pay the judgment. Specifically, Dr. Foakes agreed to make a present payment of £500 and future installments of £150 every six months until the original sum was paid off, and Ms. Beer agreed to accept that stream of payments as satisfaction of the judgment.

This agreement ran afoul of the legal-duty rule because, in promising to pay £500 followed by installment payments of £150, Dr. Foakes was promising to do something he already had a legal obligation to do—namely, to pay Ms. Beer £2090 in total. Ms. Beer, on the other hand, gave something up under the new contract; specifically, she agreed to accept total payments of £2090 to satisfy her debt, thereby forgoing her right to interest payments.

---

[49] [1884] 9 App. Cas. 605 (H.L.). The discussion of this case is drawn from Shawn J. Bayern, *Against Certainty*, 41 HOFSTRA L. REV. 53 (2012), which covers doctrinal stability in more detail.

The case arose because Ms. Beer sought to rescind the agreement and insist on her original right to interest. In the House of Lords, the Earl of Selborne, Lord Chancellor, disposed of the case largely on doctrinal grounds, observing that regardless of the legal-duty rule's merits, it was too late in history to change the doctrine:

> The doctrine itself, as laid down by Sir Edward Coke, may have been criticised, as questionable in principle by some persons whose opinions are entitled to respect, but it has never been judicially overruled; on the contrary I think it has always, since the sixteenth century, been accepted as law. If so, I cannot think that your Lordships would do right, if you were now to reverse, as erroneous, a judgment of the Court of Appeal, proceeding upon a doctrine which has been accepted as part of the law of England for 280 years.[50]

What is striking about Lord Selborne's doctrinal, stability-oriented defense of the legal-duty rule is how poorly it addresses the circumstances in which that rule operates. It does not indicate how the parties might have relied on the existing rule, how they would be harmed if the rule were to change, or why in context it matters how long the rule has been "accepted."

To be clear, as discussed in chapter 1, doctrinal stability can be an important consideration in deciding cases. When parties have relied on legal rules, it can be unfair and might potentially disrupt their ability to plan for the future if the rules change suddenly, without notice, for no good reason. The frustration of planning should count at least as a reason, though not necessarily a decisive reason, to avoid changes that disrupt settled doctrine. But as Lord Selborne's analysis in *Foakes* suggests, courts and commentators often appeal to doctrinal stability without regard for the role that stability might play—or not play—in particular cases.

Consider, to begin with, that the practical force of the legal-duty rule is to prevent some contract modifications (see section 3.1.5). As a result, we might expect that if the parties had relied on the rule, they simply would not have entered into modifications of contracts or debts. If Dr. Foakes and Ms. Beer were both honest negotiators, both aware of the legal-duty rule, and both confident that the rule was an unshakeable part of the legal regime that governed them, then their only plausible actions in reliance on the rule would have been either: (1) to recognize that the rule takes away a potentially valuable opportunity to modify their debt and resign themselves, accordingly,

---

50 *Foakes*, 9 App. Cas. at 612.

to the terms of the original debt, or (2) to find some technical way to escape the force of the rule, as discussed more in a moment.

The parties took neither of these paths. That is, they attempted to modify their contract without using any special technicalities to avoid the force of the legal-duty rule. That attempt alone makes it very unlikely that Dr. Foakes and Ms. Beer both relied on the legal-duty rule—or that future parties similarly situated will rely on the rule, at least if they are honest.

Of course, not everyone is honest. So another possibility is that Ms. Beer knew about the legal-duty rule and Dr. Foakes did not, and she attempted to get him to comply with a new payment schedule by offering a modification that she knew would be unenforceable. In that case, however, it becomes difficult to develop either a moral or a policy-based rationale to support the legal-duty rule's application to *Foakes v. Beer*. If Ms. Beer knew her promise to modify the debt was unenforceable, and if she was simply attempting to mislead Dr. Foakes to encourage him to pay his debt (rather than, for example, to declare bankruptcy) and had no intention at the time to adhere to her promise, it would have been immoral for her to make that promise. Indeed, it probably would amount to promissory fraud.[51] To put it differently, Ms. Beer could indeed have relied on the legal-duty rule when agreeing to restructure Dr. Foakes's debt, but only if she were relying on the rule specifically to deceive Dr. Foakes. If that is the sort of reliance that the rule permits, then doctrinal stability becomes simply an excuse for fraud (or, at the very least, sharp and unfair dealing) and is entirely unpersuasive.

Another possibility is that neither of the parties knew about the legal-duty rule. Indeed, this seems most likely possibility under the circumstances of the actual case. In that event, the parties' ignorance of the rule suggests they did not in fact rely on it at all.

A final possible type of reliance on the existing legal-duty rule is that in whatever transaction originally led to the £2090 debt, someone at least implicitly relied on the future operation of the legal-duty rule to refuse to allow modifications to that debt without consideration. To put it differently, when parties enter into a contract (or otherwise do anything that results in a legal duty from one to the other), they might theoretically set the price or other terms of the contract (or otherwise adjust their activity) in the shadow of the legal-duty rule, secure in the knowledge that the rule will prevent various types of contractual modifications from taking effect. But this

---

[51] *See* RESTATEMENT (THIRD) OF TORTS: LIABILITY FOR ECONOMIC HARM § 15 (2020).

sort of reliance is extremely unlikely as an intuitive matter. It is also conceptually unimportant for the following two reasons.

First, though probably less importantly, the legal-duty rule does not apply only to contract modifications. For example, it would have applied if Ms. Beer's judgment against Dr. Foakes had been for medical malpractice rather than, as it was, the result of a commercial dispute.[52] Had the debt arisen in tort, it is implausible that the parties relied on the legal-duty rule at the time the initial debt was established. The court, at least theoretically, could have set the initial judgment with the legal-duty rule in mind, although in practice such specific reliance is not plausible.

Second, more decisively, under English law at the time the legal-duty rule did not prevent all modifications without consideration. It allowed modifications that were made if certain particular formalities were followed, like the *seal*—discussed later in this chapter's coverage of gift promises (see section 3.1.7). For now, it is enough to recognize that if the parties had stamped their modification with some hot wax or something similar, the modification would have been enforceable regardless of consideration. Similarly, as discussed in the previous section, the parties could have made actual exchanges of cash to each other, rather than only promises.

Accordingly, Ms. Beer (or the judge that issued her order) could not have relied on a guarantee, backed by the stability of legal doctrine, that her original debt could not be modified without consideration; there were in fact many ways in which it could have been modified without consideration. That the legal-duty rule prevented one of those ways would almost certainly have been of exceedingly little or no value, practical or otherwise, to her or anyone else at the time the initial debt came into effect.

While *Foakes* may be distinctive in presenting such a clear combination of a bad rule and an adherence to that rule for uncompelling reasons of doctrinal stability, it is common to see "certainty" or "doctrinal stability" as an argumentative point in cases—or classroom discussions—when in fact it is hard to pinpoint any practical or moral value that certainty would have to anyone.

Though the legal-duty rule was not overruled in *Foakes* in the 1880s, as discussed in the previous section the rule has been sharply limited today.

---

[52] Beer v. Foakes, [1883] 11 Q.B. 221 at 221 ("In August, 1875, the plaintiff recovered judgment against the defendant for 2090*l*. in an action on certain bills of exchange accepted by the defendant.").

3.1.7 Gift Promises and Reliance

Gift promises are considerably less significant for the economy than bargain promises. They aren't trivial; breaking a gift promise can still be wrong and can seriously disappoint the recipient. And gift promises can have a systematic economic role, too: they tend to transfer money from wealthier people either to charities (which help the public) or to relatively poorer beneficiaries (who are likely to value gifts more than wealthy donors because they have less money).[53] But these effects, on their own, amount to less than the full weight of the market economy that bargain contracts have in their favor. Gift promises, in other words, give judges less reason to take notice.

Moreover, gift promises tend to raise more significant problems of proof than bargain promises. People normally make bargains for self-interested reasons, so it may be relatively easy to convince factfinders, in the absence of other evidence, that a plaintiff who claims that a defendant made an irrational or unmotivated bargain is lying. But how is a rich aunt to deny her nephew's claim that she promised to buy him a computer when he enters college? Similarly, because gift promises are made for reasons of affection, people might make them impulsively without realizing the consequences. Gift promises also tend to occur within families, which makes it more difficult for courts to have the full picture of the relationships, history, and moral obligations between the parties—and makes it more likely that if the court enforces gift promises, they will be intruding into family affairs.

And while not getting an expected gift can sting, on its own it's not necessarily a very serious injury. The recipient isn't even normally left worse off by their combined interactions with the giver. Indeed, the recipient was probably made happier for a time because of the gift, and it's hard to say how that happiness should weigh against their later disappointment. As Tennyson put it, "'Tis better

---

[53] Economists call this concept *diminishing marginal utility*. It is familiar in many settings. For example, moving from earning $0 a year to earning $50,000 a year tends to change a person's lifestyle more than moving from $50,000 a year to $100,000 a year. Even more obviously, having one dinner is much better than having no dinners; having two dinners, for most people, isn't much or any better than having one.

Diminishing marginal utility sometimes provides a theoretical explanation for *risk aversion*. Most people would not gamble away one dinner on a particular evening just for a 50% (or even a 55%) chance at two dinners. Similarly, most people would value $100,000 more than a 50% (or, say, a 51%) chance at $200,000. The extra $100,000 if the gambler wins is not as valuable to most people as the value of the lost $100,000 if the gambler loses. As usual with theoretical economic explanations, however, the explanation is not perfect in the real world. Many people *are* gamblers and seek out risks, possibly for the psychological thrills they provide, because of addiction, or for other reasons.

to have loved and lost / Than never to have loved at all."[54] To be sure, disappointment is real and can sometimes be psychologically devastating, but mere disappointment in not receiving a gift is a smaller injury than the law usually takes notice of.

These are all no-duty rationales, just as we saw in tort law (see section 2.3.1): difficulty of telling the good cases from the bad cases, concerns that the injury isn't significant enough for the heavy institutional machinery of the courts to get involved, and perhaps the courts' sense that lawsuits would be inappropriate because of some higher social value (family harmony, or avoiding intruding too far into intrafamily matters) and a similar sense that other enforcement mechanisms (family approbation) are more suitable.[55] For these reasons, the law adopts what amounts to a no-duty rule for straightforward gift promises—that is, gift promises that have no particular special feature in their favor that the law recognizes. It is still ordinarily *morally* wrong to break a gift promise, just as it's morally wrong not to throw a life-preserver to a drowning child, but courts have decided that they shouldn't deter the wrong or compensate the victim for reasons of administration or policy. Contract law ordinarily expresses this no-duty rule simply by saying that gift promises have no "consideration." That is just formal, conclusory legal terminology to differentiate them from bargains; that is, bargains have consideration and gift promises do not.[56]

Note that the no-duty rule applies—the ordinary way to say this is simply that consideration is still required—even if a promise is put in writing, signed, publicized, and so on. The rule applies even if the promisor clearly wanted courts to enforce the promise. The policy rationales associated with consideration—again, mainly problems of proof, intruding too far into family affairs, and the absence of a sufficient injury—normally override the promisor's individual wishes at the time they made the promise. There is some reason to think

---

[54] ALFRED, LORD TENNYSON, IN MEMORIAM 44 (London, Edward Moxon 1850).

[55] The leading commentators tend to agree with this proposition, although some adopt more focused views of the implicit policies behind consideration law. For example, *Corbin on Contracts*, one of the leading modern treatises on contract law, says that consideration doctrine "is designed primarily to *protect promisors* from their own donative promises." 2 CORBIN ON CONTRACTS § 5.17 (2021) (emphasis added).

[56] The term *consideration* is used inconsistently in contract law. Sometimes it refers to *anything* that can make a promise enforceable, but in most cases it refers simply to the price that each side has given up in a bargain contract. For more information about the various uses of the term, see LON L. FULLER ET AL., BASIC CONTRACT LAW 12 (10th ed. 2018). The legal term *consideration* more or less derives from the natural usage of the term in modern English: one might do something after considering it; the list of things one has considered might be called considerations; *consideration* then comes to mean something like "reason" or "motivation," consistently with the notion of a price for a contract. *See* "consideration, n.," OED ONLINE, https://www.oed.com/view/Entry/39602.

that concerns about meddling in or misjudging family affairs are particularly important, because—though the law is inconsistent on the matter—gift promises to charities are often enforceable.[57]

Historically, there have been several factual features of gift promises that have sometimes persuaded courts that they should be enforced for technical reasons. The two most important are what is commonly called *nominal consideration* and a device known as the *seal*.

"Nominal" consideration simply means consideration "in name only," and the notion applies to a gift promise that is put into the form of the bargain but still lacks the substance of one. "I will pay for your college tuition if you give me $2 today." That has the form of a bargain, but nobody with any experience in the world would regard it as a self-interested deal on both sides. Parties might put a gift promise into the form of a bargain in the hope that doing so will get the courts to enforce it. They would once have succeeded, but under modern law, nominal consideration is not ordinarily sufficient to form a legally enforceable contract. Note that there is no price threshold that marks off a nominal bargain from a real one; it is not specifically the amount of money that matters but whether the parties saw the items being exchanged as the *price* for each other's performance (or promised performance). A particular promise or item could well be nominal consideration on one set of facts but real consideration on another.

There are two significant exceptions to the rule that nominal consideration is insufficient for a legally enforceable contract to have been formed. The first is that nominal consideration is sufficient to enforce *option* contracts—another term simply for a promise to keep an offer for a bargain contract open.[58] This is probably because most options are related to commercial affairs, because they are often relied upon, and because option contracts can often legitimately have very small prices that might *appear* nominal but aren't. For example, an option that lasts a week and confers the right to buy a share of a stock for $120 when the stock is currently trading at $80 might sell for a penny, but that penny is not nominal consideration; it is a real market price. (The option has some value because, in the next week,

---

[57] *See* RESTATEMENT (SECOND) OF CONTRACTS § 90(2) (1981). That said, the same Restatement subsection also enforces "marriage settlements," which are of course family-related promises. *See also* FULLER ET AL., *supra* note 56, at 23–24 (discussing the problem of "ingratitude" in an intrafamily context and other legal systems' responses to that problem).

[58] *See* RESTATEMENT (SECOND) OF CONTRACTS § 87(a). The Restatement calls nominal consideration "purported consideration."

the price of the stick might rise above $120.)[59] The second is that nominal consideration is sufficient for a promise to be a *surety*, or stand in for someone else's obligation if they fail to meet it.[60] Such promises are also likely to be commercial, and they are particularly likely to be relied on.

The *seal* was another mechanism by which gift promises could sometimes be enforced. Historically, a seal was the result of pouring a piece of hot wax on a document and stamping it with a family ring, but it could also be "a wafer or other substance affixed to the document or . . . an impression made on the document."[61] In historical and aristocratic England, the seal was a "natural formality"[62] that drove home to parties that what they were doing had legal significance. Seals provided proof that a promise had occurred, and it was unlikely that a seal would be used impulsively. As a result, it was perhaps sensible for courts to enforce promises made with a seal (commonly said to be "under seal"). To say that differently, in historical aristocratic England, the seal addressed the no-duty rationales against enforcing gift promises. In the United States, which didn't import England's aristocracy, the practice of using seals disintegrated, eventually turning into people scribbling the word "seal" or marking a document in some other way. This reduced practice had little social significance; it provided little proof and didn't serve as a check on impulsive gift promises. All the concerns about gift promises—intruding too far into the family and so on—remained. Statutes and courts responded accordingly by, in most states, effectively eliminating any legal significance from the seal—thereby preserving the general no-duty rule for gift promises. (Some states still preserve the role of the seal.)[63]

To summarize the rules so far, then, there is ordinarily no way for parties to make a gift promise enforceable even if they want to do so—unless it's an option or a promise to be a surety, in which case nominal consideration will suffice. But there is one important factor we have yet to discuss in detail that does make some gift promises enforceable.

---

[59] The conventional formula for valuing options is known as the Black-Scholes formula. *See* Fisher Black & Myron Scholes, *The Pricing of Options and Corporate Liabilities*, 81 J. POL. ECON. 637 (1973). The formula is complex, but it is also intuitive: it depends on the duration of the option, the expected volatility of the underlying asset, and the riskfree rate of return (because while one holds an option the money used to purchase it is not earning interest).

[60] *See* RESTATEMENT (SECOND) OF CONTRACTS § 88 (1981).

[61] *Id.* § 96(2) (1981).

[62] FULLER ET AL., *supra* note 56, at 22.

[63] *See generally id.* at 22–24.

That factor is *reliance*. Reliance is a term of art in contract law—and, as is commonly the case in learning the common law (see section 1.5.2), it is important not to take the term at face value. People often say they were "relying on" something to mean they were just hoping for it to occur. This is not necessarily inaccurate in casual English; it is commonplace to refer to psychological reliance, for example. Contract law uses the term *reliance* in a more specialized way: for there to be reliance, a promisee must change their position in some way as a result of the promise. In other words, the promise must be the *factual cause* of some action or inaction by the promisee. As a brief example, if an aunt promises her nephew when he's 12 that she'll buy him a car when he turns 17, his longstanding hope and the fact that he was perhaps "counting on" his aunt is not legal reliance. But if he pays for driving lessons that would be useful only if he gets a free car from his aunt (because he otherwise would not be able to afford a car and wouldn't plan to use one), that constitutes reliance.

Reliance, defined this way, is a real injury. It is just as real as the injuries people suffer in tort law: after their interaction with the promisor, those who have relied on a promise are worse off than they started. Their injury is tangible, often reflecting out-of-pocket economic expenses, and ordinarily has made them materially worse off. For that reason it is very different than a merely disappointed expectation or hope. Indeed, the relative significance of the injury is enough to override the other no-duty rationales that have made courts hesitant to enforce gift promises. Since at least the time of the first *Restatement of Contracts* in 1932, the law has enforced gift promises that have been relied on. As the Restatement originally put it:

> A promise which the promisor should reasonably expect to induce action or forbearance of a definite and substantial character on the part of the promisee and which does induce such action or forbearance is binding if injustice can be avoided only by enforcement of the promise.[64]

When someone sues to enforce a gift promise that has been relied on, the governing legal doctrine is normally called *promissory estoppel*. *Estoppel* is a needlessly obscure term from what has come to be called *Law French*, a result of the influence of the French language on the upper classes of England after the Norman Conquest of 1066.[65] In general, though not universally, when the term *estoppel*

---

64 RESTATEMENT OF CONTRACTS § 90 (1932).

65 Law French is not particularly good French. Someone I used to work with was once served a sandwich on an airplane and asked the flight attendant what meat was in the sandwich. The flight attendant simply replied, "airplane meat." In the phrase "Law French," the word "Law" has the same function as the word "airplane" does in

appears in the common law it connotes reliance of some kind. For example, in the law of agency—one person acting for another—an agent may lack authority to act for a principal (one for whom an agent acts) but nonetheless cause that principal to incur liability if the principal is aware of the agent's activity, remains silent, and others *rely* on that silence. Estoppel or similar principles can also create liability under partnership law, even when a partnership does not exist. The historical details are not particularly important for our purposes, except to note that estoppel comes originally from doctrines of England's courts of *equity*, which are historically associated with a discretionary character. That discretionary character explains, in part, the Restatement's use of phrases like "if injustice can be avoided only by enforcement of the promise."[66]

Having decided that gift promises are enforceable when relied upon, the law faced a further question: how are they to be enforced?[67] If the reason for enforcing relied-upon gift promises is that that real injury associated with reliance is significant whereas the psychological injury associated with a disappointed hope is not, restoring the promisee to the situation they were in before they received and acted on the promise should be sufficient. In other words, the promise caused some harm, and compensating that harm should be enough. That is more or less the state of the law today.[68] As we will see later in this chapter, the damages that enforce promises according to their terms are called *expectation damages*, whereas restoring the promisee to a situation as close as possible to they one they were in before the promise was made is achieved by *reliance damages*. So we might say that relied-upon gift promises should lead to reliance damages.

---

the phrase "airplane meat": is a noun used as an adjective to mean "artificially processed beyond recognition."

66 Promissory estoppel can be traced to a doctrine known as *equitable estoppel*, under which one who makes a statement of *fact* (rather than a promise) that someone else relies on is estopped—that is, prevented—from denying that fact later in court. Equitable estoppel is sometimes called *estoppel in pais*. The *pais* in that phrase has the same origin as *país* in Spanish, meaning "country." The term *pais* was historically used in that same sense to refer to acts that were not formally recorded but just took place "in the country," outside court.

67 *See* FULLER ET AL., *supra* note 56, at 37–41.

68 The modern Restatement adds, to the first Restatement's formulation, "The remedy granted for breach may be limited as justice requires." RESTATEMENT (SECOND) OF CONTRACTS § 90(1) (1981). That language is rather general and reflects the general character of *equity*, the historical system from which promissory estoppel arose. The Restatement further adds, in a comment:

> [T]he same factors which bear on whether any relief should be granted also bear on the character and extent of the remedy. In particular, relief may sometimes be limited to restitution or to damages or specific relief measured by the extent of the promisee's reliance rather than by the terms of the promise.

Id. § 90 cmt. d.

But in this area, remedies are discretionary, just like liability in the first place. In particular, courts may choose to enforce a relied-upon gift promise by requiring the promisor to pay the value of what was promised, not just the reliance losses of the promisee. Expectation damages may be easier for a court to compute—they can simply look at the terms of the promise—or they may be the only way to ensure that promisees are fully compensated for their losses.

A numerical example may help make reliance and expectation damages, and the policies behind them in this context, clearer. Suppose that a grandparent promises their grandchild that they will pay $150 for tennis lessons in the coming summer. The grandchild buys a tennis racket for $40, spends some time practicing and reading the rules of tennis in advance of the lessons, and also forgoes an opportunity to take a vacation with a friend for a few weeks because of the lure of the tennis lessons. If the grandparent doesn't pay for the lessons, expectation damages would simply be $150. A simple view of reliance damages would lead to damages in the amount of $40 (the money that the grandchild spent on the racket) reduced by the resale value of racket. But the grandchild has more complex reliance losses—personal time and the opportunity cost of a forgone vacation. A court could conceivably determine that expectation damages of $150 are the fairest way to make sure the grandchild's full reliance losses are compensated. This might be particularly likely if, instead of buying the tennis racket for $40, the grandchild had bartered something of indeterminate value for it. It may be hard to come to a reliable valuation of what the grandchild bartered away, but we know that whatever the value was, $150 in tennis lessons were enough of a lure to motivate the grandchild to make that exchange.[69]

As a historical note, the tension between expectation damages and reliance damage serves as a useful lesson of the need for legal imagination and creativity. In an often-quoted debate on the floor of the American Law Institute in advance of its adoption of the first *Restatement of Contracts*, Samuel Williston, the reporter (or main drafter) for the project seemed not to recognize the possibility of reliance damages or even to consider the policy rationale in their favor:[70] as discussed above, reliance damages get rid of the injury that leads the law to enforce relied-upon gift promises in the first place, so they are probably sufficient to solve the problem that the law is trying to solve when a relied-upon gift promise is breached, at least if reliance damages can be easily and reliably computed. As just discussed, expectation damages sometimes may have reasons of policy, fairness, and administrability in their favor over reliance

69 *See* FULLER ET AL., *supra* note 56, at 40–41.

70 *See id.* at 39–40.

damages, even for relied-upon gift promises, but Williston did not cite those potential advantages. He simply said: "Either the promise is binding or it is not. If the promise is binding it has to be enforced as it is made."[71] Williston's view reflects the conceptualism of his era; it appears he simply could not recognize the doctrinal development that others were suggesting would be fairer.[72] The proper response to that sort of limited view is simply to point out that the law is in fact under no practical or logical constraint that dictates the particular result that someone is assuming. Clearly it is *possible* to award reliance damages instead of expectation damages; to respond to that possibility, there must be some *reason* to choose expectation damages or else the choice would be unjustified. As the old dean of Yale Law School, Grant Gilmore, wrote in a different context: "The vice of the formalistic approach to law, on the level of serious scholarship as on the level of political slogans and advertising campaigns, is that it leads to a disastrous overstatement of the necessary limits of law."[73]

3.1.8 Conditional Gift Promises and Bargains

As a test of what we have seen so far about consideration doctrine, and to demonstrate further that it is hard to reduce the doctrine to purely formal propositions, suppose that a gift promise is put into a conditional form: "If you send me your bank details, I'll wire you money for college tuition." This looks like it might be an offer for a bargain, in much the same way a homeowner might say to a child in the neighborhood, "If you clear my driveway of snow, I'll pay you $50." The two cases have very similar forms, but the first is still a gift promise because we know that account numbers for someone's bank account are almost certainly not a price to be exchanged for college tuition. The promisor simply needs those bank details to effect a wire transfer; they don't separately desire those details.[74]

In a famous example, Samuel Williston, the reporter of the first *Restatement of Contracts*, recognized this:

> If a benevolent man says to a tramp,—"if you go around the corner to the clothing shop there, you may purchase an overcoat on my credit," no reasonable person would understand that the short walk was requested as the

---

[71] *Proceedings at the Fourth Annual Meeting Held at Washington, D.C.*, 4 APPENDIX A.L.I. PROC. 5, 103 (1926).

[72] *See, e.g.*, *id.* (in which Judge Alfred R. Page asked Williston, of a hypothetical promisee who was promised $1000 for a car but had paid only $500 for it, "how is injustice going to be done [to the promisee] if he is not going to get the other $500; how is he going to be done an injustice, if he only paid $500 for the car?").

[73] GRANT GILMORE, THE AGES OF AMERICAN LAW 108 (1977).

[74] *See* FULLER ET AL., *supra* note 56, at 63–64.

> consideration for the promise, but that in the event of the tramp going to the shop the promisor would make him a gift. Yet the walk to the shop is in its nature capable of being consideration. It is a legal detriment to the tramp to make the walk, and the only reason why the walk is not consideration is because on a reasonable construction, it must be held that the walk was not requested as the price of the promise, but was merely a condition of a gratuitous promise.[75]

Suppose that in a contrasting example, a callous property developer rather than a "benevolent man" tells a homeless man that they'll buy him a coat if he moves down the street, and the property developer's goal is simply to clear the homeless person out of a publicity photo for the opening of a new building. In that case, the same words—"if you go around the corner to the clothing shop there, you may purchase an overcoat on my credit"—would be a bargain rather than a gift. Similarly, requesting bank details, so readily treated as a gift in the example earlier, could easily be part of a bargain: suppose an employer sends an email to all its employees saying, "If you register for direct deposit online by this Friday, we will add a one-time bonus of $100 to your paycheck because direct deposit is much less expensive for us than sending you checks each weeks."

The question is not whether a particular item or action constitutes consideration but whether the parties see that item or action as the inducement for their own performance, rather than as the means for a gift to be made. That is not a question that can be answered with regard to form alone or any particular words the parties have used, in the general case; it requires a substantive, fact-sensitive analysis based on experience.

In his discussion of this hypothetical case, Williston added: "In case of doubt where the promisee has incurred a detriment on the faith of the promise, courts will naturally be loath to regard the promise as a mere gratuity, and the detriment incurred as merely a condition."[76] This comment, written before the first *Restatement of Contracts* and before the doctrine of promissory estoppel had taken hold, shows the erosion of the older rule that reliance was *not* sufficient to enforce a gift promise. Still, even today it is probably correct, not as a matter of specific announced doctrine but of predicting courts' decisions: if there is significant doubt about whether a situation is a bargain or a gift promise, courts will probably err on the side of enforcing the promise. It is better to accidentally enforce a gift promise than to fail to enforce a bargain. Again,

---

[75] SAMUEL WILLISTON, LAW OF CONTRACTS § 112, at 232–33 (1924).

[76] *Id.* at 233.

bargains have the full weight of the market economy behind them—they enable productive and fair trade—whereas the policies against enforcing gift promises come from a milder caution against interfering in matters where courts are not necessary and might not be good at judging intrafamily matters. Much as with the no-duty-to-rescue rule in tort law, where the slightest hint of activity rather than inaction tends to lead to liability, courts tend to impose standards of conduct instead of relying on no-duty rules too aggressively.

3.1.9 Past Consideration

Sometimes a promisor makes what is effectively a gift promise but is motivated to do so because of a benefit they previously received. For example, in *Webb v. McGowin*,[77] the president of a company promised to provide financially for the life of an employee who was very seriously injured while preventing an accident that could have killed the company president. The law traditionally says that the company president's promise was given for *past consideration* because, though his promise is not part of a bargain (it is not meant to induce anything), there is at least a metaphorical sense in which it is being "exchanged" for something provided in the past.

Past consideration is probably not very important in the real world, but it is typically taught in Contracts courses, and it is a helpful illustration of the no-duty nature of consideration rules. Though the law is murky,[78] a promise based on past consideration is typically enforced today as long as it is not too disproportionate to the value of the past consideration—that is, not too much like a pure gift promise. To see why the law might prefer that result, consider a case like *Webb*. Many but not all of the policy rationales associated with enforcing gift promises don't apply in cases like that: it is not an intrafamily promise, so there is no risk of interfering with or misjudging family affairs; there is *some* risk that the promisor acted hastily, but that is perhaps why the law cares whether the promise based on past consideration is disproportionate to the benefit received; there is little risk of fraud; the promisee's injury is no greater than any other promise that hasn't been relied on, but the moral tenor of the case is different because breach would involve both the breaking of a promise and the disvaluing of the prior benefit. These have appeared to be enough, in modern contract law, to permit enforcement of at least many promises that are given for past consideration.

Courts occasionally say that the benefit in a past-consideration case must be "material" for it to permit a later promise in "exchange"

77 168 So. 196 (Ala. Ct. App. 1935).

78 *See* RESTATEMENT (SECOND) OF CONTRACTS § 89 (1981).

for it to be enforceable, but that rule seems to add nothing to the doctrine and has not been consistently applied. It causes the court in *Webb* to go through rhetorical gymnastics—referring to life insurance, actuarial tables, and such[79]—to explain that saving someone's life is a "material" benefit!

3.1.10 Summary

In short, consideration doctrine serves a similar role in contract law as duty does in negligence law. It gives courts an opportunity to look at problems of proof, the gravity of the plaintiff's injury, and superseding social values in order to determine that bargain promises are enforceable but gift promises, without some extra factor like reliance, are not. Gift promises that are relied on are enforceable, ordinarily up to their reliance harms, although for administrative reasons sometimes expectation damages are available even for gift promises. Bargain promises—those in which each party gives up something as the price for the other's participation—are enforceable by expectation damages simply for being bargain promises.

Classical contract law would sometimes incorrectly treat deals that were real bargains as if they were gift promises. For example, in an illusory-promise case like *Wood*—recall, the contract where Lucile agrees to license her name exclusively through Wood and Wood doesn't agree to anything specific but takes her on as a client—there was a commercial relationship between the parties, and the argument that consideration is missing on Wood's side is nothing more than a mechanical argument that Lucile's promise was in fact a gift promise. But it was not. Lucile wasn't making Wood her exclusive agent out of kindness; she was doing it because those were the terms on which the parties negotiated their deal. Similarly, in contract-modification cases like *Foakes*—the case of a renegotiation of debt between a creditor and a debtor to make it more likely that the debtor will pay something rather than nothing—the fact that only one side is giving up something new does not mean they are doing so as a way to give a gift to the other party. They are doing so because the modification improves their own likely outcome.

The classical rules of consideration, in other words, used to operate mechanically to treat promises as gift promises when they were not really gift promises. Importantly, cases like *Wood* and *Foakes* have none of the no-duty policies associated with the law's hesitation to enforce gift promises: they do not involve intrusion into family affairs, for example, or present any special problems of proof or impulsive action. Also, in both *Wood* and *Foakes* a promisor has breached a contract, which is morally wrong. There is no reason of

79 *Webb*, 168 So. at 198.

policy or morality to fail to enforce such agreements, and the common law has adjusted accordingly—though admittedly slowly and without always repealing the classical rule outright.

Moreover, even when rules of classical consideration might seem coincidentally to do some good by withholding enforcement of a promise (for example, in the case of contract modifications extracted under duress—or perhaps in cases of illusory promises where the presence of only an illusory promise on one side happens to correspond with a contract that is extremely lopsided and thus grossly unfair), they are ineffective in policing contracts on substantive grounds. A bad contract modification that is not enforced only because of the legal-duty rule—as in *Lingenfelder*, the case of the architect who abuses the position that the contract gives him to extract more money than he could originally negotiate from the other party—would become enforceable as long as the party engaging in duress relies on the promise. This is because the legal-duty rule is merely a rule of consideration—merely an incorrect labeling of a promise as a gift promise. The legal-duty rule also cannot stand in the way of completed exchanges—for example, if the architect in *Lingenfelder* had demanded immediate payment of the extra sum he extorted—only promises.

The most important lesson from the coverage of consideration is to see it as an example of how the common law changes and of the intricacy of the common law. Understanding how courts will decide illusory-promise or legal-duty-rule cases today requires understanding all of the following: the classical axioms of consideration; the way those axioms apply to various facts; the reason that mechanical application is a poor fit with justifications of morality and policy; and what modern courts have done to prevent that result.

3.2 Other Promises That the Law Does Not Enforce

Despite the general rule that bargains are enforced according to their terms, the law refuses to enforce some bargains. Just as no-consideration rules operate like no-duty rules in tort law, rules that treat some even some bargains as unenforceable remove classes of promises from the legal system on grounds of policy or principle. For example, courts may be ill-equipped to deal with some bargains, or the parties themselves may not have wanted the courts involved. Or perhaps including the cases in the legal system will cause undesirable results in view of some policy that supersedes the enforcement of individual contracts.

In some cases, the parties have made a bargain but don't want the courts involved. In English contract law, courts and commentators frequently say that contracting parties need to exhibit an *intent to be legally bound* or an *intent to establish legal relations* for a court to enforce even a bargain promise.[80] This principle is made explicit less often in US contract law, and some influential sources have purported to reject it in principle. For example, the Restatement's black-letter rule is

> Neither real nor apparent intention that a promise be legally binding is essential to the formation of a contract, but a manifestation of intention that a promise shall not affect legal relations may prevent the formation of a contract.[81]

Nonetheless, the case outcomes are similar between the US and other common-law jurisdictions. For example, in general US courts won't enforce an informal agreement between spouses about cooking schedules or who will drive the kids to school.[82]

In a related type of case, courts refuse to get involved when the subject matter of an alleged contract is too personal. Some statutes declare explicitly that promises to marry will not be legally enforced.[83] In related contexts, courts have suggested they won't intrude too far into intimate personal relationships, even when the parties have made bargains.[84] These are classic no-duty rationales.

Many of the traditional defenses to contract formation—fraud, incapacity, and the like—are probably easiest to understand as clear judicial determinations that some promises are not wrongful for the promisee to break in the first place. Breaking a promise extracted through fraud or at gunpoint is not morally wrong. As for incapacity, it *is* probably morally problematic for most sixteen-year-old children to break their promises, but for administrative reasons the law picks a general age of majority rather than trying to analyze the particulars of each child's situation. So, in other words, fraud and duress are like judicial bright-line determinations of breach;

---

80 *E.g.*, Jones v. Padavatton, 1 W.L.R. 328 (C.A. 1968).

81 RESTATEMENT (SECOND) OF CONTRACTS § 21 (1981).

82 *See id.* cmt. c illus. 6 ("A, a husband, is living in harmony with his wife, B. Before A leaves on a trip, A and B assess B's financial needs and agree that A will remit a fixed sum per month to support her. There is no contract.").

83 *E.g.*, CAL. CIV. CODE. § 43.5(d) (West 2022); *see also* Boyd v. Boyd, 39 Cal. Rptr. 400 (Cal. Ct. App. 1964).

84 *See, e.g.*, Perry v. Atkinson, 240 Cal. Rptr. 402, 405 (Cal. Ct. App. 1987) ("In essence, Perry seeks judicial enforcement, by way of damages, of a promise to impregnate. The courts should not undertake the adjudication of promises and representations made by consenting adults regarding their sexual relationships.").

incapacity, at least in the case of children, is like an administrative no-duty rule (see section 2.3.1).

Promises under duress implicate other policies too. At least in theory, a promisor under duress might very keenly want their promise to be enforced at the time they make it. For example, imagine an armed burglar who thinks a house is empty and is surprised by a homeowner's presence in the middle of the night. The burglar says, "I was hoping to do this quietly and slip away unnoticed, but now that I've seen you, I'm going to have to kill you." The homeowner responds by promising not to go to the police and, moreover, to transfer a large amount of money to the burglar when the banks open in the morning. At that moment, the homeowner probably very much wants a way to make binding commitments, because otherwise there is no way to bargain successfully with the burglar. Nonetheless, the law will not enforce such a promise, and the generally understood reasons are (1) that it would not be morally wrong to for the homeowner to break the promise (a no-breach rationale), and (2) that enforcing promises like this would both reward and encourage crime (a no-duty rationale).

Unconscionability is a very broad, open-ended doctrine that can render some apparent bargains unenforceable. "Unconscionable" has never been clearly defined; for example, the statutory UCC uses the concept but never defines it.[85] Based on an article by Arthur Leff, courts have partitioned the concept into two categories: procedural and substantive.[86] What has come to be called *procedural unconscionability* reflects a defect in the bargaining process, a notion that serves as a generalization of the classical contract defenses like fraud, duress, and incapacity. In other words, in some settings—a long and complicated form contract that nobody reads, a pressured and intrusive door-to-door sale that takes advantage of someone's hospitality and lack of commercial sophistication—there is no bargain even when fraud, duress, incapacity, or the other classical defenses don't literally apply. Because there in fact is no bargain (or because there is a suspect bargain), the rationales in favor of enforcing bargains don't apply (or apply with less force) to such cases. By contrast, *substantive unconscionability* refers simply to extremely uneven or oppressive terms—conceptually the same sorts of problems addressed by some statutes, like minimum-wage laws or rent control.

---

[85] U.C.C. § 2–302(1) ("If the court . . . finds the contract or any clause of the contract to have been unconscionable at the time it was made the court may refuse to enforce the contract, or it may enforce the remainder of the contract without the unconscionable clause, or it may so limit the application of any unconscionable clause as to avoid any unconscionable result.").

[86] *See* Arthur Allen Leff, *Unconscionability and the Code—The Emperor's New Clause*, 115 U. PA. L. REV. 485 (1967).

Substantive unconscionability is also functionally very similar to an older doctrine that contracts that are *void as against public policy* are not enforceable.[87] For example, for different reasons, people can't sell votes, kidneys, their lifetime future services as laborers, their present services as assassins or thieves, or their Social Security pensions, even if they knowingly try to do so through bargains.

Unconscionability may serve as a helpful kind of simplification and generalization from a series of smaller, less coordinated doctrines—exactly the sort of thing the common law has been heading toward in other areas (like emotional harms in tort; see section 2.6.1 and compare Figure 2.2). As White & Summers put it in their leading treatise on the UCC, both procedural and substantive unconscionability have "cousins" in older law: "procedural unconscionability looks like fraud or duress"—or, they might have added, incapacity—"during contract formation, and substantive unconscionability reminds us of contracts or clauses contrary to public policy or illegal."[88]

It may be okay that unconscionability is so open-ended. Its longstanding presence hasn't threatened to overturn the contracting system in general, and the vast majority of contracting parties don't need to rely on the precise boundaries between morally acceptable contracts and unconscionable ones; most contracts are nowhere near the line. Its lack of a definition permits courts to develop the doctrine to suit new types of harsh dealing. As with the general determination of reasonableness in tort law, the range of possible facts is perhaps too broad to try to specify all the wrongful ones in advance. And perhaps those near the border of unconscionability shouldn't rely too heavily on their harsh dealing in the first place.

3.3 The Statute of Frauds

In general, contracts in the common law don't have to be in writing; oral promises are just fine. People without business experience often have the impression that every business deal is written down, but that's just not true. Not even every important business deal is written down. There just isn't time, and there's enough trust not to make it worthwhile in many cases. There is also often other evidence of a contract—preliminary emails, partial performance, past dealings, and so on. Of course, many deals *are* in writing, but people who study law and business abstractly rather

---

[87] *See* RESTATEMENT (SECOND) OF CONTRACTS § 178(1) (1981) ("A promise or other term of an agreement is unenforceable on grounds of public policy if legislation provides that it is unenforceable or the interest in its enforcement is clearly outweighed in the circumstances by a public policy against the enforcement of such terms.").

[88] 1 JAMES J. WHITE ET AL., UNIFORM COMMERCIAL CODE § 5:4 (6th ed. 2017).

than in real-world settings often overestimate the importance of writings.

In 1677, the Parliament of England passed the Statute of Frauds to prevent "many Fraudulent Practices which are commonly endeavoured to be upheld by Perjury and Subornation of Perjury."[89] Even the original Statute of Frauds never required that all contracts be in writing; it identified only particular types of contracts that required a signed writing to be enforceable. The original statute was poorly written, but it has remained, at least in the background, as a part of contract law. So much caselaw has built up around the statute that it is effectively a part of the common law, even though it has a statutory origin and has corresponding specific statutes in most or all US states.

Overall, the statute of frauds has not been a success. As Mel Eisenberg puts it in his casebook:

> The best general guide to the judicial interpretation of the Statute of Frauds is to remember this simple truth: The courts have not favored the Statute of Frauds. Generally—although certainly not invariably—whenever the words of the Statute leave any leeway (and often when they do not), the courts have restricted its meaning and found ways of making an oral agreement enforceable.[90]

Courts have long been sensitive to the possibility that strict "application of the statute of frauds [can] work a fraud or a gross injustice upon the promisee."[91] As a result, many exceptions to the statute have developed. One way to think about this development is that courts already have available the rules of evidence and other procedural rules to evaluate unsupported claims, and they can use judicial sanctions to impose penalties on those who would use courts for fraudulent purposes. And if a contract is objectionable or invalid, courts have other ways to strike it down. So in many or most cases, when the statute of frauds arises it would render unenforceable an otherwise unobjectionable contract that probably has sufficient evidence in its favor—for formal reasons that date to a poorly drafted statute enacted more than four hundred years ago. This general pattern may explain the courts' narrowing of the statute over the centuries.

---

[89] 29 Car. 2 c. 3 (1677) (Eng.).

[90] FULLER ET AL., *supra* note 56, at 1097.

[91] Fireworks Spectacular, Inc. v. Premier Pyrotechnics, Inc., 147 F. Supp. 2d 1057, 1064 (D. Kan. 2001). The notion and language that the statute of frauds can "work a fraud" is commonplace and appears in hundreds of cases.

As background, the statute of frauds does not apply to all contracts; as I noted at the outset, in general promises don't need to be written in order to be enforced. Indeed, most statutes of frauds do not require *any* promises or contracts to be written; all that is necessary is *some* writing sufficient to indicate that there was a contract. This can be a memorandum written long after a contract was formed. Though a "writing" is necessary, this includes electronic records in the modern world, including emails, recorded voicemail messages, and so on. Moreover, though a "signed" writing may be necessary, the law has interpreted "signed" extremely broadly; any recorded intent to authenticate a document can count as a signature. For example, as the California Supreme Court has pointed out, "a party's printed or typewritten name in a telegram has been held to satisfy the statute of frauds," and "[e]ven a tape recording identifying the parties has been determined to meet the signature requirement."[92] And "[w]hen an advertisement constitutes an offer, the printed name of the merchant is intended to authenticate the advertisement as that of the merchant" and therefore satisfies the statute.[93]

The modern statutes of frauds applies to several specific categories of cases—and states' statutes differ, so for planning and litigation it may be important to consult an individual state's statute.[94] One of the important general categories, dating back to the original statute, includes contracts to buy and sell real estate. This is probably an unobjectionable application of the statute of frauds in general because real-estate deals are ordinarily slow and financially significant, and real-estate deeds are in writing and formally recorded anyway. Courts can perhaps apply the rule too vigorously if they would use it to strike down parties' actual real-estate deals because a writing isn't complete or clear enough, but otherwise it would not surprise most people to learn that real-estate purchases need a writing to be enforced.

Another important category is the sale of goods, because Article 2 of the Uniform Commercial Code, which applies to the sales of goods, has its own modern statute of frauds.[95] The UCC's statute of frauds has many exceptions: *receiving* a signed writing can be enough to satisfy the statute and render an otherwise oral contract enforceable; contracts that involve "specially manufactured" goods that are "not suitable for sale to others in the ordinary course of the

---

[92] Donovan v. RRL Corp., 27 P.3d 702, 713 (Cal. 2001).

[93] *Id.*

[94] For example New York's applies to finder's fees for those who help put business deals together. N.Y. GEN. OBL. LAW § 5–701(a)(10) (Consol. 2014).

[95] U.C.C. § 2–201.

seller's business" and that the seller has committed resources to are exempt from the statute and enforceable even if oral; and goods that have been paid for or received and accepted do not require a writing. The result is that many cases beyond very simple *executory*—that is, entirely unperformed—contracts are exempt from the force of the UCC's statute of frauds. The UCC's statute of frauds is, however, particular that the *quantity* of goods must be written down.

The last significant modern category worth discussing here involves contracts that may take a long time to be completed. The original Statute of Frauds from 1677 covered contracts "not to be performed within the space of one yeare from the, makeing thereof."[96] Probably the statute would have done better to require written proof of contracts after a certain duration between contract formation and a *lawsuit*—because after a long time, oral evidence may tend to become less accurate as witnesses become unavailable and memories fade—but a formalistic principle of traditional English common law was that all rights and duties of the parties needed to be known from the time a promise was made. (Modern promissory estoppel, as an example, violates that rule; rights can develop after a promise is made if reliance later occurs—a principle that earlier formalists would have rejected.)

What the drafters of the statute actually meant, however, is unclear; what is a contract "not to be performed within the space of one year"? Partly because of their general opposition to the statute of frauds, courts have interpreted those words extremely narrowly, including within the force of the modern statute only those contracts that essentially *cannot* be completed within a year, even if such quick completion is very unlikely. For example, a contract to build a huge stadium that will almost certainly take three years as a practical matter does not need to be in writing. Normally the provision applies only when the express terms of a contract would require that it take more than a year to perform. It does not matter whether the contract *actually* takes more than a year; what matters is the logical *possibility* that it could have been completed within a year at the time it was made. If there is such a possibility, no signed writing is ordinarily needed.[97] Compare the structure of the *rule against perpetuities* (see section 4.4.3); as discussed in chapter 4, a lot of the complexity of that rule comes from the requirement that the legal effect of a conveyance be determined at the time the conveyance was made. A rule that developed today could easily, by contrast, depend

---

96 29 Car. 2 c. 3 (1677) (Eng.).

97 *See* 4 CORBIN ON CONTRACTS § 19.1 (2022) ("In its actual application, the courts have been perhaps even less friendly to this provision than to the other provisions of the statute. They have interpreted its words . . . very narrowly.").

on whether a contract *actually* takes a year to perform or not (as determined after the fact), but that sort of thinking was unnatural to classical lawyers.

The statute of frauds in general is probably inconsistent with modern policies, particularly in an era with a robust set of evidentiary and procedural rules. It is unclear why contracts should need to be in writing when evidence in many other settings can be oral. There is no rule in tort law, for example, that a negligence claim can't proceed without documentary evidence, camera recordings, or skid marks. Some have suggested that the rule has a *channeling* function, encouraging contracting parties to produce reliable evidence so as to reduce the severity of disputes later on. But this too is probably just a retroactive explanation for a bad centuries-old statute, and if people don't know the law, any channeling function of the rule will be ineffective, and the rule will just serve as a trap for the unwary. As a study group on the revision of the UCC found in 1990:

> Despite its ancient lineage, there is no persuasive evidence either that the statute of frauds has prevented fraud in the proof of the making of a contract or that its presence has channeled behavior toward more reliable forms of record keeping. . . . On the other hand, there are claims that the statute of frauds is anachronistic . . . .
>
> . . .
>
> On the other side of the Atlantic, England repealed the statute of frauds for sales in 1953. Since then there has been little discussion and no reports about the impact, if any. In short, the statute of frauds has apparently sunk in England without an adverse trace.[98]

As that report also noted, other statutes and international frameworks do not have a statute of frauds—and they seem to operate just fine. For example the UN Convention on Contracts for the International Sale of Goods (CISG)—covering commercial sales of goods between parties in nations that have signed a common treaty—simply reads, "A contract of sale need not be concluded in or evidenced by writing and is not subject to any other requirement as to form. It may be proved by any means, including witnesses."[99]

---

[98] PEB STUDY REPORT ON ARTICLE 2, at 50–51 (1990) (quoted in FULLER ET AL., *supra* note 56, at 1142).

[99] United Nations Convention on Contracts for the International Sale of Goods, U.N. Doc. A/CONF.97/18 Annex I (1980), S. TREATY DOC. NO. 98–9 (1983), 19 I.L.M. 668 (1980), *available at* https://uncitral.un.org/sites/uncitral.un.org/files/media-documents/uncitral/en/19-09951_e_ebook.pdf [https://perma.cc/LB88-Y6CW] (2010 ed.).

Other similar domestic legal domains that have considered the question tend not to require writings; for example, the Revised Uniform Partnership Act (RUPA) defines "partnership agreement" as "the agreement, whether written, oral, or implied, among the partners concerning the partnership, including amendments to the partnership agreement";[100] the Revised Uniform Limited Liability Company Act (RULLCA) has a similar rule for LLCs, an even more formal business organization than general partnerships.[101]

In the end, there is little more reason to require contracts to be evidenced in writing than there is for car crashes to be evidenced by tire tracks or cameras. Recorded evidence can be helpful but isn't generally demanded by the purposes of accuracy or administrative efficiency.

3.4 Contract Interpretation

If consideration rules in contract law are like duty rules in tort law—focused on eliminating whole classes of cases from the court system—we can think of the rules of interpretation (and the related rules of formation, discussed in the next section) as intricate, case-specific ways the courts determine what counts as *breach* of a legally enforceable promise. Like tort cases involving breach of duty, individual contract cases vary widely. Contract interpretation is probably the most frequently litigated question of contract law precisely because it is so hard to pin down to general rules; the most fundamental goal of interpretation is simply to try to figure out what the parties wanted.

Sometimes nonlawyers expect that there are "magic words" that have special meaning in legally enforceable contracts. With a small number of relatively unimportant exceptions, this is not true. The language of contract law does not need to be very different from any other forms of communication.

3.4.1 Subjective and Objective Features of Contract Interpretation

Hundreds of cases refer to the "objective theory" of contract interpretation, which is the idea that parties' contracts are to be interpreted by objectively determining the reasonable meanings of their communications—rather than what they may have subjectively intended or actually had in mind. Saying there is an objective standard of interpretation is like saying there is an objective standard for reasonableness in tort law: reasonable behavior is not

---

100 UNIF. P'SHIP ACT § 101(7) (1997).

101 REV. UNIF. LTD. LIAB. CO. ACT § 102(13) (2006).

determined by what individual parties intended or had in mind but by whether their behavior, which can be seen by others, lived up to a particular standard (see section 2.2.1).

It is possible to imagine a fully objective system of contract interpretation—one in which the intentions of the actual parties to a contract case are *never* relevant—and indeed classical contract law was nearly such a system. But it is not the system of contract law we have today. Instead, it is more accurate to say that while contract interpretation is *largely* objective, it depends on a complex interplay between subjective matters (what parties actually had in mind) and objective ones (what reasonable people would think the parties were trying to communicate to each other).

The *Restatement (Second) of Contracts* covers the most common case of interpretation with the following rule: "Where the parties have attached different meanings to a promise or agreement or a term thereof, it is interpreted in accordance with the meaning attached by one of them if at the time the agreement was made . . . that party had no reason to know of any different meaning attached by the other, and the other had reason to know the meaning attached by the first party."[102] That section has both subjective and objective features: it refers to the meanings that "the parties have attached" (subjectively) and favors whichever of these is reasonable (objectively). In referring to a party that "had reason to know the meaning attached" by the other party, the Restatement is simply saying that that party was unreasonable not to know of the other party's meaning. In other words, if the parties (subjectively) have two different meanings in mind but only one of them is reasonable, the (objectively) reasonable party wins. This principle can and probably should be generalized to the principle that whichever party's interpretation is *more* reasonable wins the interpretive battle.[103]

The typical interpretive dispute involves two parties who assign different meanings to a communication (typically some action or some spoken or written word or phrase) under circumstances where one of them is more reasonable (or at least the court thinks so). For example, in *Lucy v. Zehmer*,[104] the owner of farmland agreed to sell it to another after a negotiation that was relatively informal but that the court believed was an actual deal. It is important to say that the court did not in fact know what happened precisely during the negotiations; it needed to construct what we might think of as an authoritative hypothetical movie reel of the events of the negotiation,

---

[102] RESTATEMENT (SECOND) OF CONTRACTS § 201(2) (1981).

[103] *See* FULLER ET AL., *supra* note 56, at 400 ("If the parties subjectively attach different meanings to an expression . . . the more reasonable meaning prevails.").

[104] 84 S.E.2d 516 (Va. 1954).

based on the testimony it heard and chose to believe. Based on that hypothetical movie reel, the court believed the owner of the farmland agreed to sell it to an acquaintance for a fair price after having considered and worked out several impediments to the deal, such as requiring his wife's assent. Having constructed that hypothetical movie reel of the negotiations, the court effectively concluded that a reasonable person watching it would determine that an earnest contract negotiation had occurred. The owner of the farmland sought to get out of the contract by arguing that he was kidding: the whole thing was a joke, and he had never intended to sell the farm; he was just trying to get the other party to admit he was boasting about having the money ready to buy it. On the Restatement's principle, the owner's subjective view of the situation as a joke doesn't matter; the other party was serious, and a reasonable interpretation of events (according to the court) was that a real contract negotiation had taken place.

Reaching that conclusion requires paying some attention to the subjective interpretations of the parties because the legal conclusion is not that the parties meant whatever a reasonable third party might have thought they meant; the choice of possible interpretations is specifically between the two subjective interpretations that the parties happened to hold. In other words, the more objectively reasonable of the two parties' subjective interpretations is the one that wins the interpretive dispute—the one that contract law pays attention to in determining the obligations of the parties.

A fully "objective theory" would instead ignore the parties' subjective interpretations and assign an objective meaning to their communications regardless of either of their intents. Doing that would substitute the court's judgment for that of *both* parties, rather than only the one who was the least reasonable. As Arthur Corbin, one of the leading contract scholars of the 1900s, put it, "No contract should ever be interpreted and enforced with a meaning that neither party gave it."[105] Giving a meaning to the contract that neither party wanted would potentially surprise both of them, could create a deal that neither of them would have agreed to, and probably has worse effects on parties whose uses of language are further from the courts' (because of industry, geography, class, or other factors).

The parties' subjective interpretations have other roles to play in contract interpretation. Another principle in the Restatement is that "Where the parties have attached the same meaning to a promise or agreement or a term thereof, it is interpreted in accordance with that meaning."[106] An older and imprecise notion in

---

105 6 CORBIN ON CONTRACTS § 25.1 (2023).

106 RESTATEMENT (SECOND) OF CONTRACTS § 201(1) (1981).

contract law that contracts require a "meeting of the minds" is often properly criticized because it is inconsistent with any use of objective principles in interpretation—for example in *Lucy* there is a contract even if there was no "meeting" of actual human "minds"—but it is important to note that when there *is* in fact a meeting of the minds, that meaning governs.[107] So a variation of *Lucy* in which *both* parties believed that an apparent transaction was a joke should not be enforced as a serious contract just because a court thinks that reasonable people observing the transaction would have thought it was a real transaction.[108] Obviously, two actors who perform the formation of a fictional contract on stage haven't really entered a contract—and this is true even if they're engaged in less formal performance art (or, say, a public prank) where the audience does not know that it's a joke.

There is another type of interpretation case worth noting; some casebooks include it along with their coverage of interpretation, although it is often treated separately as a *mistake* doctrine called *mutual misunderstanding*. These are cases in which two parties have different meanings in mind for a communication but they are *equally* reasonable. The Restatement covers this in a section in its chapter on contract formation: "There is no manifestation of mutual assent to an exchange if the parties attach materially different meanings to their manifestations and . . . neither party knows or has reason to know the meaning attached by the other"[109]—that is, the two meanings are both reasonable (or, perhaps more clearly, equally reasonable), so that there is no way to break the tie. This pattern includes the famous *Peerless* case:[110] under circumstances where the date of a shipment matters, two parties make a deal to buy and sell cotton to be delivered on a ship called *Peerless*. Despite its name, there were in fact many ships named *Peerless*. One of the parties meant the *Peerless* arriving in October; the other meant the *Peerless* arriving in December. The court decided that there was no contract.

Because this principle is often not treated as a principle of interpretation, its scope has never been entirely clear. The

[107] *E.g.*, Advent Sys., Ltd. v. Unisys Corp., CIV. A. 88–3100, 1992 WL 185606, at *4 (E.D. Pa. July 23, 1992) ("[T]he evidence at the second trial, including evidence of the conduct of the parties, makes clear that both parties thought they had a contract, and that the defendant, at the very least, bound itself to make reasonable efforts to market the product. This is not a situation in which the issue is whether the defendant's conduct measured up to some vague standard of reasonableness as to which there was no meeting of the minds. Rather, it seems that the parties had a reasonably well-understood notion of what would be required of each of them, and were proceeding to carry out their obligations . . . .").

[108] *Cf.* Keller v. Holderman, 11 Mich. 248 (1863).

[109] RESTATEMENT (SECOND) OF CONTRACTS § 20(1) (1981).

[110] Raffles v. Wichelhaus, 159 Eng. Rep. 375 (Ex. 1864).

Restatement says there's no "mutual assent to an exchange"—that is, no contract at all—but that is probably too strong in the general case. For example, if two parties both believe they have a deal on all important matters, but they use a term in a three-page written contract that has two equally good meanings, and we genuinely believe each party adopted one of those meanings, the parties probably do have a contract even if the two interpretations are, as the Restatement puts it, "materially different." Courts generally avoid this problem simply by breaking the tie among the meanings somehow; it is rare that words or other communications have different meanings that are each *exactly* as reasonable as the other. Even if one meaning is slightly better as an objective matter, the party who used language more carelessly—who "had reason to know" of the other party's meaning—will likely lose. A different possibility is to say the parties have a contract but to cancel the particular disputed term, treating the contract as if it doesn't have that term. That may require courts to fill in the resulting gap using reasonable defaults, which is ordinarily what happens when contracts have gaps because the parties failed to address some matter that later becomes important.

In a case like the *Peerless* case, we might imagine that neither party is at fault—they both used language reasonably and ran into a hard-to-avoid problem. But it is probably more likely that both were careless—they *both* used language in an unreasonable way, not anticipating an ambiguity that reasonable businesspeople probably should have been able to see in advance. The Restatement doesn't care whether *neither* party was negligent or *both* were negligent; it reaches the same result if "each party knows or each party has reason to know the meaning attached by the other."[111] In tort law, if both parties were negligent in this way—in the *Peerless* case, each using language in a way that they had "reason" to avoid, which is just to say using language carelessly or negligently—we would apply a principle of comparative fault (see section 2.7.1) and allow the parties to split the reliance losses they had each incurred because of their shared negligence. Nothing prevents that principle from being applied to contract cases. But it is not an established part of contract doctrine. It didn't come up in the *Peerless* case because the law had a more rigid character at the time, but it would be a more flexible solution that is worthwhile to consider today.

The Restatement also covers cases in which two parties adopt different meanings but one *actually* knows that the other is adopting a different meaning. In these cases, which are less important overall as a matter of practice, the general rule is that a party cannot profit

[111] RESTATEMENT (SECOND) OF CONTRACTS § 20(1)(b) (1981).

from that kind of misunderstanding. If you know that the other party to a contract is making an interpretive mistake, you should tell them. Contract law lets people profit from skill in valuation, timing, and so on, but it is very easy to correct another person's *interpretive* mistake, and there is no convincing moral or economic justification for permitting people not to do so.[112]

Note that because of the objective features of contract interpretation, parties who use language carelessly—unreasonably, or negligently—can find themselves bound by contracts even though they never (subjectively) intended to be. Using language negligently can cause real harm, just like driving a truck negligently can cause harm, but if a party didn't intend to form a contract and can convince a factfinder of that lack of intent, why don't we think reliance damages are sufficient (as in cases of promissory estoppel)? In other words, why expose someone to full contractual liability (including expectation damages; see section 3.6) just because they used language in a way that the other party reasonably interpreted as contractual—when they themselves weren't even contemplating contractual liability? The answer to that question is probably administrative—that is, contractual liability in such cases is justified by the need to have regular rules that support the contracting system as a whole. In particular, the answer seems to be that we don't have a reliable way to determine parties' subjective intents well enough to reduce their damages from expectation damages to reliance damages just because they maintain that they never intended to enter a contract. Many parties in breach of a promise would claim they didn't really mean to enter a contract, and it would be hard to separate those parties from those who simply had made bad decisions and wanted to avoid contractual liability. Maybe if a party could convincingly show that they never contemplated entering into a contract (i.e., that they never even thought they were making a promise), however, their unreasonable use of language should be treated only as a tort, not as the basis for a contract.

3.4.2 The Role of Writings in Contract Interpretation

An unfortunate feature of US common law is that the rules governing the effect and interpretation of writings are needlessly complex. They make up some of the hardest material in contract law to learn. Some commentators may regard the problem they pose as difficult, but the messiness of the rules is not justified by the problem

---

112 RESTATEMENT (SECOND) OF CONTRACTS § 201(2)(a) (1981); *cf. also id.* § 20(1)(b).

itself; the messiness comes from a reason we have seen before: formal old rules get whittled away slowly and inconsistently.

The core problem in interpreting writings is that parties may say one thing but write down another. Maybe they've used a standard form contract and have forgotten what it says. Maybe parties write down most of their deal, but as they're about to sign it, one says to the other, "I know this document says that we're supposed to perform by March 1, but as we discussed you'll give us to March 5, right?" and the other party agrees.

As we saw with the statute of frauds (see section 3.3), it is important to resist the temptation to favor writings automatically over all other forms of communication and negotiation. Business deals are often factually complicated, and it is difficult and expensive—indeed, impossible—to write everything down. No written contract, no matter how carefully drafted, is complete. Particularly in smaller deals, parties don't have lawyers; all they might have is a standard form agreement written ages ago into which they are filling in numbers or other details. Maybe parties without lawyers have downloaded a form from the internet thinking it is standard and not understanding the possible interpretations of all the provisions it includes. It is easy to approach all these parties hard-heartedly with a very rigid rule like "you should have read and understood everything you signed," but that doesn't match reality or business norms. And paying too much attention to a writing threatens to run into the same problem we tried to avoid in the previous section: "No contract should ever be interpreted and enforced with a meaning that neither party gave it."[113]

This all raises the problem of what to do when there's a discrepancy, as there often is, between the deal that the parties thought they had and the one that they have written down. There is, maybe counterintuitively, no easy way to avoid this problem entirely: a written agreement can say "this agreement is the parties' final word on the matter," but the parties might have said exactly the opposite (in similarly strong words) as they signed it. Or, more fancifully, a writing could say "this agreement was not negotiated at gunpoint," but that doesn't mean that it wasn't.

An obscure old *Saturday Night Live* sketch illustrates this point evocatively. A passerby drops money into the guitar case of a subway musician, who objects: "I'm an artist! I'm not doing this for money!" The passerby takes the money back, at which point the subway musician begins to sing songs whose lyrics complain of the musician's desperate circumstances and beg for money. The passerby tries once

---

[113] 6 CORBIN ON CONTRACTS § 25.1 (2023).

again to give money to the musician: "Here, go ahead and take it; you need it more than me." The musician strenuously objects again: "That's just a song, man!" The passerby seems convinced. The musician then starts singing, "It wasn't just a song. / I really need the money. / I was just too embarrassed to let you give it to me," eventually including lyrics that specifically identify and address the passerby.[114] When the passerby tries to respond to the ambiguity by leaving the money near the musician's guitar case, the musician replies: "I don't want your money, you arrogant yuppie creep!" and throws the money away.[115] The potential tension between oral communications and written communications can be similar.

It may seem that written contracts should generally be considered more reliable than oral agreements. But every written contract has a context and a potential backstory and explanation. Consider this admittedly stylized illustration from the *Restatement (Second) of Contracts*:

> *A* and *B* are engaged in buying and selling shares of stock from each other, and agree orally to conceal the nature of their dealings by using the word "sell" to mean "buy" and using the word "buy" to mean "sell." *A* sends a written offer to *B* to "sell" certain shares, and *B* accepts. The parties are bound in accordance with the oral agreement.[116]

Classical contract law would have favored the written agreement over the oral one.[117] The only justification for the classical rule is a kind of general administrative blockade of information in order to make sure writings are absolutely followed. But writings can never be absolutely followed—even classical law would not uphold them, for example, when evidence outside the writings proves that they came about through fraud or duress. And it is not clear *why* it is so important to anyone that writings be absolutely followed even if that would go against the intention of both parties based on reliable evidence.

This type of situation, in any event, is addressed in common law, in part, through an overly complicated rule called the *parol-evidence rule*. The parol-evidence rule is badly named, badly motivated, and inconsistently applied from state to state. It is, however, definitely

---

114 *Saturday Night Live* (NBC television broadcast, Oct. 9, 1993), *available at* https://www.youtube.com/watch?v=UWNiT5A5thQ [https://archive.org/details/saturday-night-live-s-19-e-03-jeff-goldblum-aerosmith].

115 *Id.*

116 RESTATEMENT (SECOND) OF CONTRACTS § 212 cmt. b illus. 4 (1981).

117 RESTATEMENT OF CONTRACTS § 231 illus. 2 (1932); FULLER ET AL., *supra* note 56, at 619–20.

still part of the law in at least some form, though it has been significantly weakened over time in at least many states.

The word *parol* just means "oral" or "spoken word." It is the same word as *parole* in a punitive context; the origin of that term is that when a defendant is out "on parole," they're out on their *word* that they will behave well. *Parol* shares roots with *parable*, for example. So you might begin by thinking of the parol-evidence rule as being about "oral evidence" instead of "parol evidence." But even if you did that, the name would still be misleading because the rule is not a rule of evidence or even one that is particularly about evidence; it is a rule of contract law. For reasons I'm about to describe, it would be clearer if it were called the *side-agreement rule*.

At its core, the basic rule is not that complicated. Sometimes there is a written agreement that cancels, "discharges," replaces, or otherwise renders unenforceable (1) earlier agreements between the parties and (2) any simultaneous oral agreements the parties have made, often as "side agreements" to the main deal they have written down. When a court finds that a writing does this, it calls the writing (as a conclusory matter) an *integration* or an *integrated agreement*—another way of saying "this writing includes or brings together several agreements." To put that differently, *integration* is simply the term a court gives to a writing that triggers the parol-evidence rule.

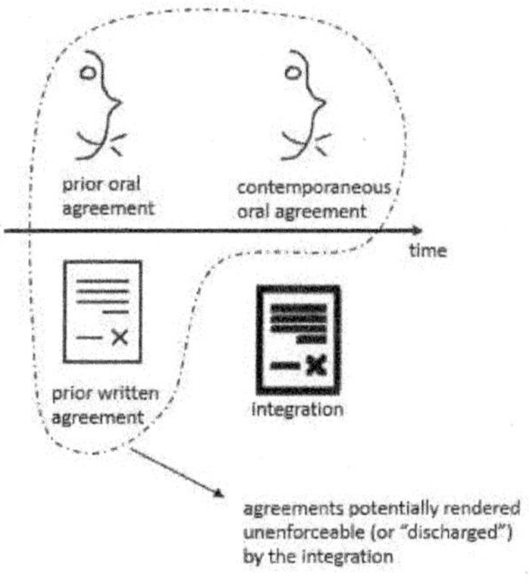

Figure 3.3

Note that the parol-evidence rule does not cancel or replace or discharge *future* agreements, only ones that are earlier or simultaneous with the integration.[118]

[118] Written contracts may separately have *no-oral-modification* clauses, which are commonly enforced today, although one concern is that they may appear in standard

As a simple matter of ordinary interpretation, a court could find that a writing is in fact an integration—that is, both parties intended it as one, or the party who did is more reasonable than the party who didn't (see section 3.4). If a court did this, it wouldn't need a special rule to give the writing that effect. For example, suppose on Monday the parties enter one deal, and then on Tuesday the parties replace that deal with a new deal (with consideration on both sides, and without any hint of an unfair contract modification). They write down Tuesday's deal in a document that says, "This is the final agreement between the parties, and it replaces all our prior deals." (Such a written provision is commonly called an *integration clause.*)[119] The Tuesday deal would be enforceable and would replace the Monday deal, and no special rule is required to reach that result: newer deals can replace older ones if that is what the parties want. The core application of the parol-evidence rule is simply that: a writing whose binding legal interpretation is to cancel or replace prior agreements (or simultaneous oral ones) does so.

We could, and perhaps should, end the matter there. It would certainly be easier, and it would be consistent with the rules of interpretation we have studied so far. One further rule that is not particularly objectionable is that because judges have special expertise in reading documents, it is a judge, rather than a jury, that determines whether a writing is an integration—that is, whether the parol-evidence rule applies and causes the writing to cancel or replace prior agreements (or simultaneous oral ones). Some states do not have a much stronger parol-evidence rule than that.

The classical, sharper versions of the parol-evidence rule go further, and they are the source of much doctrinal confusion because they probably go too far, leading courts to apply the rule inconsistently and to develop exceptions. Much like the statute of frauds, the classical forms of the parol-evidence rule could strike down agreements even when there's good evidence for them, just because of the formal consequences of the rule. In other words, the

---

form terms and not reflect the real intention of the parties. *See, e.g.*, U.C.C. § 2–209(2) ("A signed agreement which excludes modification or rescission except by a signed writing cannot be otherwise modified or rescinded, but except as between merchants such a requirement on a form supplied by the merchant must be separately signed by the other party."). In classical contract law, for axiomatic reasons no-oral-modification clauses were not enforced because an oral modification, if made for consideration and valid under the statute of frauds, was a new contract by the parties and therefore had legal effect. *See* MELVIN A. EISENBERG, FOUNDATIONAL PRINCIPLES OF CONTRACT LAW 813–14 (2018).

[119] Other labels are *entire-agreement clause* and *merger clause*. Note that such clauses are not necessarily enforceable exactly as written, partly because they often appear as standard terms and may not in fact reflect the parties' intent. *See* RESTATEMENT (SECOND) OF CONTRACTS § 216 cmt. e (1981); FULLER ET. AL, *supra* note 56, at 604.

conceptual difficulties of the parol-evidence rule—and the mismatch between the stronger forms of the rule and the moral and other functional goals of modern contract law—arise because the rule is pushed beyond the role it would have as a regular rule of contract interpretation aimed at figuring out what the parties meant. In this respect it is much like cases in tort law in which judges artificially declare particular behaviors as reasonable or unreasonable rather than letting that determination remain a factual question.

A typical feature of the older, harsher form of the parol-evidence rule (which is still sometimes applied in modern cases) is that any document that reasonably appears to the court to be an integration, regardless of whether either party intended it as one, counts as an integration. A particularly forceful version of the rule would require judges to determine whether a writing is an integration just by looking at the writing itself—not by looking at other contextual features of the situation. In other words, just like classical contract law's insistence that "buy" means "buy" even if the parties have chosen to speak in code and have it mean "sell," a document that appears on its face to a judge to be an integration can, under the harshest form of the classical rule, be treated as an integration. That sort of rule has little in its favor except perhaps very general arguments about institutional regularity—courts should be predictable and so on—but its defenders rarely explain why courts couldn't pay more attention to factual context and still be predictable. Moreover, as discussed in chapter 1, it is predictability for the contracting parties (not for academics reviewing cases) that matters—and that is not achieved by making parties subject to a judge's whimsical interpretation of their writings without regard to the parties' intent in producing the writings. It is these sorts of concerns that have caused the older form of the parol-evidence rule to erode and to be applied inconsistently. As the Corbin treatise puts it, "No writing, whatever its form and content, is sufficient to establish its existence and operation as an 'integration' assented to as such by the parties."[120] In other words, courts properly need to look at more than the writing itself if their goal is to determine the role that the parties intended for the writing to have.

The classical, more forceful version of the parol-evidence rule also differs from the more modern versions of the rule in the precise *effects* that it causes an integration to have. Without any special parol-evidence rule, we could simply say something like "a writing modifies or cancels prior agreements if, under normal interpretive rules, that is how the writing is to be interpreted." Then, whenever we encounter an integration, we could simply interpret it and figure

---

[120] 6 CORBIN ON CONTRACTS § 25.1 (2023).

out whether and how the writing modifies or cancels earlier agreements. That would more or less match the modern approach to the parol-evidence rule: "There is no way to determine whether evidence of an antecedent agreement or negotiation varies or contradicts an 'integration' until after the 'integration' has been interpreted."[121] Even under the most modern and flexible forms of the parol-evidence rule, a side agreement or a prior one that directly contradicts an integration is still usually not enforceable, but there is significant (though disputed) room for agreements that "supplement" the integration.

Different versions of the parol-evidence rule have more or less rigid rules for striking down prior agreements (or contemporaneous oral ones) that don't contradict but merely "supplement" the writing. The classical rule, which was the most rigid, is that once a court determines that a document is an integration, any oral agreements or prior agreements that *would ordinarily, if they had been made, have been included in the integration* are rendered unenforceable.[122] To put it more simply, under that version of the parol-evidence rule, an integration cancels all prior agreements and oral agreements that the judge thinks should be included in the integration's scope—that is, in the single agreement that the integration "integrates" or reduces to a single writing—after simply looking at the writing.

An example may shed light on this needlessly complex point. In *Mitchill v. Lath*,[123] parties entered a routine agreement to buy and sell land. Across the street from the land was an "ice house"—a small and in this case ugly structure used to store ice before electrical refrigeration was common—that the sellers owned and had the right to remove. The sellers promised to remove the ice house as part of the land deal, but they did not include that promise in the written purchase-and-sale agreement. They then refused to honor their oral agreement to remove the ice house. That agreement, though oral, is not within the statute of frauds because it is not itself a contract to sell real estate. It would normally have been enforceable. The *Mitchill* court (in New York in 1928) held that the oral promise was unenforceable because the writing was an integration and, essentially, the justices (given their own experiences) would have expected any promise to remove the ice house to have been included in the integration. A dissenting judge adopted a more modern view: refusing to enforce the oral agreement

---

121 *Id.*

122 *See* Mitchill v. Lath, 160 N.E. 646, 647 (N.Y. 1928) (for an oral side agreement to remain enforceable despite an integration, "it must be one that parties would not ordinarily be expected to embody in the writing").

123 *Id.*

> on the ground that it varies the contract embodied in the writing may be based only upon a finding or presumption that the written contract was intended to cover [i.e., include or replace] the oral negotiations for the removal of the icehouse which lead up to the contract of purchase and sale. To determine what the writing was intended to cover "the document alone will not suffice. What it was intended to cover cannot be known till we know what there was to cover. The question being whether certain subjects of negotiation were intended to be covered, we must compare the writing and the negotiations before we can determine whether they were in fact covered."[124]

One way to evaluate *Mitchill* is to ask what the local practices were involving written real-estate contracts. In a world in which buyers and sellers use a standard form to make such contracts, it is hard to imagine they would go out of their way to mention the removal of an ice house from an adjacent property that wasn't even for sale. If such contracts are frequently and heavily customized in the locale, then it would be useful to ask why the parties in *Mitchill* didn't include that term in their written agreement.

The law has tried out a few alternative standards for determining the scope of an integration. The UCC, in a comment, suggests integrations should invalidate prior or oral agreements only when "they would certainly have been included in the document in the view of the court."[125] This leads to a much less forceful version of the parol-evidence rule because few prior or oral agreements would *certainly* or *necessarily* have been included in an integration. In other words, the UCC seems to be suggesting that if there is any plausible explanation for why a prior or oral agreement was left out of an integration, the integration should not invalidate that agreement. Some courts have given the UCC's version of the parol-evidence rule somewhat more teeth, invalidating prior or oral agreements only when there is "the absence of reasonable harmony in terms of the language and respective obligations of the parties" between the integration and the prior or oral agreements.[126]

Again, this is all needlessly unclear and confusing. We could use a simple rule of interpretation to recognize and then give effect to integrations, but the presence of the classical parol-evidence rule creates a more ornate structure in the common law that persists even

---

124 *Id.* at 649 (Lehman, J., dissenting) (quoting a contemporaneous edition of *Wigmore on Evidence*).

125 U.C.C. § 2–202 cmt. 3.

126 Snyder v. Herbert Greenbaum & Assocs., Inc., 380 A.2d 618, 623 (Md. Ct. Spec. App. 1977).

today. One way to understand the difference between a classical approach like *Mitchill* and a more sensitive modern approach is that the modern approach is *individualized* and pays attention to the parties' business reality, whereas the classical approach is *generalized* and constructs an "objective" reality for them. In other words, the classical parol-evidence rule is concerned with what hypothetical abstract parties would have wanted the integration to do, even though the court has actual parties in front of it. The mismatch between the abstract and the actual is the main tension in this area of law.

Much is sometimes made of the difference between *partial integrations* and *complete integrations*, but this distinction never seems to have been useful to the law; it is just a needlessly complex route for the law to have gone down, like *res ipsa* (see section 2.2.3). Any integration has some scope: it will strike down some prior or oral agreements and leave others untouched. No agreement is really "the complete and final deal of the parties" in a way that means it replaces *every* deal they might have with each other. A real-estate contract that the parties treated as their "final and complete deal" wouldn't cancel a prior, unrelated catering order between the seller, who happens to own a bakery across town, and the buyer, who has ordered several cakes for a party. There is always a spectrum, and the terms *complete* and *partial* do not appear to help here.

In addition to the parol-evidence rule, there is a separate rule that applies to writings that is called the *plain-meaning rule* or the *four-corners rule*. Though the rule is separate, courts and commentators often confuse it with the parol-evidence rule—sometimes conceptually and sometimes just as a matter of terminology. The plain-meaning rule is much simpler than the parol-evidence rule, however, and can easily be kept distinct. The plain-meaning rule is simply a rule that when a document has a single, "plain" meaning, that meaning is how the document should be interpreted. The rule applies to documents regardless of whether they are integrations; even a writing that is not an integration needs to be interpreted and could have an apparent "plain" meaning, and a writing that is an integration may also still need to be interpreted so that it can be given effect. Though the two rules are separate, their pattern in common law has been similar: like the parol-evidence rule, the plain-meaning rule (1) used to be much stronger; and (2) has been inconsistently applied by modern courts, probably for much the same reasons we have already seen: looking at a writing, without more, is not always enough to figure out what the parties intended their deal to be. The rule is stronger in some states than others. A fair statement of the typical modern force of the rule is that legal interpretations of a written agreement must be chosen from among those that are *reasonably susceptible* to its text—but consider again the "buy means sell" example. Some courts continue to apply more rigid versions of the rule that lead to very poor results.[127]

The plain-meaning rule should not be mistaken for a suggestion that every writing must have a plain meaning. The rule, even in its classical form, is that *if* a writing has a single, plain meaning, that meaning governs. The dispute in courts is often about whether a document has a plain meaning—often with both sides somewhat implausibly insisting that their own favored meaning is the single plain meaning. Many commentators believe that few or no documents have a single plain meaning; the "buy means sell" example is an abstract vindication of that view, but many real-world cases involve written contracts that appear to mean one thing until one of the parties raises a new fact or argument. Accordingly, one critique of the plain-meaning rule is that it should rarely apply. Another is that it is based on an unsound policy and that, instead, the regular rules of interpretation should govern written documents. Nobody suggests written documents should be ignored, just that they should be used, along with other evidence, to determine what the parties intended (or, if they disagreed, which of them had a more reasonable interpretation of their bargain). In any event, modern US jurisdictions each have their own versions and statements of the rule, and the forcefulness of the rule varies from jurisdiction to jurisdiction.

Even in states that adopt a strong version of the plain-meaning rule, there is room for *trade usages* and other forms of evidence, such as the parties' prior dealings, to explain their writings. For example, the word "white" may carry a particular dictionary definition, but nobody would think that "white wine" needs to look like milk or that "white chocolate" needs to be the color of laser-printer paper. The rules on course of dealing, course of performance, and trade usage are often taught in Contracts courses and appear in both the Restatement and the UCC,[128] but professors sometimes don't make explicit that these rules are very large exceptions to the plain-meaning rule in that they can override what a judge might think of as the single clear meaning of a writing. As the UCC's statutory command to judges puts it, "the express terms of an agreement and any applicable course of performance, course of dealing, or usage of trade *must* be construed whenever reasonable as consistent with each other."[129]

---

[127] *See, e.g.*, Steuart v. McChesney, 444 A.2d 659 (Pa. 1982).

[128] *See* RESTATEMENT (SECOND) OF CONTRACTS §§ 219–223 (1981); U.C.C. § 1–303.

[129] U.C.C. § 1–303 (emphasis added).

Given the law's inconsistency in determining the force of writings in contract law, the best approach to the rules in this area is probably to keep an open mind. Perhaps different rules ought to apply to different types of interpretive situations. For example, maybe the plain-meaning rule makes more sense when interpreting a 300-page agreement for the acquisition of a large company than it does for two people in a local trade who know each other and have negotiated deals on particular terms before.[130] It is also important not to let your views on "text" in constitutional law or statutory interpretation drive your views on contract interpretation; the policies in those areas can be very different.

In summary, like rules in tort law where judges opine from the bench about what is reasonable or not, purportedly as a matter of law, rules like the parol-evidence rule and the plain-meaning rule are ways for judges to retain control over litigation—and perhaps prevent cases from surviving motions for summary judgment. Courts have tended not to apply the more formalistic versions of these rules consistently, which has led to many inconsistent exceptions and differences among the states. Mainly that is because of a general tension: writings may be good evidence of agreements but are never perfect evidence, and often they convey exactly the wrong impression. Paying special attention to writings may channel parties' efforts into documents that avoid or reduce the impact of later disputes, but many parties are not aware of the precise rules of contract law, so the channeling function of such rules is suspect. Maybe writings, like the seal (see section 3.1.7) are a natural formality—but many people today think of text messages as considerably *less* formal and significant than phone calls, a fact that was not true even a few decades ago.

3.5 Contract Formation: The Rules of "Offer and Acceptance"

Hundreds of cases say that for a contract to be formed, there needs to be an *offer* (some communication that a reasonable person would think they could accept and thereby form a contract) and an *acceptance* (a definite "yes" in response to an offer). Contract formation—specifically the rules related to "offer and acceptance"—may seem to be foundational to the study of contracts, so it may seem odd that the topic appears so late in this chapter.[131] The reason is

---

[130] For more analysis along these lines, see Shawn Bayern, *Contract Meta-Interpretation*, 49 U.C. DAVIS L. REV. 1097 (2016).

[131] Consideration is often treated as a matter of contract formation, but it is distinct from rules of offer and acceptance. Moreover, it is a matter of contract "formation" only on formalistic grounds, because doctrinally courts *say* that parties have not "formed" a contract if it lacks consideration. Little is to be gained from

that the study of contract formation depends on the rules of contract interpretation discussed in the previous section.

The rules of offer and acceptance have something important in common with some features of negligence law in tort: they are much too complicated, and the law is easier to learn and apply if the rules are dramatically simplified. In other words, contract-formation doctrine has functional similarities with *res ipsa* (see section 2.2.3) or assumption of risk (see section 2.7.2) in that it adds complexity without often achieving much that is useful. We might get rid of a lot of contract-formation doctrine simply by applying the interpretive rules we have just studied.

For example, if two parties both think they have a contract, then they should have a contract—that is just an application of the rule that the parties' shared subjective interpretation governs. It shouldn't matter whether we can call something one of them said an "offer" and something the other one said an "acceptance." Similarly, if one party thinks they formed a contract and the other party doesn't, the more reasonable party should win. That too is just an application of general interpretive rules (see section 3.4). If the rules of contract formation do anything else, they violate sound interpretive principles and risk favoring the *unreasonable* party.

3.5.1 Formation as a Simple Extension of Interpretation

Consider the straightforward case of *Lonergan v. Skolnick*.[132] A seller was looking to sell land at a discount and posted an advertisement ("need cash, will sacrifice"). A potential buyer replied by mail. After some further discussion by mail, the seller wrote a letter on April 8 to the buyer that confirmed some details the buyer had asked about and added: "If you are really interested, you will have to decide fast, as I expect to have a buyer in the next week or so."[133] On April 14, the buyer received this letter, and he replied on April 15 purporting to accept an offer for a contract to sell the land. Unfortunately, on April 12, the seller had already sold the land to a third party.

The legal question in this case is conventionally taken to be "was the seller's letter a legally significant offer?" Though that is not a terrible question to ask, it slightly obscures the actual dispute

framing the question that way. As discussed earlier in this chapter, the questions addressed by consideration really concern what promises the law determines to enforce, and when there is "no consideration" courts are essentially saying, as a general matter, that there is no enforcement of those promises.

132 276 P.2d 8 (Cal. Ct. App. 1954).

133 *Id.* at 9.

between the parties, which is just a dispute about whose interpretation is more reasonable. In writing a letter on April 15 thinking that he was forming a contract, the buyer presumably thought that the two parties had reached a deal. In selling the land on April 12 to someone else, the seller presumably didn't think he had communicated any willingness to this buyer to be bound into a specific deal. In other words, the two parties have assigned different interpretations to their communications. Of their two different subjective meanings, the more reasonable one should win (see section 3.4).

That is exactly what the more conventional question—did the buyer make an offer?—is aimed at determining. An offer is defined as a communication that a reasonable person thinks they could accept.[134] So, to determine whether the seller's letter constitutes an offer, we ask if the buyer was reasonable in thinking that it was an offer. That is the same kind of question that the general interpretive inquiry would ask.

Regardless of whether we focus on general interpretation or on the presence of an offer, the reason there's potential ambiguity (that is, a potential interpretive dispute) in *Lonergan* is that, in the seller's letter, "If you're really interested, you will have to decide fast, as I expect to have a buyer in the next week or so" could mean either "You have about a week to send me a decision about my particular offer here, after which time I make no promises" or "I might sell the property to someone else, and soon, so if you really want this property you should move toward negotiating a final contract quickly." Which of the two parties' interpretations is more reasonable depends on how we interpret the seller's language, in view of the circumstances of the case. As a purely interpretive matter, that is potentially a close question—reasonable people can probably see it either way—which may mean the parties' interpretations are nearly enough tied, as a matter of objective reasonableness, that we should conclude there was no contract. The important point, however, is that using the language of "offer" and "acceptance" doesn't add much to the inquiry.

Incidentally, as a matter of legal realism, there is probably another reason that the courts in *Lonergan* determined that there was no contract: holding that there was a contract would be very harsh to the seller. The seller is trying to get cash quickly and is willing to sell his property at a discount in order to do so. There is no reason to think that anything the seller has done is intentionally

---

[134] That is just a more casual version of the Restatement's slightly more stilted definition: "An offer is the manifestation of willingness to enter into a bargain, so made as to justify another person in understanding that his assent to that bargain is invited and will conclude it." RESTATEMENT (SECOND) OF CONTRACTS § 24 (1981).

dishonest or misleading; at worst, he has used language carelessly. He certainly does not desire to be bound to two different contracts to sell his land; surely his sale of the land on April 12 to a third party means he didn't think he was bound to the potential buyer who ended up suing him. The buyer's expectation damages, if there was a regular contract under general principles of contract law, would be the difference between the market value of the land and the contract price. In this case, the putative market price of the land was about $6,100, and the price that the buyer thinks he was offered was $2,500, so his suit was for about $3,600. Supposing the seller sold the land to a different third party for a similar discount, that would mean the seller pocketed $2,500 and would now owe even more than that to the plaintiff in the case—merely because that buyer was, in the abstract, skilled at making a deal quickly. That is not a risk that the seller likely would have been willing to accept. As a clue that this is a result that courts oppose and try to avoid, the lower court in *Lonergan* found that the seller's letter of April 8 *was* an offer but that the buyer didn't respond quickly enough—even though his reply was sent only a day after he received the offer. Often, when two courts reach the same result on different and inconsistent grounds, that is an indication that they were motivated to reach that particular result for reasons that are not fully captured by the doctrine.

A further indication that imposing a contract (with full expectation damages) on the seller is too harsh in *Lonergan* is found in a doctrine that is the law in many (but not all) states that a buyer of real estate is not entitled to expectation damages against a seller who hasn't acted in bad faith.[135] The rationale for such a doctrine is that, as in *Lonergan*, expectation damages for accidentally selling land twice—or, for example, for agreeing to sell land but forgetting that you don't really have the power to do so, because you co-own it with someone else who refuses to sell—could be financially ruinous. As we saw earlier (see section 3.4.1), perhaps when it is clear that parties don't want a contract and have only used language carelessly, the lower measure of reliance damages is sufficient.

In any event, whatever the result in *Lonergan*, it would be easy to express it without bothering with the terms *offer* and *acceptance*, though those terms don't do any harm in the general case. They are just a more complicated way to say that the party with the more reasonable interpretation of events prevails, even if the precise sequence of contract formation has become hard to determine by the time a case reaches a court. And the concepts of offer and acceptance may obscure the fact that if both parties subjectively believe there is a contract, then there should be one even if we can't easily identify

---

135 *See* MELVIN A. EISENBERG & SHAWN BAYERN, CONTRACTS 261 (15th ed. 2020).

an offer or an acceptance. Those general principles have more or less become the modern law. For example, as the UCC puts it: "An agreement sufficient to constitute a contract for sale may be found even though the moment of its making is undetermined."[136]

The terminology of offer and acceptance remains commonplace, but it often makes little difference. For example, even though hundreds of cases still repeat the proposition that "contract formation requires offer and acceptance," there has long been a rule that contracts may be *implied in fact*, and this label is sometimes used to refer to situations where it is clear that the parties have a contract even though they didn't go through any procedures to form it that easily map onto the notion of "offer" or "acceptance."[137] This is much like *res ipsa loquitur* in tort (see section 2.2.3), where we know that someone was negligent even if we don't know how. Perhaps neither the particular offer nor the particular acceptance is clear because the parties' contract resulted from an extended conversation and a shared sense as they left the conversation. Or maybe a party receives a formal offer and then acts for a long time as if they have accepted it without ever sending any clear or discrete communication saying that; there too the parties can have a contract.[138] As a result, the actual rule is more like "contract formation requires offer and acceptance except when it doesn't"; more important than "offer" or "acceptance" are the parties' reasonable beliefs about whether they have a contract. Indeed, the paradigmatic examples of contract formation in the popular imagination—shaking hands or signing a document together—don't involve a clear or discrete offer or acceptance.

3.5.2 Rules That Assign Special Significance to Particular Types of Communications

Some of the more particular rules of contract formation do get in the way of sensible interpretation. As Mel Eisenberg has pointed out, the law of contract formation has many rules that assign formal meanings to communications between the parties. He calls these *expression rules*;[139] perhaps *communication rules* would be a clearer term today. Just like situations in negligence law where judges give

---

[136] *E.g.*, U.C.C. § 2–204(2).

[137] See RESTATEMENT (SECOND) OF CONTRACTS § 4 (1981) ("A promise may be stated in words either oral or written, or may be inferred wholly or partly from conduct.").

[138] *See* U.C.C. § 2–207(3) ("Conduct by both parties which recognizes the existence of a contract is sufficient to establish a contract for sale although [i.e., even though] the writings of the parties do not otherwise establish a contract."); *see also* RESTATEMENT (SECOND) OF CONTRACTS § 19 cmt. a (1981).

[139] *See* Melvin Aron Eisenberg, *Expression Rules in Contract Law and Problems of Offer and Acceptance*, 82 CAL. L. REV. 1127 (1994).

opinions about whether a particular defendant's behavior was reasonable or not, rather than letting the question go to the jury, many rules in contract formation try to dictate to parties what counts as reasonable. The rules can all be evaluated (in terms of policy and morality) simply by asking whether they allow the more reasonable party to win or cause the more reasonable party to lose.

Many of the particular rules in this area are sound, though they don't add much. For example, when an offer is made, by default it lapses after a reasonable time.[140] That rule reaches exactly the same results as a general interpretive rule: if I make an offer on Monday, you accept on Thursday, and we disagree about whether you waited too long to accept, the more reasonable of us should win, and that is all that the general rule about the lapse of offers does. There is a more particular rule—and this is very much like rules that courts have laid down in negligence law about what behavior counts as reasonable "as a matter of law"—that an offer made in a face-to-face conversation lapses, by default, at the end of the conversation.[141]

Some rules are more formalistic but still on balance justifiable. For example, a rejection by an offeree causes an offer to terminate.[142] In general, people don't reject offers and then quickly change their minds and accept them, so someone who does so probably shouldn't count on the fact that they have formed a contract.[143]

There is also the famous *mailbox rule*, more commonly called the *dispatch rule* in other common-law countries—and maybe calling it the *acceptance rule* would be clearer, because it applies only to acceptances. As a matter of background law, delayed communications (and communications in general that are sent over slow delivery systems like the mail) are usually effective when they are received, not when they are sent. But the mailbox rule treats acceptances differently: it declares that acceptances are effective as soon as they are irrevocably sent. The usual justification for the rule is that it accelerates possible performance by the offeree to its earliest reasonable point. As the judges in the case that established the mailbox rule[144] recognized, two parties communicating at a distance over a delayed and not-fully-reliable communications channel can never be *sure* that the other party is on the same page as they are, so it would be counterproductive to wait for any such assurance. It may

---

140 RESTATEMENT (SECOND) OF CONTRACTS § 41 (1981) (adding that "reasonable time is a question of fact, depending on all the circumstances existing when the offer and attempted acceptance are made").

141 *See id.* cmt. d.

142 *Id.* § 38.

143 *See* Eisenberg, *supra* note 139, at 1157.

144 Adams v. Lindsell, 106 Eng. Rep. 250 (K.B. 1818).

be tempting to say that the party who accepts should wait for confirmation, but then the party sending confirmation would not be sure that the confirmation was received, so they would need to wait for confirmation of the confirmation, and so on. The general result that perfect coordination is impossible was proved as a logical matter by computer-network theorists more than 150 years later.[145]

The main force of the mailbox rule is that an acceptance that crosses paths with a revocation by the offeror in the mail is effective even if the revocation happens to arrive first. Given that, probably a clearer justification for the mailbox rule is simply that acceptances are commonplace but revocations of offers by offerors are rare. So if there has to be a general rule, we should not let the rare case of revocations drive the results. Overall, the mailbox rule seems useful, though it is less and less important in a world of quick and reliable communication where parties can clarify any discrepancies with a phone call.

Some rules of contract formation are harder to justify.[146] There is a rule in the common law that offers and acceptances must match perfectly, or else the purported acceptance (even if it clearly says "yes!") is a *counteroffer* and acts as a rejection. If that rule has any function, it is to prevent people from being in deals that they don't want. But many other legal systems have a more adaptive modern rule that pays attention to whether any differences between the offer and counteroffer are *material*, rather than just whether they exist.[147] And the UCC has repealed the rule in modern US law for contracts within its scope.[148]

3.5.3 Revocation and "Firm Offers"

A particularly problematic rule of contract-formation law comes from an overly aggressive application of consideration doctrine (see

---

145 *See* E.A. Akkoynunlu et al., *Some Constraints and Tradeoffs in the Design of Network Communications, in* SOSP, PROCEEDINGS OF THE FIFTH ACM SYMPOSIUM ON OPERATING SYSTEMS PRINCIPLES 67, 70 (J.C. Brown & Juan Rodriguez-Rosell eds., 1975) ("In an arbitrary distributed facility, it is impossible to provide complete status."); Jim Gray, *Notes on Data Base Operating Systems, in* OPERATING SYSTEMS 393 (Michael Flynn et al. eds., 1978).

146 *See* Eisenberg, *supra* note 139, at 1158–66.

147 *E.g.*, UNIDROIT PRINCIPLES OF INTERNATIONAL COMMERCIAL CONTRACTS Art. 2.11.1, at 50–51 (2010) ("[A] reply to an offer which purports to be an acceptance but contains additional or different terms which do not materially alter the terms of the offer constitutes an acceptance, unless the offeror, without undue delay, objects to the discrepancy.").

148 U.C.C. § 2–207(1) ("A definite and seasonable expression of acceptance or a written confirmation which is sent within a reasonable time operates as an acceptance even though it states terms additional to or different from those offered or agreed upon, unless acceptance is expressly made conditional on assent to the additional or different terms.").

section 3.1) that, like the illusory-promise rule, would erroneously treat promises made for commercial reasons as if they were gift promises. That rule prevents parties from making "firm offers"—that is, irrevocable ones—without consideration, and in fact it overlaps significantly with the illusory-promise rule (see section 3.1.4) and is an undesirable rule for very similar reasons.

It may be surprising at first, but under classical contract law, even someone who promises explicitly not to revoke an offer (until, say, a particular time) can still later legally revoke it at will. An offer made with words like "You have until Friday at 5:00 p.m. to consider this offer, and I firmly promise that I will not revoke it before then" could still be revoked on Thursday. The reason is simply that no consideration was given for the promise to hold the offer open—that is, the promise not to revoke it. The underlying deal could have consideration, but the offer to hold the promise open does not.

Promises to hold an offer open are not ordinarily gift promises, made for reasons of love or affection. They are ordinarily made in order to improve the likelihood of commerce.[149] An offeree who knows they have a fixed period of time to consider an offer is more likely to take the offer seriously and to invest resources in evaluating it. (For example, if someone knows they are not competing with other potential buyers to buy a house, they may be more willing to pay for an inspection to evaluate it.) And a promise to keep an offer open is still a promise and has reasons of morality in favor of its enforcement. In other words, there is no reason in morality or policy not to enforce a promise to keep an offer open; the rule results only from a mechanical application of classical consideration doctrine.[150]

Because the rule has little or no justification, it has eroded sharply in modern law. We have already seen, in section 3.1.7, one interesting way that the rule has eroded. Recall that an *option contract* is enforceable even when given only for nominal consideration—that is, even when it is only part of a nominal bargain. An option contract is simply a promise to keep an offer open. As a result, a well-advised offeror who wants to make an enforceably firm offer could simply say "I'm giving you this offer in exchange for a penny"—and, to be even surer under a quirk in the doctrine, they could actually exchange the penny. As a result, this is one of the few areas in modern law where a particular meaningless trick of form can drive legal outcomes and serve as a useful transactional-planning technique.

---

149 *See* Eisenberg, *supra* note 21, at 1018–23.

150 *See* Eisenberg, *supra* note 34, at 1751.

Moreover, the UCC explicitly repeals the rule, although only in a limited way:

> An offer by a merchant to buy or sell goods in a signed writing which by its terms gives assurance that it will be held open is not revocable, for lack of consideration, during the time stated or if no time is stated for a reasonable time, but in no event may such period of irrevocability exceed three months; but any such term of assurance on a form supplied by the offeree must be separately signed by the offeror.[151]

Finally, if an offeree relies on a firm offer, it becomes enforceable on that basis. That is just an application of the general rule of promissory estoppel, although it has separate explicit support in the Restatement.[152]

As with other unhelpful classical rules that we've seen, a clean and outright repeal would be easier. Instead, understanding the old rule, the reasons it does not function well to achieve goals of morality and policy, and the mechanisms by which it has been limited is needed in order to achieve a complete picture of the modern state of the rule.

3.6 Important Problems in Contract Remedies

Contract law is one of the few subjects in the common law where there is significant dispute over even the basic goal of remedies—that is, over the conceptual "position" into which we're trying to put the promisee:

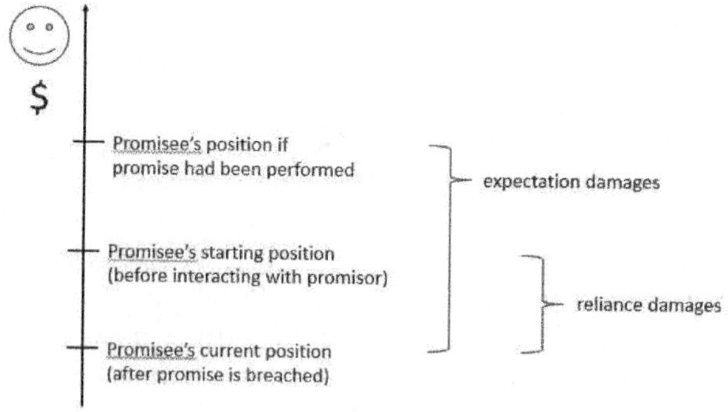

Figure 3.4: On a scale of personal happiness, or sometimes money—the law is not always clear—*reliance damages* aim to restore a promisee to the point on the scale where they were before the promise was made, and

[151] U.C.C. § 2–205.

[152] RESTATEMENT (SECOND) OF CONTRACTS § 87 (1981).

expectation damages push them forward to the point on the scale they'd have occupied if the promise had been performed.

We have already seen *reliance damages* (see section 3.1.7). Their goal is to put the promisee back, as nearly as possible—in terms of money or general happiness or satisfaction, and the law is not always clear on which—into the situation they were in before any promise was made. If a promise was made and the promisee has not relied on it in any way, there will be no reliance damages: the promise won't have caused any harm and the promisee will occupy the same position as they were in before the contract was made. (Of course, other circumstances for the promisee may have changed, but we ignore those and focus only on the changes caused by the promise.) Reliance damages are the most appropriate general remedy for the breach of gift promises, subject to the discussion in section 3.1.7. Contract law also occasionally uses *restitutionary* measures of damages.[153]

By contrast, *expectation damages* are damages that aim to put the promisee in the situation they'd occupy if their promise had been performed. Expectation damages are the normal remedy for breach of bargain contracts. Their precise justification in that context (over reliance damages) remains disputed, but they have many reasons in their favor.[154] Expectation damages give the promisor incentives to do what they promised, so they give the promisee assurance, which enables productive planning. Expectation damages are usually clearer and more reliable to calculate than reliance damages. They also may be necessary to fairly backstop the parties' deal.[155]

Though damages measures can sometimes have rules or applications that appear complicated, they tend to rest on straightforward principles. Professor Larry Garvin, in his teaching, compares damages problems to "spot the difference" puzzles in children's books.[156] When awarding damages, courts have in mind a position into which they aim to put the plaintiff—for example, the situation in which the promise had been performed (for expectation damages) or the situation in which the promise had never been made (reliance damages). The job of damages is simply to identify what factual features are different between the plaintiff's current state and that target state and then convert those differences into money.

---

153 *See* RESTATEMENT (SECOND) OF CONTRACTS § 344 (1981).

154 *See* Robert Cooter & Melvin Aron Eisenberg, *Damages for Breach of Contract*, 73 CAL. L. REV. 1432, 1475–77 (1985).

155 *See* Shawn J. Bayern & Melvin A. Eisenberg, *The Expectation Measure and Its Discontents*, 2013 MICH. ST. L. REV. 1, 5.

156 *See* Wikipedia, *Spot the Difference*, https://en.wikipedia.org/wiki/Spot_the_difference.

For example, in *Hawkins v. McGee*,[157] a doctor made an unusual promise to a patient that surgery would give the patient a "perfect hand." When the surgery failed dramatically, the court awarded damages that aimed to measure, conceptually, "the difference between the value to him of a perfect hand or a good hand . . . and the value of his hand in its present condition."[158] That is simply an application of the principle of expectation damages. Of course, money for physical injury and its emotional consequences is always imprecise, but courts do the best they can, as with pain-and-suffering damages in tort law.

In *Hawkins*, the court denied damages for the patient's pain during the operation itself. That pain would have been present even if the doctor had done what he promised, so it is not a "difference" that expectation damages aim to address. But, for example, if reliance damages had been used in *Hawkins*, the pain from the operation *would* be a "difference" between the promise's actual state and their target state because if the promise had never been made, the promisee wouldn't have undergone any medical procedure.

As another example, the fee that the patient paid to the doctor to perform the operation should not be included in expectation damages in a case like *Hawkins* (because even if the doctor had met the terms of his promise, the patient would have paid that fee). But the fee would be included in reliance damages in such a case (because if the doctor had never made a promise to the patient, there would have been no operation and no fee). Note that while reliance damages are sometimes described as tort-like, they are not identical to tort damages. For example, in a medical-malpractice case, a patient cannot recover the doctor's fee because the malpractice didn't cause that fee to be paid. The baseline to which damages are meant to restore a patient in a malpractice case isn't based on a promise or on restoring the patient to a situation before they'd never interacted with the doctor; it is something more like "the situation the patient would have been in had the doctor met the standard of care for medical professionals" (see section 2.2.4), in which case the fee still would have been paid.

In a more typical contract case than *Hawkins*, substitute performance is usually physically possible for the promisee to purchase. Then, expectation damages typically resolve to the cost of finding and then purchasing a substitute for performance (minus any

---

[157] 146 A. 641 (N.H. 1929).

[158] *Id.* at 644.

costs that the promisee saved by not having to pay the original promisor).[159]

The notion of saved costs is an important one in determining expectation damages. A promisee ordinarily loses something from breach, but the breach may also save them money too—because it means they do not need to complete their own performance. For example, if a homeowner contracts for a kitchen renovation for $14,000 but then refuses to pay before the work starts, the renovator loses $14,000 from the breach but saves the cost of construction (which they no longer need to complete because of the breach). If the costs of construction would have been $12,000—so the renovator's profits from the contract would be $2,000—damages are simply $2,000. One way to understand that result is to recognize that the breach caused the contractor to lose its profit from the contract; that is, its *net* loss from breach, as compared to performance, is its lost profit. Another way to understand the contractor's damages is to say that the breach cost it $14,000 but saved it $12,000, leading to a difference of $2,000. The result is, of course, the same. Contracts courses often work through slightly more complicated examples where partial payments have been made, some work has already been done, some supplies have been purchased that the contractor might (or might not) use or resell, and so on, but the "spot the difference" principle remains.

Another type of remedy is available in contract law: a court injunction commanding the promisor to do what they promised, otherwise known as *specific performance*. (*Specific* here means *in kind*, as suggested by the word *species*—much as how assets between two modern brokerage accounts can be transferred "in kind" instead of being converted to cash. An older term was *performance in specie*.) Specific performance arose historically from equity courts, much like promissory estoppel (see section 3.1.7), and its history explains much of its modern character. First, following the historical rule that courts of equity acted only when courts of law weren't sufficient to achieve justice, the general rule is that specific performance isn't awarded when damages are good enough to put the plaintiff in the position they'd have been in had their promise been performed (by allowing them to purchase a substitute performance).[160] Second, specific

---

159 In the context of goods, substitute performance is called *cover*. *See, e.g.*, U.C.C. § 2–712. The cost of finding substitute performance is one type of a general kind of damages called, relatively informally, *incidental damages*—essentially the costs of routine mechanical responses to a breach of contract, like taking care of goods until they can be resold or otherwise mitigating losses.

160 *See generally* Melvin A. Eisenberg, *Actual and Virtual Specific Performance, the Theory of Efficient Breach, and the Indifference Principle in Contract Law*, 93 CAL. L. REV. 975 (2005) (calling substitute performance purchased with damages "virtual specific performance").

performance retains a discretionary character that is typical of doctrines that derive from equity; instead of operating strictly on principle, judges need to decide that specific performance is a good idea in the case in front of them—all things considered, including in principle public policy—before awarding it.

The reason for that discretion is largely historical, but it may make sense because of the strong force of judicial orders. Courts can attempt to compel parties to follow orders by holding them in *contempt of court* and threatening them with time in jail. This sort of "jail" is conceptually different from "prison" in that it is not meant to be punish, only to compel the defendant to comply with the court's order. But it is still a very forceful response exhibiting an unusual degree of compulsion for civil cases.

By contrast, damages are not as personally compulsive. The term *damages* always refers to a court *judgment* declaring that some amount of money is due. If a defendant doesn't pay a claim for damages, the plaintiff can try to *execute* the judgment by asking a government official to seize the defendant's property. But that process is slow and difficult. In principle, if a defendant has the means to satisfy a judgment but is choosing not to (by purposely putting funds outside the reach of a jurisdiction, for example), a court may issue a *turnover order* that requires the defendant to pay. Like an order for specific performance, a turnover order comes with the threat of jail.

This whole arrangement is largely historical, but it is functional enough. In a market economy, money is usually a good remedy because it permits contracting parties to select their own suitable substitutes for performance and it avoids the threat of jail, which courts and contracting parties would probably usually prefer to avoid if they can.[161] Other legal systems, like Germany's, tend to make specific performance more readily available as a matter of law, but even in those systems it appears that plaintiffs frequently request damages because damages are so often "adequate."[162]

The main remaining upshot of the historical difference between law and equity is that plaintiffs aren't in general said to have a *right* to specific performance, because the adequacy of damages needs to be determined and the judge's discretion needs to be applied. In some situations, like employment, specific performance is essentially never awarded—it is seen as too intrusive even if an employee is so distinctive that damages don't let the employer hire an adequate

---

161 *See generally id.*

162 *See* KONRAD ZWEIGERT & HEIN KÖTZ, INTRODUCTION TO COMPARATIVE LAW 505–09 (Tony Weir trans., 3d rev. ed. 1998) (excerpted in GORDLEY ET AL., *supra* ch. 1, note 17, at 273–75).

substitute employee. (Orders to remain employed are too much like slavery.) In other cases, like contracts to sell real estate, specific performance is almost always available. The traditional rationale for the rule that specific performance is available when a seller breaches a real-estate contract is that real estate is unique and that damages therefore are never sufficient to let the buyer purchase an alternative performance that serves as a genuine substitute. In modern land developments and condo buildings, that proposition is doubtful, and the older rule that makes specific performance available automatically in real-estate cases has been slowly eroding.[163] But the easy availability of specific performance against real-estate sellers may still be justified for a different reason: such orders are very easy for courts to execute and involve no real threat of jail. In at least many common-law jurisdictions, a court's order of specific performance against a real-estate seller can simply be recorded as a real-estate deed itself, thereby automatically transferring title and fully resolving the dispute.[164]

Courts sometimes say they avoid specific performance when it would be difficult for them to oversee or "superintend" performance of the contract.[165] This has never been an important principle, however, and it is unpersuasive for at least two reasons. First, while the power of courts to oversee ongoing activity may have been limited in the days when courts involved a few judges who rode into town on horseback, dispensed justice, and left, courts are much more significant and durable institutions today. Modern courts desegregated the schools and can oversee the administration of prisons after their conditions are determined to be unconstitutional.[166] Second, more specifically, an order of specific performance simply tells a party to follow through on its promise. Determining whether a party has done this involves exactly the same type of reasoning, with the same kind of institutional competencies, as determining that there was a breach of contract in the first place. The range of contracts may take courts into varied, often specific subject matter, but if they can determine that a party has breached

---

163 *See* 12 CORBIN ON CONTRACTS § 63.8 (2023).

164 *E.g.*, Marshall v. Floyd, 664 S.E.2d 793, 796 (Ga. Ct. App. 2008) ("[A] decree for specific performance operates as a deed . . . .").

165 *See, e.g.*, London Bucket Co. v. Stewart, 237 S.W.2d 509, 510 (Ky. 1951) ("It is the general rule that contracts for building construction will not be specifically enforced because ordinarily damages are an adequate remedy and, in part, because of the incapacity of the court to superintend the performance.").

166 *See, e.g.*, Coleman v. Schwarzenegger, 922 F. Supp. 2d 882, 890 (E.D. Cal. 2009) ("Following that hearing, the . . . court concluded that it had no choice but to place the [California Department of Corrections and Rehabilitation] medical health care delivery system in receivership.").

a contract, they can also determine that a party has violated an injunction based on a contractual obligation.

Another remedy that is sometimes available in contract cases is *disgorgement* of the profits that a promisor earned from breach. This was not a traditional remedy in classical contract law, so it is left out of many Contracts courses even today, but it is exhibited in modern cases. The *Restatement (Third) of Restitution and Unjust Enrichment* lays out one general principle under which disgorgement of profits may be available:

> If a deliberate breach of contract results in profit to the defaulting promisor and the available damage remedy affords inadequate protection to the promisee's contractual entitlement, the promisee has a claim to restitution of the profit realized by the promisor as a result of the breach. Restitution by the rule of this section is an alternative to a remedy in [expectation] damages.[167]

Cases in which "the available damage remedy affords inadequate protection" for the promisee can include those where expectations damages are very hard to quantify because they are subjective or reputational.[168]

Disgorgement in contract cases serves as another reminder of the presence and ongoing need for imagination in the common law. There is no *logical* constraint that prevents disgorgement from being available; if it wasn't available in the past, maybe it was simply because courts hadn't yet realized the role it could play.[169]

3.6.1 Competing Conceptions of the Promisee's Harm from Breach

In many cases, the "spot the difference" approach is sufficient to resolve questions of damages: simply compare all features of the hypothetical universe that would have materialized if the promise had been performed and those in the real universe that have resulted from breach. A recurring set of cases in contract law complicates the picture a little because the promisee's expectation interest is unclear. That is, even though the terms of the promise are clear, the value of the situation the promisee would occupy if the promise had been performed is disputed.

---

167 RESTATEMENT (THIRD) OF RESTITUTION AND UNJUST ENRICHMENT § 39 (2011).

168 *E.g.*, *id.* cmt. d illus. 4.

169 For more discussion of disgorgement in contract law, see Melvin A. Eisenberg, *The Disgorgement Interest in Contract Law*, 105 MICH. L. REV. 559 (2006).

For example in *Peevyhouse v. Garland Coal & Mining Co.*,[170] two individuals owned a farm and agreed to allow a coal company to strip mine the farm as long as the coal company restored it to its previous condition. The coal company refused to conduct this restoration and admitted breach. In a lawsuit, the promisees asked (roughly) for damages that would measure the cost of completing the renovation—essentially, enough money to let them purchase a substitute performance. In response, the coal company argued that damages should be computed by taking a snapshot of the difference between (1) the value of the farm with renovations and (2) the value of the farm without renovations. This difference would be much less than the cost of completing renovations because the market did not value those renovations as much as the promisees did. Indeed, because the market value of the farm was relatively low, the cost of completing renovations would have far exceeded the market value of the property. The court awarded the lower measure of damages suggested by the coal company.

The case is poorly reasoned. The main problem in the opinion is that the court fails to recognize the subjective value of the farmland to the owners. In theory, *all* homes and similar land are valued more by the present owners than by the market—or else the owners would have chosen to sell (putting aside the transaction costs of selling the real estate, which in practice can of course be significant). Market value is not the only type of value. It may be the only kind of value that matters to some parties; for example, if Willie and Lucille Peevyhouse, the promisees in *Peevyhouse*, had been property speculators interested in "flipping" property, their only concern would indeed have been the market value of the property. But if they were living nearby and cared specifically about restoring their land—as some later reporting on the case has suggested[171]—then paying attention only to the market value of the land fails to implement expectation damages properly. That is, it fails to restore the promisees as nearly as possible to the situation they would have occupied if the promise had been performed.

Very often, subjective value exceeds market value; this is the case with most home renovations and pool installations, and, as another example, most specialized adaptations of property (such as modifications to a car) for people with disabilities. Subjective value is the ultimate source of market value but is not fully captured by market prices. For example, suppose I'm buying a newly constructed condo, and the builder tells me that it normally installs granite countertops. Because of newspaper reporting, I know that granite can

170 382 P.2d 109 (Okla. 1962).

171 *See* FULLER ET AL., *supra* note 56, at 216–17.

sometimes be radioactive; I also know that it can sometimes become hard to clean over time. So I negotiate with the builder to install engineered quartz countertops instead of ones made of granite. Suppose quartz costs about the same as granite and will not adjust the market value of the property in any way; most buyers won't notice the difference or care about it—my preferences about radioactivity and cleaning are, let us imagine, idiosyncratic to me. If the builder breaches this contract by installing granite, should there be no damages? The right way to approach this case is not to be limited by the market value of the property but to consider what harm breach actually causes, as against my expectation interest. If I'm a property speculator buying the condo just to resell it, I have no damages. If I am going to live there and care about the granite, and would use damages—if awarded—to tear out the granite and reinstall quartz, the cost of doing that reflects my true damages, even though it may be expensive and may appear "wasteful" to outsiders—just like any bathroom renovation or pool installation might be "wasteful" if it were judged only by its contribution to the market value of the house.[172]

The doctrine in this area has been inconsistently applied.[173] The Restatement's rule is essentially that damages based on the cost of completion can be awarded unless they are "clearly disproportionate" to "the probable loss in value,"[174] although what that means is not clear—there is little basis on which we can know what counts as disproportionate or what sort of "value" matters. If the rule is to depend on disproportion of some kind, paying attention to the plaintiff's actual valuation rather than market values or objective values alone would be helpful.[175] Deciding these cases too generally, without sufficient individualization to the parties, threatens (as in *Peevyhouse*) to misunderstand the parties' bargains and provide the wrong incentives to perform them.

A similar kind of tension arises when a buyer breaches a promise to a seller, who then resells the item to a third party. For example, if I agree to buy a used car for $18,000, then back out of the deal in breach of contract, and the seller finds another buyer for the car for $18,100, it may seem that the seller has no damages. My breach, in other words, may have caused no harm, just as a negligent driver who happens not to hit anyone has caused no harm. The seller may

---

172 *See* Melvin Aron Eisenberg, *The Responsive Model of Contract Law*, 36 STAN. L. REV. 1107, 1156–65 (1984).

173 *See id.*

174 RESTATEMENT (SECOND) OF CONTRACTS § 348 (1981).

175 *See* Eisenberg, supra note 172, at 1165; see also Melvin A. Eisenberg, *Conflicting Formulas for Measuring Expectation Damages*, 45 ARIZ. ST. L.J. 369 (2013).

have *incidental* damages in, for example, maintaining the car until they can resell it, but the seller appears to have lost no profit because of the successful resale. That may be the correct analysis, particularly for a used car.[176] With new or otherwise standardized merchandise, however, the seller may be what is called a *lost-volume seller*, meaning that the breach costs the seller its profit on the car by reducing the number of its total sales by one car. In other words, if a new-car dealership enters a contract with a buyer who breaches, the expectation interest for the dealership may rest on the lost profit on that individual contract; the fact that the dealer happens to sell the "same" car to another party isn't enabled (in a causal sense) by the breach, so it shouldn't reduce the seller's lost-profit damages.[177]

3.6.2 Limitations on Expectation Damages

Damages are rarely perfect in restoring promisees to any particular level of happiness or wealth that they target. In the United States, they typically do not include attorney's fees. They also systematically neglect types of harms that are treated as noncognizable—for example, the wasted time of individuals. If a bank breaches an agreement with the customer in a way that causes the customer to need to waste most of their free time over a week resolving the problem but ultimately restores all the customer's money, the customer probably has no damages that the law would recognize. (The time of employees in companies can be recoverable, however, in a lawsuit by the company.)[178] Damages frequently miss out on other subjective losses.

The imperfection of damages was one theme of a famous article coauthored by a major legal theorist of the 1900s, Lon Fuller.[179] As the article put it, "it is not always wise to make the defaulting promisor pay for all the damage which follows as a consequence of his breach."[180] This may reflect a principle similar to one of comparative responsibility in tort law. There are many doctrines in contract damages that, though they do not explicitly implement a comparative-fault principle, may approximate it in at least some situations. Perhaps one goal of these doctrines is to develop alternatives to all-or-nothing rules, like the old rule of contributory

---

176 *Cf.* Lazenby Garages Ltd. v. Wright, 1 W.L.R. 459 (C.A. 1976).

177 For more discussion, see Eisenberg, *supra* note 175, at 391–96.

178 *See, e.g.*, Sec. Stove & Mfg. Co. v. Am. Ry. Express, 51 S.W.2d 572, 574 (Mo. Ct. App. 1932) (upholding an award that included in reliance damages "$150.00 for the time of the [corporate] president [and] $40.00 for wages of plaintiff's other employee").

179 L.L. Fuller & William R. Perdue Jr., *The Reliance Interest in Contract Damages*, 46 YALE L.J. 52 (1936).

180 *Id.* at 84.

negligence, under which a plaintiff either receives their full damages or nothing.

At least three doctrines in contract law allow for there to be a spectrum rather than an all-or-nothing result in contract damages. One is a doctrine of *mitigation* that limits remedies in most legal subjects: even a party who has a legitimate legal claim is not permitted to run up their expenses at the other party's expense. In contract law, the "duty to mitigate"—not really a duty, because it is not an affirmative obligation but just a limit on damages—is relatively thin. Ordinarily, to avoid seeing their damages reduced, promisees must only avoid running up expenses needlessly or take minimal steps to try to reduce their damages. Wrongly fired employees, however, may need to look for alternative work.

A second doctrine is the rule that, in order to be recoverable, damages must be reasonably foreseeable at the time the contract was originally made. This doctrine usually is associated with the nineteenth-century English case *Hadley v. Baxendale*[181] and is a bit sharper in the common law that in some other legal systems. The major force of the rule is that the promisor isn't liable for harms (typically some or all of the promisee's lost profits) that the promisor had no reason to know were likely at the time the contract was formed. *Hadley* laid out a particular formulation of the rule that was unnecessarily complicated,[182] and the complication has persisted. For example, the Restatement starts with a relatively simple, general rule: "Damages are not recoverable for loss that the party in breach did not have reason to foresee as a probable result of the breach when the contract was made."[183] It then, following the cumbersome distinction laid out in *Hadley*, elaborates upon what "foresee as a probable result of the breach" means in that sentence:

> Loss may be foreseeable as a probable result of a breach because it follows from the breach
>
> (a) in the ordinary course of events, or

---

[181] 156 Eng. Rep. 145 (Ex. Ch. 1854).

[182] *Id.* at 151 ("Where two parties have made a contract which one of them has broken, the damages which the other party ought to receive in respect of such breach of contract should be such as may fairly and reasonably be considered either arising naturally, i.e., according to the usual course of things, from such breach of contract itself, or such as may reasonably be supposed to have been in the contemplation of both parties, at the time they made the contract, as the probable result of the breach of it.").

[183] RESTATEMENT (SECOND) OF CONTRACTS § 351(1) (1981).

> (b) as a result of special circumstances, beyond the ordinary course of events, that the party in breach had reason to know.[184]

That specific list of two ways that harms can be foreseeable probably isn't helpful. (We could equally well break foreseeability down into two other arbitrary categories, like "Loss may be foreseeable based on data or based on intuition" or "Loss may be foreseeable because of (a) the reasonable business experience of a promisor or (b) developments unrelated to the promisor's business experience that give the promisor a reason to think the loss may occur.") But the split between "ordinary course" and "special circumstances" tracks a conventional distinction between *general* damages (those anyone might foresee) and *special* or *consequential* damages, which are particular to the promisee or their circumstances and, under *Hadley*, ordinarily need to be communicated to the promisor before the contract is made in order for the promisee to recover them after a breach.

If a promisor learns new information *after* contract formation about the promisee's likely losses from breach, under a strict version of the *Hadley* rule they are free to ignore that information: the damages they pay will depend only on what they knew (or should have known) when the contract was formed. Other legal systems are not always so solicitous of the wrongful promisor's interests. For example, under the *Principles of European Contract Law*—a sort of pan-European analogue to the Restatement—breaches that are "intentional or grossly negligent"[185] are exempt from a rule like that of *Hadley* and are limited only by rules of remoteness, proximate causation, and the like typically found outside contract law—which tend to depend on what was foreseeable at the time of the *wrong*.[186]

Even in the common law, the *Hadley* rule may be eroding somewhat, though very quietly, in several ways. First, much more is foreseeable now than it used to be. With increased experience with commercial cases and a much better understanding of probability than in the past, it is likely that courts today would find more particular consequences of breach to be foreseeable than they did 150

---

[184] *Id.* § 351(2); *cf. also id.* § 351 cmt. b ("These terms are often misleading, however, and it is not necessary to distinguish between 'general' and 'special' or 'consequential' damages for the purpose of the rule stated in this Section.").

[185] PRINCIPLES OF EUROPEAN CONTRACT LAW PARTS, I AND II, Art. 9:503 (Ole Lando & Hugh Beale eds., 2000), https://www.trans-lex.org/400200 [https://perma.cc/2DQE-9ANM].

[186] *See* Melvin Aron Eisenberg, *The Principle of* Hadley v. Baxendale, 80 CAL. L. REV. 563, 577 (1992) ("The principle of proximate cause, like the principle of *Hadley v. Baxendale*, normally turns on foreseeability, but foreseeability in proximate cause is measured at the time of the wrong . . . .").

years ago. Indeed, on its facts, the *Hadley* case would probably itself have the opposite result today: the owner of a mill presented a shaft to a carrier and said the mill was stopped and the shaft needed to be sent quickly; it would probably be considered foreseeable today, based on that communicated information, that the mill would be closed and lose profits as the result of shipping delays.

Second, even if particular damages are not easily foreseeable, courts recognize that productive goods, like industrial equipment—the shaft in *Hadley*—have a market value. At least in theory, in a well-functioning market, the rental value of goods will approximate their productive value. So the cost of a delay in delivering industrial equipment, measured by its rental value, may approximate the lost profits of the promisee, which is usually the type of damages *Hadley* would exclude. As one court wrote:

> Capital goods such as machinery have a use value, which may equal the rental value of the equipment or may be an interest value. The latter is ordinarily interest at the market rate on the value of the machine. It might be quite foreseeable that deprivation of the machine's use because of a carriage delay will cause a loss of rental value or interest value during the delay period.[187]

On that principle, the mill in *Hadley* could recover *something* for the delay, even if not its own idiosyncratic lost profits.

A third doctrine that generally limits full recovery (and sometimes prevents recovery entirely) is that damages must be "reasonably certain"—an apparently oxymoronic phrase that nonetheless comes up frequently in law—to be recoverable. That rule has been under pressure and does not usually have much force today, although it can occasionally come up in unexpected ways, perhaps as an indirect method for courts to limit damages that seem disproportionate to the contract at issue. For example, the New York high court refused to let a company that had a contract to operate a stadium be awarded decades of profits on the contract when the stadium was not built.[188] The court held that its damages were too uncertain despite voluminous proof:

> The quantity of proof is massive and, unquestionably, represents business and industry's most advanced and sophisticated method for predicting the probable results of contemplated projects. Indeed, it is difficult to conclude what additional relevant proof could have been submitted by [the plaintiff] in support of its attempt to establish, with

[187] Hector Martinez & Co. v. S. Pac. Transp. Co., 606 F.2d 106, 109 (5th Cir. 1979).

[188] Kenford Co. v. County of Erie, 493 N.E.2d 234 (N.Y. 1986).

> reasonable certainty, loss of prospective profits. Nevertheless, [the] proof is insufficient to meet the required standard.[189]

Perhaps the court was expressing a general skepticism of financial models; the best learning of business schools or economics departments was perhaps genuinely not good enough to meet its standard—although the use of financial models to support damages is extremely commonplace in general, and the adversarial litigation system should be enough of a safeguard to protect the defendant if the plaintiff's model is unrealistic, overly hopeful, or otherwise problematic. Maybe the court sought to protect the public fisc, because the defendant was a county in New York. Perhaps its goal, as I suggested earlier, was to avoid disproportionate damages rather than uncertainty.

The rules limiting expectation damages have relaxed somewhat overall in modern law. This trend may just reflect a moderately friendlier view toward liability over time; as Grant Gilmore once jokingly wrote, classical contract law was "dedicated to the proposition that, ideally, no one should be liable to anyone for anything."[190] So, for example, a new business could not recover lost profits under classical contract law because the law declared those profits to be too uncertain. That rule is tantamount to saying that startups are statistically worthless, and it is no surprise that that rule has tended to be overturned.

But courts may still be skeptical of disproportionate damages. A little-known principle related to disproportion, often omitted from Contracts courses, is buried in the *Restatement (Second) of Contracts*:

> A court may limit damages [even] for foreseeable loss by excluding recovery for loss of profits, by allowing recovery only for loss incurred in reliance, or otherwise if it concludes that in the circumstances justice so requires in order to avoid disproportionate compensation.[191]

The comment to that principle in the Restatement is instructive in helping to notice the difference between what courts say and what they do (see section 1.5.1)—and of the notion that a legal principle may be real but covert rather than explicit, a practical pattern rather than an announced one:

> Typical examples of limitations imposed on damages under this discretionary power involve the denial of recovery for

---

[189] *Id.* at 236.

[190] GRANT GILMORE, THE DEATH OF CONTRACT 15 (2d ed. 1995).

[191] RESTATEMENT (SECOND) OF CONTRACTS § 351(3) (1981).

> loss of profits and the restriction of damages to loss incurred in reliance on the contract. Sometimes these limits are covertly imposed, by means of an especially demanding requirement of foreseeability or of certainty. The rule [included in the Restatement] recognizes that what is done in such cases is the imposition of a limitation in the interests of justice.[192]

The principle here is similar to the one that Fuller and Purdue described in the article discussed earlier; as the comment to the Restatement justifies it:

> It is not always in the interest of justice to require the party in breach to pay damages for all of the foreseeable loss that he has caused. There are unusual instances in which it appears from the circumstances either that the parties assumed that one of them would not bear the risk of a particular loss or that, although there was no such assumption, it would be unjust to put the risk on that party. One such circumstance is an extreme disproportion between the loss and the price charged by the party whose liability for that loss is in question. The fact that the price is relatively small suggests that it was not intended to cover the risk of such liability. Another such circumstance is an informality of dealing, including the absence of a detailed written contract, which indicates that there was no careful attempt to allocate all of the risks. The fact that the parties did not attempt to delineate with precision all of the risks justifies a court in attempting to allocate them fairly.[193]

It would of course be better, all else equal, if courts laid out this reasoning explicitly rather than covertly. But even if it is a covert principle, it may well reflect the actual state of the law: recognizing the principle allows lawyers to plan and to predict cases better than a strict adherence to more rigid doctrinal rules, and it probably comports better with the actual expectations of business parties because it is more sensitive to terms that might be implied from the context of their actual bargains. An illustration from the Restatement may be helpful:

> *A*, a private trucker, contracts with *B* to deliver to *B*'s factory a machine that has just been repaired and without which *B*'s factory, as *A* knows, cannot reopen. Delivery is delayed because *A*'s truck breaks down. In an action by *B* against *A* for breach of contract the court may, after taking

---

192 *Id.* § 351 cmt f.

193 *Id.*

> into consideration such factors as the absence of an elaborate written contract and the extreme disproportion between *B*'s loss of profits during the delay and the price of the trucker's services, exclude recovery for loss of profits.[194]

One other limit on contract damages is that, just as in tort law (see section 2.6.2), courts are skeptical of purely emotional harms. To address emotional harms, contract law has adopted a clearer, more unified principle than tort law has—the sort of clearer principle I suggested in section 2.6.2. Instead of categorizing cases into unrelated pockets of emotional-harm liability without much coordination, as in tort law, the contract-law principle is that contracts or breaches where emotional harms are *especially* foreseeable may lead to recovery of emotional harms. Not just foreseeability but unusually high levels of foreseeability are required. For example, the emotional harms that come from wrongfully firing an employee or breaking up a general partnership are probably readily foreseeable under *Hadley*, but such breaches don't normally lead to recovery for emotional harms. As the Restatement puts it:

> Recovery for emotional disturbance will be excluded unless the breach also caused bodily harm or the contract or the breach is of such a kind that serious emotional disturbance was a particularly likely result.[195]

Tort law's treatment of emotional harms could do with a single, relatively clear principle like that.

3.6.3 Liquidated Damages

Liquidated damages are those that the parties have agreed to in their contract—for example, "If you breach, you will pay me $1000/day until you perform." The term *liquidated damages* may be confusing today. People now think of financial *liquidity* as if it applies a metaphor involving fluidity: cash can (metaphorically) flow freely and easily anywhere, so it is "liquid"; real estate is hard and expensive to sell, so it is *illiquid*. But that is not the original sense of the terminology, which originally depended on a different metaphor: water (and some other liquids) are *clear* because light travels through them. The original legal and financial senses of the word *liquid*—preserved today in the term *liquidated damages*—refers specifically to that clarity. In traditional law, a "liquidated" sum or amount is simply one about which there is no dispute—one that has been clarified or reduced to a particular figure or formula. When parties *liquidate* damages, that is all they have done: they have listed a

194 *Id.* cmt. f illus. 17.

195 *Id.* § 353.

specific amount of damages or a formula for computing one, thereby (in theory) removing a dispute about how damages are to be determined. Amusingly, in idiomatic English today we might use exactly the opposite metaphor: if we were inventing new terminology today, we might speak of a "crystallized sum" or "crystallized damages"—damages that are clear and in a fixed form.

The rule about liquidated damages serves as an interesting limit on the principle that bargains are enforced. The rule is essentially that liquidated-damages terms in contracts won't be enforced unless they are a reasonably good estimate of the promisee's actual damages. Parties can normally agree about what their obligations are, but the courts scrutinize remedial provisions more closely. The principal reason for the rule's existence may just be historical—the early courts simply may have resisted being directed by parties about what orders or judgments to enter because they saw the determination of remedies as a role that was exclusively theirs—but the rule would need to have some useful function for it to have lasted as long as it has, particularly in the face of general arguments that bargains should normally be enforced according to their terms.

The rule probably continues to make sense just because, in the real world, liquidated-damages provisions tend to be poorly written and to have arbitrary effects.[196] They often amount to what the courts call a *penalty*, and the courts are reluctant to award large damages when real damages are in fact small or nonexistent. In evaluating liquidated-damages rules, it may help to remember that US law ordinarily does not allow gambling in the general case; the arbitrary and speculative results of liquidated-damages clauses may well seem to mirror some of the problems that gambling can lead to. Courts also tend to avoid or temper situations where a large amount of money turns on very little—where millions of dollars might depend on an arbitrary fact that has no practical significance to either party—and liquidated-damages terms can cause that to happen.

Courts also don't let parties opt into specific performance as a remedy. Courts don't ignore a term in a contract that asks for specific performance, but they don't consider themselves bound by such a term.

3.6.4 The Theory of Efficient Breach

The so-called *theory of efficient breach* is one of the worst mistakes in US legal education in any subject. Despite being

---

[196] For more analysis of liquidated damages, see Melvin Aron Eisenberg, *The Limits of Cognition and the Limits of Contract*, 47 STAN. L. REV. 211 (1995).

disavowed by modern economists, it is still often uncritically accepted by many law professors and taught as if it is true.

The idea behind the theory is that expectation damages provide an efficient deterrent against nonperformance of contracts, whereas any greater measure of damages will supposedly deter promisors from breaching their contracts even if it is efficient for them to do so. The theory, if correct, would mean that the law should never award specific performance or any damages beyond expectation damages, like disgorgement.

Richard Posner, in the most recent edition of his textbook on law and economics, lays out the argument in the following widely quoted passage:

> Suppose I sign a contract to deliver 100,000 custom-ground widgets at 10¢ apiece to A for use in his boiler factory. After I have delivered 10,000, B comes to me, explains that he desperately needs 25,000 custom-ground widgets at once since otherwise he will be forced to close his pianola factory at great cost, and offers me 15¢ apiece for them. I sell him the widgets and as a result do not complete timely delivery to A, causing him to lose $1,000 in profits.[197]

Of this scenario, Posner says "awarding damages not will deter a breach of contract. It should not. It is an efficient breach."[198] This is the most aggressive application of the theory of efficient breach, and it is deeply mistaken even on grounds of economics alone, for reasons that many have pointed out over the years.[199] Consider: when the seller of the widgets breaches by selling to *B*, the seller has no way to be sure that *B* in fact values the widgets more than *A*. All the seller knows is that *B* is willing to pay more today than *A* has paid in the past; the seller hasn't even checked with *A* again! Maybe prices in general have risen. Maybe *A* originally negotiated a particularly good deal. Maybe *A*'s valuation of the goods has sharply risen for private reasons.[200]

And even if efficient allocation of resources demands that *B* rather than *A* end up with the goods, breach is not necessary to achieve that result; *A* could sell them to *B* just as easily as the seller could.[201] Posner tried to address this objection: "True, had I refused to sell to B he could have gone to A and negotiated an assignment to him of part of A's contract with me. But this would have introduced

197 POSNER, *supra* ch. 2, note 122, § 4.10, at 131.

198 *Id.*

199 *See, e.g.*, Eisenberg, *supra* note 160, at 997–1013.

200 *See id.*

201 *See id.*

an additional step, with additional transaction costs—and high ones because it would be a bilateral-monopoly situation."[202] But Posner appears to have assumed that the breach will somehow be a "friendly" one, with *B* providing damages to *A* that *A* gladly accepts; if that is not the case—and it is likely not to be[203]—there will be litigation, which has a much higher transaction cost than any difference in costs between *A* reselling the widgets to *B* and the seller doing so. (Indeed, if the relationship between *A* and *B* would be a bilateral monopoly—which is to say, a negotiation between two parties who have no other negotiating partners—then logically the relationship between the seller and *B* would be one as well. That is, if *B* needs the widgets and can't get them from anyone else, *B* will need to deal with either *A* or the seller. There is no reason to think negotiating with one of them is more expensive than negotiating with the other.)

Posner writes that breach along with the seller's payment of damages is "Pareto superior"[204]—that is, everyone benefits, and nobody is made worse off, from breach plus the payment of damages compared to performance: "Having obtained an additional profit of $1,250 on the sale to B, I am better off even after reimbursing A for his loss, and B is also better off."[205] But as we have seen (see section 3.6.2), legal measures of damages are limited by various contract-law doctrines—and they are imperfect for other reasons, such as, in the United States, not including attorney's fees. Even if *A* sues the seller and wins, *A* will not be in the same position as if the seller had fully performed.[206]

Moreover, as Mel Eisenberg has pointed out, breach is fortunately relatively rare, and the theory of efficient breach would make weaken the contracting system by making it more common, thereby increasing costs for everyone:

> Given the dilution or elimination of the moral force of bargain promises under the theory of efficient breach, that theory, if widely adopted, would decrease the efficiency of the contracting system in three ways. First, it would increase the need to resort to litigation, which is very expensive, as opposed to achieving performance of contracts through the internalization of the moral norm of promise-

---

[202] Posner, *supra* ch. 2, note 122, § 4.10, at 131.

[203] *See, e.g.*, Egerer v. CSR W., L.L.C., 67 P.3d 1128 (Wash. Ct. App. 2003) (an apparently efficient breach resulted in litigation and damages much higher than the promisor initially predicted).

[204] Posner, *supra* ch. 2, note 122, § 4.10, at 131.

[205] *Id.*

[206] *See* Eisenberg, *supra* note 160, at 997–1013.

> keeping, which is very inexpensive. Second, it would lead contracting parties to make greater use of costly noncontractual measures, such as security deposits, to ensure performance. Third, it would diminish the force of reputational constraints, because such constraints rest in significant part on moral norms.[207]

So the theory of efficient breach fails even on its own economic terms. I have been at legal conferences where at least one leading law-and-economics scholar, when pressed, has apologized for the theory, admitting that the law-and-economics movement was overzealous in defending it in its earlier years. And the theory is even worse when analyzed in non-economic terms; it tells people that it's fine to do immoral things as long as they profit from their actions.

I've cast the analysis of the theory of efficient breach in this section in relatively argumentative terms because, as I said at the outset, it is one of the leading mistakes in US legal education. Its teaching is widespread in Contracts courses even though scholars have recognized its deep problems. Therefore, it deserves, at the very least, vigorous debate and discussion, whereas it is often taught as an economic truth. Fortunately the theory has not had much influence on the courts. Even Posner rejected the theory once he became a judge and it was argued to him, calling it "a beguiling argument that contains much truth," but adding "we do not think it should carry the day"[208] and upholding an award for specific performance. In fact, in tort law it can be an actionable economic tort to cause someone to breach a contract, as in Posner's example. As the *Restatement (Third) of Torts: Liability for Economic Harm* describes, it is a tort to lead someone to breach a contract by acting "for the purpose of appropriating the benefits of the . . . contract."[209]

To be clear, rejecting the theory of efficient breach does not imply that no breach is ever efficient. There can be individual situations in which it is efficient to breach a contract, particularly in scenarios other than ones where sellers opportunistically breach in order to sell commodities to third parties. That was never in dispute. What is in dispute is the validity of a theory that would justify breach more broadly in contract cases and would limit contract remedies to expectation damages.

---

207 *Id.* at 1013.

208 Walgreen Co. v. Sara Creek Prop. Co., 966 F.2d 273, 275 (7th Cir. 1992).

209 RESTATEMENT (THIRD) OF TORTS: LIABILITY FOR ECONOMIC HARM § 17 (2020).

3.7 Summary

The basic model of legal claims that chapter 2 developed in the context of tort law (see section 2.10) applies quite well to contract law. In general, liability arises for doing something wrongful—we call this in the tort context *breach* or being *at fault*. In the case of contract law, the wrongful behavior is breaking a promise and is called, more formally, *breach of contract*. The law of contract interpretation and contract formation ("offer and acceptance") are the main areas of contract law that determine what counts as failing to live up to the requirements imposed by a promise. The law of consideration, the statute of frauds, and a few other doctrines fill the same role as no-duty rules in tort law: for reasons of policy or principle courts have decided that, as a matter of law, certain promises are not legally enforceable even if it wrong to break them.

Causation in contract law is not usually very interesting, which makes sense: if the main role of causation in tort law is to make sure there is an adequate connection between plaintiffs and defendants, in contract law the parties clearly have a connection because they've made a contract with each other. That said, though damages in contract law are more complicated that in most subjects because there are multiple baselines against which damages can be computed—multiple positions to restore plaintiffs to—fundamentally the main two contract measures, expectation damages and reliance damages, involve changes *caused* by breach of a promise. Contract law also has principles that broadly resemble "scope of liability" principles: the *Hadley* rule operates as a fairly (and probably overly) strong scope-of-liability limitation.

Overall, the story of modern contract law is one of significant change, from a formalistic system to a functional one that responds to morality, policy, and business needs. Many Contracts books are still stuck in the past—they report rules from the 1880s or 1920s, like the illusory-promise rule or the legal-duty rule, uncritically, as if they are still in force without any modifications today. This chapter has aimed to teach deeper lessons: that the law is more than a set of black-letter rules and that it often requires understanding an old rule, the reasons it was a poor rule, and the way it has changed. For example, a statement about the illusory-promise rule that does not recognize it is a "faltering rampart to which a litigant retreats at his own peril" (see section 3.1.4) is a misleading statement about contract law. Such a statement is too credulous—too eager to believe a straightforward rule rather than to study how it has been applied. Missing out on the deeper levels of potential learning would neglect a significant part of what Contracts courses in the United States are trying to teach.

Chapter 4

PROPERTY LAW

Contents

The range of Property courses in American law schools is so broad that a course called Property could cover almost anything, from a grand theoretical discussion about the nature and history of human societies to the details of local deed-recording laws for real estate. In that mix, too, is environmental law and intellectual property—which are often the research focuses of the people who teach the Property course today.

The most interesting of the grand theoretical courses on property try to give students enough perspective to see how property law is both a cause and an effect of the basic decisions we make about social organization. For example, before studying law, people are apt to talk about "private property" as if it has some definite abstract meaning and can be taken for granted; the Property course can help people see that the full picture is more complicated.

My approach in this chapter focuses, for the most part, on several particular legal questions that judges have to answer in property law. When seen as a series of particular decisions for a common-law judge, property law starts to seem more similar to tort law and contract law—and many of the same concepts and struggles that we've seen so far (strict liability versus negligence; the role of comparative responsibility; the need and tendency for the common law to respond to changes in the world) apply to property law as well.

4.1 Stolen Property

Suppose a thief breaks into someone's house, steals their couch (admittedly not the typical target of thieves, just given the ratio between value and weight), and resells it to an innocent third party—

someone who didn't know, and had no reason to know, that they were buying it from a thief. The thief then disappears or is insolvent, but the original owner of the couch discovers that the couch is in the innocent buyer's home and seeks its return. The good-faith buyer defends on the basis that they paid a fair market price for the couch and that the original owner's claim should be only against the thief. Does the original owner or the good-faith buyer prevail?

A bad way to go about answering that question is to try to derive the answer formalistically. Many sources, in addressing the question, rely on general propositions like "a thief can't convey title to property that they never had, so the thief's sale of the couch to a third party is ineffective as against the original owner." It should be clear by now that that sort of reasoning isn't helpful because it doesn't address any considerations of morality or policy; it is just a *conclusory* statement that pretends the answer can be derived purely from logic. Indeed, *title* is just the label we give to the property claim of the winning party. The law could—and in fact does—just as easily adopt a principle like "some sales of property create good title even if the seller did not have title." The important thing for law students, lawyers, and judges to do is to figure out which of those two *logically* possible principles is the more suitable one, in view of considerations like fairness and the incentives of the opposing rules. It is helpful to recognize, too, that the law need not—and does not—choose a single answer in all situations; nothing prevents the law from adopting a more granular or particularized approach, where on some facts the original owner recovers the property and on other facts they don't. Moreover, maybe these two principles aren't the only ones the courts could use; for example, the courts could, at least as a matter of logical possibility, adopt some principle of loss-splitting or comparative responsibility (compare section 2.7.1).

If the buyer knew or should have known that they were buying from a thief, the situation is quite easy to resolve: the buyer is at fault, the original owner is innocent, and so the original owner should recover. Though it is not normally discussed this way, that result is simply the application of the *fault principle* or *negligence principle* that we saw in tort law (see section 2.1). In other words, if the buyer who bought the couch should have known—was unreasonable in not knowing—that the couch was stolen, they have acted negligently. We can make that reasonableness determination by looking at all the facts: the price that that the buyer paid, whether the thief presented the sale in a reputable fashion, and so on. For example, if we're dealing with a more realistically stolen item, like a gold watch, a sale at a seventy percent discount out of the trunk of a car behind a deserted mall should easily give any reasonable buyer enough of a basis to know that the transaction isn't legitimate. By contrast, if the sale is at a fair market price from a reputable local store that deals in used goods and vouches for them, a buyer is much more likely to be innocent. In any event, a simple application of the same fault principle from tort law can be used to address questions where only the buyer is at fault. In other words, the original owner's claim has many of the same principles in its favor as a negligence claim in tort law would: "you have behaved unreasonably," the original owner might say to the third-party buyer from the thief, "and would be causing me harm as a result of your own bad behavior if you continued to keep the stolen item."

When the third-party buyer is innocent, however, the situation is much harder to resolve. In that case, the original owner's claim is effectively a strict-liability claim against the third party (compare section 2.8.1). The original owner, in other words, would file a claim against someone who has done nothing wrong, asking the law to impose a kind of liability against that innocent person. Normally, when the law does that, there ought to be some particular reason for it, because we can't reach that result on a general fault-based analysis alone given that neither party is at fault (see section 2.1).

The general rule in the common law here *is* in fact one of strict liability: under the prevailing common-law rule, the original owner does get most goods back from an innocent third-party buyer. Perhaps we presume that third-party buyers of used goods should really have known better, so we assign at least a small level of fault to them. The law's rule is more than a presumption, though, or a shift of a burden of proving fault (see section 2.2.3); the innocent buyer simply loses as a matter of law in the general case. Maybe judges are concerned that the opposite rule would do too much to encourage theft, indirectly, by supporting the market for stolen goods. Maybe denying the original owner's claim feels too much like re-victimizing the original owner, who already suffered a theft and has lost the use of the property for some amount of time already.

Some in the law-and-economics movement would analyze this situation by comparing the *incentives* of the two opposing rules here (owner wins vs. innocent third-party buyer wins, which again is the same thing as saying strict liability vs. negligence). For example, if the owner wins, that could conceivably cause potential third-party buyers of goods to take more precautions—to investigate property they're buying in order to determine whether it is legitimate or stolen. By contrast, if the third-party buyer wins, owners may have more of an incentive to protect their property against theft by (for example) installing burglar alarms.[1] This reasoning is unpersuasive

1 *See* COOTER & ULEN, *supra* ch. 2, note 146, at 151–53.

for two reasons, however. First, it is implausible to imagine that a rule favoring third-party buyers will really encourage owners to protect their property better, just on the off-chance that property is stolen but then located in the possession of a good-faith buyer. Most personal property is not even easily tracked, for example: if an electronic good is stolen, it would be very hard for most original owners to prove that the good was originally theirs even if it is eventually found in the home of a third-party buyer, which itself is unlikely to begin with. Second, because even a rule that favored buyers would favor them only if they had acted in good faith, without fault, buyers still have an incentive to conduct reasonable checks on the goods they were seeking to buy even without a rule that's supposed to promote that incentive. Indeed, as we saw in tort law (see section 2.8.1), strict liability and negligence provide similar incentives for people in the buyer's position.

As the economists rightly point out, however,[2] it is unclear which of the two rules here is most efficient, and a fairness-based analysis too is difficult to resolve when both parties are innocent. As usual, in that kind of situation it is difficult to determine whether the rule should be one of negligence or of strict liability. The difficulty in determining which rule is fairer or rests on a better policy may explain the law's refusal to adopt a single rule in this area. For one thing, different legal traditions have different rules to address this situation.[3] For another, even common-law systems tend to treat currency differently from other property: "Currency allows the title in money to be renewed whenever the money passes to a person who receives it in good faith and in return for a valuable consideration."[4] It is also important to note the role of statutes of limitations in this area. However powerful the arguments might be that a good-faith buyer should restore property to the original owner, for example, they will not normally have to do so fifty years after a purchase—a fact pattern that commonly arises in cases of stolen artwork.[5]

---

2 *See id.* at 153.

3 *See id.* at 152; John Henry Merryman, *The Good Faith Acquisition of Stolen Art, in* CRIME, PROCEDURE AND EVIDENCE IN A COMPARATIVE CONTEXT: ESSAYS IN HONOUR OF PROFESSOR MIRJAN DAMASKA 275, 277 (John Jackson et al. eds.) ("In the civil-law world the precise rules vary from nation to nation, but in general the law is significantly kinder to the good faith purchaser and less so to the owner.") (citing sources).

4 David Fox, *Bona Fide Purchase and the Currency of Money*, 55 CAMBRIDGE L.J. 547, 547 (1996).

5 *See, e.g.*, Ashton Hawkins et al., *A Tale of Two Innocents: Creating an Equitable Balance Between the Rights of Former Owners and Good Faith Purchasers of Stolen Art*, 64 FORDHAM L. REV. 49, 50 (1995) ("At the heart of the stolen art problem—virtually dispositive in many cases—is the question of the appropriate statute of limitations, i.e., how long after the theft can the former owner sue the current holder of the art?").

Additionally, the Uniform Commercial Code (UCC) includes a rule that "A person with voidable title has power to transfer a good title to a good faith purchaser for value."[6] What this means has never been precisely clear; as the leading treatise on the UCC puts it, " 'Voidable title' is a murky concept. The Code does not define the phrase. The comments do not even discuss it."[7] Whatever the rule means, it strongly suggests that some sales can give greater "title" than the seller has, which shows the brittleness of the conceptualistic rule that a buyer's title cannot be greater than the seller's. Under the UCC, merchants may also create title by erroneously selling goods that have been "entrust[ed]" to them,[8] presumably on the thought that customers shouldn't have to second-guess whether a merchant selling a good really has authority to do so.

A conceptually possible alternative to either of the two all-or-nothing rules discussed here is comparative responsibility, where the parties split the loss somehow. For example, one party could retain the stolen property but have to pay partial damages to the other. But that rarely arises as a possibility in cases like this, perhaps because courts are disinclined to blame the original owner for theft even if the owner didn't take "reasonable" precautions.

4.2 Adverse Possession

It is possible to imagine a world where recordkeepers at different governmental levels try to record the ownership of everything. It would be so difficult to keep that system of records up to date, however, that there would inevitably be some law about who "really" owns something—a pen or an old couch—even though the title-recording system wasn't properly updated.

We do have a recording system for land, given the economic importance and relatively slow speed of land transactions. In other words, while nobody thinks it is worthwhile to create a registry of who owns every copy of every book, we have made the effort to record ownership of land. Most of the time, those ownership records are basically correct. But a doctrine known as *adverse possession* has arisen, and its main function probably is to respond to the situation when reality drifts away from even the relatively careful records of land ownership. As anyone who has ever worked with a database knows—and this applies to software databases just as to the "official records" of a county—the database never perfectly reflects reality;

---

6 U.C.C. § 2–403(1).

7 WHITE ET AL., *supra* ch. 3, note 88, § 4:33.

8 U.C.C. § 2–403(2)–(3).

there are always ways that it can record errors, not be updated appropriately, or otherwise drift so that it becomes out of date.

For example, suppose at a boundary between two three-acre properties, a fence has been at slightly the wrong place, as compared to the county's formal land-title records, for thirty years. When the fence was built, perhaps someone measured the land incorrectly or misunderstood the formal description of land ownership recorded in the books and records of the county. We can easily imagine that the builder of the fence, or perhaps their neighbor or other third parties, have relied on those boundaries for decades—in making a garden, paying for landscaping, or maybe just valuing and publicly listing their property for sale. Should we rely on the old land records or the actual use of the land? The doctrine of adverse possession lets us rely on the actual use under some circumstances. Under the terms of that doctrine, someone who actually uses land and does so exclusively, continuously, and openly acquires title to the land as long as they weren't doing so with the owner's permission or something similar (e.g., as a tenant or licensee).[9]

Courts and commentators often justify adverse possession in other ways, but those arguments tend to be implausible or too formalistic. The most common doctrinal justification rests on the statute of limitations—the idea that if you have a claim and don't file it, you lose the claim. The statute of limitations is said to apply to the right to *eject*, or force someone who has no right to be there, from land. But it would take an unusual application of the statute of limitations to justify a change in land ownership; for example, why wouldn't we say that a statute of limitations eliminates the right to recover damages that arose too long ago, rather than declaring that if you don't sue for unlicensed land use in time, you lose all rights to the land? As an analogy, if a doctor has been committing the same malpractice on a patient—say, a long-running error in the amount of a drug the doctor has prescribed, or a long-running misinterpretation of a diagnostic scan—a three-year statute of limitations in tort law could prevent claims for individual acts of malpractice older than three years but still allow the patient to recover for more recent violations of the doctor's standard of care. (Indeed, some doctrines have arisen in medical-malpractice cases that even permit patients to recover for old but ongoing malpractice.)[10] Why wouldn't a statute

---

[9] 16 POWELL ON REAL PROPERTY § 91.02 (2022) ("To establish title by adverse possession, a claimant must demonstrate actual, open and notorious, exclusive, continuous and hostile possession of the premises for the prescribed statutory period often under a claim of right or color of title."). On the element confusingly called *hostility*, concerning the owner's permission or "something similar," see *id.* § 91.05.

[10] *E.g.*, Dickey v. Vermette, 960 A.2d 1178, 1180 (Me. 2008) ("Under the 'continuing negligent treatment' doctrine, the limitations period would begin to run for

of limitations for land work similarly if the usual policies of the statute of limitations were the only purposes for the doctrine of adverse possession? Moreover, courts have tended, at least covertly, not to permit those who have acted in bad faith from profiting from adverse possession, so it is not clear that the doctrine is importantly about the delay in responding to a wrongful act;[11] in other words, if the policies in this area were typical of those of the statute of limitations, the state of mind of the adverse possessor probably wouldn't matter as much as it does in the real cases.[12]

An even worse justification for adverse possession is a naive one from the law-and-economics movement that suggests that adverse possession moves land to its more productive uses. As Cooter and Ulen have described that historical argument:

> Another efficiency justification for adverse possession was emphasized in the past: adverse possession prevents valuable resources from being left idle for long periods of time by specifying procedures for a productive user to take title from an unproductive user. Under such a rule, persons who neglect to monitor their property boundaries run the risk of losing idle parts of them to someone who makes use of them. In this respect the rule tends to move property from idleness to productive use.[13]

This is a transparently bad argument; it is equivalent to saying that anytime someone steals property, we can infer that they value it more than the rightful owner. It also almost seems quaint, coming from a time when apparently active development of land was considered necessarily more valuable than more passive uses related to conservation or long-term stewardship; that is, the economic argument appears to be motivated by an assumption that one who is

---

all claims on the last act of negligence, as long as that act occurred within three years before the legal action was initiated.").

11 *E.g.*, R.H. Helmholz, *Adverse Possession and Subjective Intent*, 61 WASH. U. L.Q. 331, 347 (1983) ("[T]he results of most cases show that where courts allow adverse possession to ripen into title, bad faith on the part of the possessor seldom exists. Where the possessor knows that he is trespassing, valid title does not accrue to him simply by the passage of years. Courts thus admit the possibility of a truly hostile claimant acquiring valid title, but they do so chiefly to contrast the unfairness of treating him better than the honest possessor. Their purpose in making the contrast is to permit the honest possessor to acquire title."); *accord* 16 POWELL, *supra* note 4, at § 91.05(1)(b) (discussing a trend toward requiring good faith on the part of adverse possessors).

12 Consistently with the themes we have seen in this book, Professor Helmholz nicely concluded: "We write about human beings. Though a reasonable preference for an objective view of adverse possession militates in favor of a pure possession and an 'availability of ejectment' test, if we consequently describe that test as the law, or even as the dominant rule, we underestimate the complexity of the matter." *Id.* at 357–58.

13 COOTER & ULEN, *supra* ch. 2, note 146, at 154.

letting land lie "unused" deserves to have it taken away by someone else who would build something on the land. But that would ignore a more modern recognition that development of land isn't always productive, given the externalities of such development that have been increasingly recognized since the mid-1900s. Even on the argument's own terms, if the new user really values the land more than the old user, they can simply purchase it in the market. If they don't, we have no reason to think they value the new use more than the old owner values the old use (even if that old use is passive) in the first place. In this respect, this old economic defense of adverse possession is much like the theory of efficient breach (see section 3.6.4) in essentially making up or assuming the efficiency of the doctrine it is attempting to explain. In some ways, evaluated in these terms the doctrine of adverse possession would fare even worse than the theory of efficient breach because it doesn't require the wrongdoer to pay damages to the original owner of the right.[14]

Another economic justification for adverse possession is that it "clears title" to land—that is, that it "lowers the cost of establishing rightful ownership claims by removing the risk that ownership will be disputed on the basis of the distant past."[15] Perhaps this justification is meant to be the same as the one I gave above about simply recognizing the drift over time, and potential reliance on that drift, between real use and historical ownership recorded in a database. If not, it is unclear how a complex doctrine that needs to be litigated in difficult cases "clears title" more readily than a simple rule that recorded land ownership prevails.[16] In other words, if its goal is some small reduction in transaction costs as a purely economic matter, surely adverse possession doesn't really do its job.

The doctrine of adverse possession, instead, appears to give effect to actual uses and expectations as compared to formal, text-based ones. In that respect it serves the same functions as the *erosion* of doctrines like the parol-evidence rule in contract law (see section 3.4.2) because it recognizes that reality is often more important than what has been written down, even if the writings are quite formal.

4.3 New Property

Much as in the case of stolen property (see section 4.1), many cases that raise questions about new property rights—addressed by doctrines that go under the labels of *found* property, *creation*, and *capture*—are susceptible to analysis as tort problems. That is, many

---

[14] *See* Thomas W. Merrill, *Property Rules, Liability Rules, and Adverse Possession*, 79 NW. U. L. REV. 1122, 1145–53 (1985).

[15] *See id.*

[16] I am indebted to Joseph Singer for discussion of this point.

questions in these cases can be decided on a fault-based analysis—an innocent party prevails over those who were negligent or worse—with a residual question of what to do when both the plaintiff and the defendant are innocent, in which case we face the usual tensions between strict liability and negligence (see section 2.8.1).

The analysis could stop there, in which case claims to shift possession of property from one from one person to another would be determined simply by reasonableness and, when necessary as a tiebreaker, by the choice to apply or decline to apply strict liability. There would probably not be much wrong with that state of affairs. Indeed, just as with rules of contract interpretation (see section 3.4), it would be hard to justify rules of capture, found property, and the like that systematically favor unreasonable parties over reasonable ones, intentional wrongdoers over innocent people, and so on.

But property law has developed with a variety of particular rules, as well as with a background assumption or tendency that the rules in property cases are *binary* (versus continuous or gradual)—which is simply to say that in a dispute between two parties the court will tend to declare which of them has a better right to the property at issue. To be clear, when a court decides a property right as between two parties, that decision doesn't on its own prevent someone with an even better claim than either of those two parties from filing that claim later—but in each case, the ordinary classical rule of property law is binary as between the two parties who have a dispute.

In contract law, Mel Eisenberg has observed the trend away from binary rules during the 1900s in favor of what he has called *multi-faceted rules*—those that "organize[ ] . . . experience . . . into several states, including an intermediate state between no liability and full liability."[17] For example, in contract law, reliance damages may serve as an intermediate position between no liability and expectation damages (see section 3.6), and doctrines of foreseeability and proportion may serve to allocate losses rather than treating them as objects of all-or-nothing decisions (see section 3.6.2).

The same thing may be happening in property law, though much more slowly. For example, the classical common law of property developed rules laying out the conditions for a person to *capture* new property. These rules varied from situation to situation, but they were aimed at specifying a moment when someone reduced *fugitive* property to their possession. For example, in the famous case of *Pierson v. Post*,[18] one hunter saw that another was pursuing a wild fox but nonetheless killed the fox himself and took it away. Siding

---

[17] *See* Eisenberg, *supra* ch. 3, note 34, at 1810.

[18] 3 Cai. R. 175 (N.Y. Sup. Ct. 1805).

with the eighteenth-century French scholar Jean Barbeyrac over the seventeenth-century German scholar Samuel von Pufendorf, the court laid down the following rule to govern property rights among hunters of wild animals:

> actual bodily seizure is not indispensable to acquire right to, or possession of, wild beasts; but . . . on the contrary, the mortal wounding of such beasts, by one not abandoning his pursuit, may, with the utmost propriety, be deemed possession of him;[19]

The court did not particularly justify this rule, except to say that with such possession

> the pursuer manifests an unequivocal intention of appropriating the animal to his individual use, has deprived him of his natural liberty, and brought him within his certain control.[20]

It is difficult to see this particular type of rule as anything more than what Oliver Wendell Holmes was trying to achieve in *B&O Railroad v. Goodman* (see section 2.2.1)—that is, laying down a particular interpretation of facts that, to the judges, determines what behavior is reasonable for all time and what is not. In tort law, the attempt tends to fail—and rapidly (see section 2.2.1). In the law of fugitive property, the declaration of relatively simple and general rules to govern what could instead be complex factual problems appears to have been more durable. Perhaps that is because the results are not usually as important: they don't concern human safety in the same direct way, aren't associated with the need for potentially life-altering compensation, and particularly in cases like *Pierson* tend to concern gains rather than losses to the parties. (Although the difference between a gain and a loss is subject to psychological framing, people tend to care more about losses than about gains.[21] See for example section 3.1.7 on gift promises.)

Property law has ended up with a variety of rules concerning this sort of situation. As a thoughtful judge described these rules in a modern case:

> These rules are contextual in nature. The[y] are crafted in response to the unique nature of the conduct they seek to regulate. Moreover, they are influenced by the custom and practice of each industry. The reason that absolute

---

19 *Id.* at 177–78.

20 *Id.* at 178.

21 *See generally* Amos Tversky & Daniel Kahneman, *Advances in Prospect Theory: Cumulative Representation of Uncertainty*, 5 J. RISK & UNCERTAINTY 297 (1992).

> dominion and control is not required to establish possession in [some cases] is that such a rule would be unworkable and unreasonable. The "nature and situation" of the property at issue does not immediately lend itself to unequivocal dominion and control. It is impossible to wrap [one's] arms around a whale, a fleeing fox or a sunken ship.[22]

That judge was called upon to decide the famous Barry Bonds baseball case,[23] where Barry Bonds had hit a record-breaking home run, one person caught it to some degree, a crowd attacked that person, and an innocent third party ended up with actual possession of the ball. Describing the dispute between the original partial catcher and the final possessor as one "where issues of property, tort and equity intersect,"[24] the court decided that "the ball must be sold and the proceeds divided equally between the parties."[25]

The baseball case isn't a pure case of capture—the property had been owned by Major League Baseball,[26] and both the plaintiff and the defendant were at the stadium as licensees of its owner, so it may be possible to conceive the whole case as largely contractual—but it shows the modern possibility of reaching a result that isn't binary but instead finds some middle ground between the two parties' claims. To reach a binary result, the case would turn entirely on arbitrary questions like precisely how the putative catcher's momentum interacted with that of the ball.[27] Because there was little evidence to bear on even that question, the case would then end up resting on the procedural burdens of proof—or perhaps on a shift of them if one were appropriate, as we have seen in occasional tort cases (see section 2.2.3). Again, maybe arbitrary questions of fact do little harm in some property cases, but a more adaptive rule on these particular facts is almost certainly fairer than an all-or-nothing one and seems very unlikely to do any harm to future parties' incentives. Similarly, Professor Helmholz argued for *equitable division* of property as a way to avoid classical and unjustified distinctions between *lost* and *mislaid* property.[28]

It is worth noting that the court's decision in the baseball case turned in part on factors alien to the classical rules of property law—

---

22 Popov v. Hayashi, 2002 WL 31833731, at *13 (Cal. Super. Ct. 2002).

23 *Id.*

24 *Id.* at *7.

25 *Id.* at *12.

26 *Id.* at *8.

27 *E.g.*, *id.* at *9–*12.

28 R.H. Helmholz, *Equitable Division and the Law of Finders*, 52 FORDHAM L. REV. 313, 322 (1983) ("It would seem sensible to treat the owner of the locus in quo and the finder under the same regime, and thus equitable division remains an attractive possibility.")

but not for that reason any less important. The judge in the case appeared to be motivated in part by a desire not to allow the unjustified and violent actions of a mob to be decisive in the case:

> The reason we do not know whether [the original partial catcher] would have retained control of the ball is not because of incidental contact. It is because he was attacked. His efforts to establish possession were interrupted by the collective assault of a band of wrongdoers.
>
> A decision which ignored that fact would endorse the actions of the crowd by not repudiating them. Judicial rulings, particularly in cases that receive media attention, affect the way people conduct themselves.[29]

Perhaps that is a direct application of public policy in the context of a private dispute (compare the doctrine of contracts that are "void as against public policy"; see section 3.2). Perhaps it is something like a partial burden shift for reasons of fair access to evidence (see section 2.2.3); in other words, if the case turns on the plaintiff's burden of proof, it can matter that the reason they can't meet that burden is that they were attacked by a mob. An unrelated third party who claimed without evidence that they had originally caught the ball but then mislaid it wouldn't be in the same position; we could hold that party's lack of evidence against them.

The most significant disputes about *creation* of new property in the modern world are left for intellectual-property courses. The classical justification for possession of new physical property comes from John Locke, who claimed that having "mixed" one's labor with unowned property confers rightful possession.[30] As a logical matter such a principle is entirely arbitrary and unpersuasive; as a practical matter, it may just be another attempt, like Holmes's in *B&O Railroad v. Goodman* or like the New York court's in *Pierson v. Post*, to try to come up with a principle that roughly matches reasonableness in some common cases at a particular time in human history.

4.4 Gifts

A surprisingly large amount of property law and many Property courses is based on gifts (usually those given by wealthy people to

---

[29] *Popov*, 2002 WL 31833731 at *14–*15.

[30] JOHN LOCKE, TWO TREATISES OF GOVERNMENT 231 (6th ed. 1796) ("Whatsoever . . . he removes out of the state that nature hath provided, and left it in, he hath mixed his labour with, and join to it something that is his own, and thereby makes it his property. . . . For this labour being the unquestionable property of the labourer, no man but he can have a right to what that is once joined to, at least where there is enough, and as good left in common for others.").

their relatives) and the disputes that surround them. A significant part of the law of landed estates arises in connection to donative transfers, as reflected in the titles and structures of the *Restatement (Second) of Property: Donative Transfers* and the *Restatement (Third) of Property: Wills and Other Donative Transfers*. In some ways, when first-year Property courses cover this material, they do so as a prelude to a later course on wills and trusts, the primary legal vehicles that people use when they want to give valuable property to others.

This emphasis may seem odd, given that as we saw in section 3.1.7, one of the reasons the common law may not enforce gift promises is simply that they are not important enough to merit the courts' attention, don't cause serious enough injuries to require legal remedies, require that courts interfere in family affairs, and so on. But property law perhaps addresses the unavoidable problems associated with badly given gifts—that is, gifts given ambiguously, poorly drafted wills, and other such missteps, again typically by wealthy donors who should have had better legal advice. Those problems aren't going away, and I don't mean to suggest they're not important—only that it is useful to keep in mind quite how much of many Property courses addresses the need to interpret the wishes of those who have poorly given gifts of very significant financial value. As another way to put it, we might expect the relative importance of this subject to vary inversely with the robustness of estate-taxation systems.

4.4.1 Distinguished from Donative Promises

The law draws a sharp distinction between an *executed* gift and a gift *promise* (see section 3.1.7). Gifts can be made legally effective immediately, regardless of the rules of contract law. Gift *promises* are ordinarily not enforced unless relied upon, however, for all the reasons discussed in section 3.1.7. Compared to an *executed*—that is, completed—gift, gift promises are said to be *executory*, which is one of the more confusing legal terms because in this context it simply means "unexecuted." (The use of the word *executory* in this sense appears originally to have meant something like "to be executed in the future"—thus, not executed now. In roughly the same sense, to say that someone is an "aspiring poet" is perhaps to deny they are currently a poet.) Understanding the difference between gifts and gift promises teaches us something both about property and about the policies associated with consideration in contract law.

Gifts can be made either by delivering property to the recipient or by making out a *deed of gift*, otherwise known as an *inter vivos donative document*. (*Inter vivos* means "between the living," as contrasted with a will.)[31] For one to make a gift, one has to have a property right—so one can give physical property, real property, intangible property, and so on, but not future personal services and not property one expects to receive in the future.[32] That said, in modern law there are in fact many ways to give gifts of property expected to be received in the future, including long-term trusts and flexible modern business organizations like limited liability companies (LLCs).[33]

So, for example, a note from a parent to a child saying "I hereby give you a painting hanging in my house; I intend to keep possession for it as long as I live, but after that it is yours" is effective immediately as a gift, without consideration.[34] Property law permits gifts without delivery, changes in physical possession, or even an immediate right to claim the gift. By contrast, "I promise to give you this painting when you turn 35" is a gift promise that lacks consideration, so it is unenforceable.

It is unclear why there should be a difference between these two cases, but the common law ordinarily lets people dispose of their property without significant legal protections, and the power to give a gift is a power that property rights confer. Promises of future income, future services, or other general creation of duties can perhaps be more dangerous for people's wellbeing, but it is important to note that the law does not vary here based on *value* or *importance* but instead based on *form*. A properly executed deed of gift can give away $10 million easily and irrevocably, whereas a thoroughly deliberative promise to assist someone with a new endeavor for a few evenings is unenforceable without consideration. Perhaps this suggests that the law does not take very seriously the policies supposedly aimed to *protect* promisors from their own ill-considered donative promises—as opposed to the other goals of consideration doctrine (see section 3.1).

The law is similarly inconsistent in other situations that involve the giving of gifts. For example, wills typically require special formalities like witnesses, but declaring a beneficiary for a financial account (which takes effect regardless of a will, effectively overriding a will as to the particular account) does not—and often can be completed without much fanfare on a simple online form. It may be

---

[31] *See* RESTATEMENT (THIRD) OF PROPERTY: WILLS AND OTHER DONATIVE TRANSFERS § 6.2 (2003).

[32] *See* FULLER ET AL., *supra* ch. 3, note 56, at 13.

[33] *See generally* SHAWN BAYERN, AUTONOMOUS ORGANIZATIONS (2021) (discussing the ways in which LLCs with durable operating agreements can control future property by agreement or immutable algorithm).

[34] *See, e.g.*, Gruen v. Gruen, 496 N.E.2d 869 (N.Y. 1986).

hard to justify that state of affairs, except perhaps that people are used to it. Lon Fuller wrote of "natural formalities" that serve cautionary and channeling functions[35]—encouraging people to be careful and to leave useful evidentiary records for their transactions—but it is hard to see any systematic purpose to the current legal state of affairs in this area. Particularly with the rise of easy online recordkeeping and the possibility to create and file online forms, it is probably time to rethink the formalities appropriate to gifts and gift promises. For example, maybe wills, gifts, *and* promises to give gifts over a certain value should all be enforceable merely by the donor's will, but only if the donor files the right form with the state, much like the procedures currently used to create new business organizations like corporations or LLCs. Such recording would aid appropriate gift and estate taxation, could serve as a natural formality, and could come with a "cooling off" period of a few days (before the gift takes legal effect) to ensure adequate deliberation. Such a regime would require statutory reform; it is probably too specific to come from common-law courts today. But it would probably be more rational that the patchwork framework for gifts that has developed.

4.4.2 Dead-Hand Control

A separate problem related to gifts is how to deal, particularly over the long term, with arrangements that try to tie up property in ways that survive the donor. For example, an owner of property might try to give a gift to their children in such a way that the children have the full power to use the property but never to sell it outside the family. Should the law enforce that sort of restriction three hundred years after the donor established it?

Though we sometimes pretend otherwise, the law is not imposed on us by the past. Past laws can of course be influential today, may be a useful default or an acceptable state of affairs, and may contain wisdom developed over years of dispute resolution. But there is no affirmative policy in law in honoring the wishes of long-dead generations. The underlying tension in the law's policies toward dead-hand control arise only from those that present generations still care about. One on hand, people alive today continue to want to impose restrictions on their property that last into the future, because doing so gives them a greater opportunity to shape the future, and that brings them some kind of happiness or comfort. On the other, people alive today want to use property they've inherited (or otherwise come to possess) without restrictions imposed on them

[35] *See* Lon L. Fuller, *Consideration and Form*, 5 COLUM. L. REV. 799, 815–16 (1941).

from the past. If there were an era in which suddenly nobody cared about preserving dead-hand control—that is, they didn't desire it themselves—the problem would become very easy to solve, and any rules favoring dead-hand control would go away. The problem persists because people who are currently alive continue to want their wishes to persist after they die.

Property law addresses dead-hand control through several complicated doctrines, such as those that permit or strike down restraints on alienation and those (like the rule against perpetuities; see section 4.4.3) that limit *future interests* in property. But the policies in all these areas all lead to a simple question: what types of limitations, if any, do we want to let people impose on the recipients of their gifts, and how long do we want those limitations to last?

The problems of dead-hand control may be less important today than they were at other times in US history. For example, during a period of rapid industrialization, it may have seemed wasteful for real property to remain unused and for other productive assets to be tied up. Today, it is hard for many people to feel the same concern if they see a parcel of real-estate remain undeveloped; perhaps its undeveloped state is the most environmentally appropriate use of the land, and the law has indeed come to recognize *conservation easements* specifically to preserve land in a more natural state. As a result, the concern that dead-hand restrictions might get in the way of property development may seem almost quaint today. For purely financial property, there is no real loss of efficiency from dead-hand restrictions: less money for some gift recipients to spend today just means more money for everyone else. For example, there is no real loss to society overall, apart from the costs associated with the physical paper, if someone wants to bury $1 billion in cash with them when they die; that is very different from wanting to bury (or shoot off into space) $1 billion in productive capital assets. In fact, burying $1 billion in cash might, for a time, serve as a tiny amount of carbon sequestration.

Moreover, developments in other areas of law have limited the opportunities for property law to impose meaningful restrictions on dead-hand control. For example, business organizations with perpetual duration have become commonplace and are extremely easy and inexpensive to set up in many US jurisdictions. Unlike the rules in many other jurisdictions, US business associations ordinarily require no reserves of capital and have extremely low initiation fees. Operating agreements for entities like LLCs can be extremely powerful—and difficult for later owners to change.[36] Statutory trusts

---

36 *See generally* BAYERN, *supra* note 33.

can last for centuries in many jurisdictions; for example, in Florida, trusts created after mid-2022 may last for a thousand years.[37] These changes in the law suggest that the theoretical policies behind restricting dead-hand control no longer seem important to many lawmakers today; they also leave little room for property law to have a meaningful influence in restricting dead-hand control.

4.4.3 The Rule Against Perpetuities

One of the traditional doctrines that developed to prevent dead-hand control, and which survives largely just as a thorn in lawyers' sides, is called the *rule against perpetuities*. Because it has been so extensively changed by modern statutes, my sense is that in courses where it is still taught, it is taught out of some combination of tradition and the desire to ensure that new lawyers get some experience working with intricate, technical material. That is the polite way to put it; the impolite way is that some professors appear to continue to teach the rule because they believe that it serves as an intelligence test. The rule has been found to be so complicated that at least one state supreme court has held that it is not malpractice for lawyers to fail to understand it.[38]

Because the rule is still sometimes taught, however, it may be useful to provide a brief guide to its general structure. The rule has something in common with the one-year provision of the statute of frauds (see section 3.3) in that a court must look back on a legally significant event and decide whether it was valid at the time it occurred, despite what has happened since then. A contract is within the one-year provision of the statute of frauds, or not, as of the time the contract was formed; the rule is not that courts wait a year to see if performance takes that long, and it is not that a contract might originally be valid but become invalid if a lawsuit is filed after a year. The legal status of the contract was said to be fixed at the time it was made. That view is consistent with classical law, which adopted "static" views of people's obligations,[39] perhaps in the interest of some overly strong notion of legal certainty and predictability. It may also be a product of the institutional limitations of early courts: in a legal system where judges ride into town on horses, hear cases, issue judgments, and leave, there is less opportunity for courts to monitor cases over longer periods of time, so there may have been more of a drive to focus on fixed points in the past in deciding cases. Today, however, courts don't have the same particular institutional limitations, and there are many doctrines of contract law (like

---

37 FLA. STAT. § 689.225 (2022).

38 Lucas v. Hamm, 364 P.2d 685 (Cal. 1961).

39 *See* Eisenberg, *supra* ch. 3, note 34, at 1748–49.

promissory estoppel; see section 3.1.7) that depend on facts that arise after a promise or contract is made.

The rule against perpetuities operates similarly to the one-year provision of the statute of frauds, having come from a time of static decisions and a more limited legal imagination. The rule applies, like the statute of frauds, to strike down certain legal arrangements—to declare that they were always invalid based on the form in which they were created. The rule applies to *interests* in property, created in a *conveyance* of some kind that purports to assign the interests to others.

As Jesse Dukeminier, a UCLA professor who in his time was seen by many as the only living person who fully understood the rule against perpetuities, wrote: "The essential thing to grasp about the [rule against perpetuities] is that *it is a rule of logical proof*."[40] That is, the rule asks a particular question, and it requires that the person who wants to establish that an interest is valid demonstrate that it meets the terms of the rule (or the opposing party show that it does not). Those terms are, as stated by John Chipman Gray, the rule's leading expert in the era before Professor Dukeminier's:

> No interest is good unless it must vest, if at all, not later than twenty-one years after some life in being at the creation of the interest.[41]

That is the form in which the rule is typically taught, even today. As its phrasing suggests, it applies only to interests that have not yet *vested*. The concept of vesting is surprisingly messy and has changed over time, but at its heart is the notion that there is no *condition precedent* for the interest—that is, no state of affairs that remains to determine whether or not the recipient will indeed have the interest. Having an interest that simply follows someone else's estate does not prevent vesting, which is perhaps a silly result of arbitrary choices made a long time ago.[42] So, for example, to borrow an example from Professor Gray, in a conveyance like "to *A* for life, then to *A*'s children for life, then to *B*,"[43] *B*'s interest is not even subject to the rule against perpetuities because it is vested in *B* immediately: there is no

---

[40] Jesse Dukeminier, *A Modern Guide to Perpetuities*, 74 CAL. L. REV. 1867 (1986) (emphasis in original). This article by Dukeminier is an excellent guide overall to the rule against perpetuities for those who want a more comprehensive introduction to that specific rule.

[41] JOHN CHIPMAN GRAY, THE RULE AGAINST PERPETUITIES § 201, at 174 (3d ed. 1915).

[42] *Accord* Dukeminier, *supra* note 40, at 1869 ("Hence, it is arguable that the [rule] should prohibit all future interest, and not merely contingent interests, that exist beyond the perpetuities period. But history has settled the question differently.").

[43] *Cf.* GRAY, *supra* note 41, § 205, at 176.

condition on which it depends, even if we don't know when it will take effect.[44]

The rule requires interests to vest within a particular period (if they vest at all). That is, it requires that, for a nonvested interest to be valid at the time it was created, any conditions on which that interest depends be certain (as of that same time) to resolve within a particular period. That period is, arbitrarily, *the lives of people currently alive, plus 21 years*. Dukeminier gives a tentative explanation for the historical choice of that particular period by suggesting that a property owner

> could realistically and perhaps wisely assess the capabilities of *living* members of his family, and so, with respect to them, [his] informed judgment, solemnly inscribed in an instrument, was given effect. But the head of the family could know nothing of unborn persons. Hence, [he was] permitted control only so long as his judgment was informed with an understanding of the capabilities and needs of persons alive when the judgment was made.[45]

Under the rule against perpetuities, interests that are not vested can be determined to be valid or not at the time of their creation—just, as discussed above, as contracts under the statute of frauds can be determined to be within the statute of frauds as of the time they are formed. A more modern and much simpler approach, adopted in the *Restatement (Second) of Property: Donative Transfers*, is called the *wait-and-see approach*[46] and permits interests to be valid if they do in fact vest within the rule's period: "a donative transfer of an interest in property fails, if the interest does not vest within the period of the rule against perpetuities."[47] This would be like a statute of frauds that required a signed writing only if a contract *in fact* takes longer than a year to perform. But the traditional rule remains one of "logical proof" about the original conveyance—leading to the possibility of imaginative demonstrations about how an interest might not vest within the perpetuities period.

Because the rule has little ongoing justification, at least in its specifics, it has been subject to reforms, like the wait-and-see test. Another reform is known as *cy pres*, Law French for "so close" (the modern French cognate is *si près*). If the rule against perpetuities

---

44 *Cf.* RESTATEMENT (SECOND) OF PROPERTY: DONATIVE TRANSFERS § 1.4 cmt. b (1983) ("An interest in property is a non-vested one if it is subject to an unfulfilled condition precedent.").

45 Dukeminier, *supra* note 40, at 1870.

46 RESTATEMENT (SECOND) OF PROPERTY: DONATIVE TRANSFERS § 1.4 cmt. a. (1983).

47 *Id.* § 1.4.

strikes down an interest, the result may be something entirely different, as a substantive matter, from what the donor wanted. *Cy pres* permits courts to make adjustments to achieve the donor's evident goals, rather than to let the rule against perpetuities operate mechanically to achieve undesirable results.

As suggested by *cy pres*, we might imagine a regime under which the donor's goals are paramount and we use their documents as a guide to what their goals were, with occasional formal rules that get in the way of that—either because they are bad mechanical rules (compare the rules of offer and acceptance to general interpretive inquiries; see section 3.5.1) or because they intend to stop owners from exercising dead-hand control. This general approach to interpreting donors' intent is already applied, with a healthy skepticism of formalistic interpretation, in the context of wills generally, so its development as a response to the rigidity of the rule against perpetuities seems sound.[48] Indeed, *cy pres* has a long history in the law of wills for this purpose.[49] The idea is simply that even if rules preventing dead-hand control are sound, we should not ignore the wishes of the donor—and therefore should seek to approximate them in developing an alternative that is permitted under a jurisdiction's rules concerning dead-hand control.

4.5 Bailments

The arcane law of *bailments* probably doesn't need to be taught anymore. But its connections to contract and tort are worth brief mention as a way to show further connections between the legal subjects covered in this book.

The precise definition of bailments is disputed, but Samuel Williston offered a general, workable definition: "the rightful possession of goods by one who is not the owner."[50] When there is a

---

48 *Accord* Dukeminier, *supra* note 40, at 1899 (responding to criticisms of *cy pres* by noting that judges already "have more discretionary power with respect to the construction of wills than is commonly recognized").

49 *See, e.g.*, 1 JOHN BOUVIER, A LAW DICTIONARY 277 (1839) ("In cases where a perpetuity is attempted in a will, the courts do not, if they can avoid it, construe the devise to be utterly void, but expound the will in such a manner as to carry the testator's intentions into effect, as far as the rules respecting perpetuities will allow; this is called a construction *cy prés* [sic]").

50 2 SAMUEL WILLISTON, THE LAW OF CONTRACTS § 1032, at 1944 (1924); *see also* RAY ANDREWS BROWN, A TREATISE ON THE LAW OF PERSONAL PROPERTY § 73, at 225–28 (1936). Consistently with this book's themes, Brown nicely discussed the problems in the definition and application of the concept of bailments:

> Much [confusion] could surely have been avoided . . . . After all it is the principal purpose of courts of law to decide the ultimate controversy that the contending parties place before it, in a way which will be most just to the parties concerned, and of the greatest general public utility. It is unfortunate when the law forgets this primary purpose and treats its function as an exercise in syllogisms, in which the decision turns on a more

bailment, the person currently in possession of the property is called a *bailee*; the person who owns the property and delivers it to the bailee is called the *bailor*.

One question that arises in the law of bailments is what level of care the bailee must use to maintain and prevent damage to the property. The law here parallels the attempt in tort law to impose specialized duties of care on particular parties, like the *extraordinary care* sometimes said to be required of innkeepers and common carriers (see section 2.2.2). Bailments were traditionally divided into three categories depending on who was meant to benefit from the bailment, and the duties of the bailee were assigned accordingly:

> When the bailment is for the sole benefit of the bailor, the law requires only *slight* diligence on the part of the bailee, and of course makes him answerable only for *gross* neglect. When the bailment is for the sole benefit of the bailee, the law requires *great* diligence on the part of the bailee, and makes him responsible for *slight* neglect. When the bailment is reciprocally beneficial to both parties, the law requires *ordinary* diligence on the part of the bailee, and makes him responsible for *ordinary* neglect.[51]

This overcomplicated and arguably even silly arrangement has eroded because it adds no more to the notion of reasonable care than did specialized supposed duties for innkeepers or railroad operators. Courts recognized this relatively early; for example, the Supreme Court of Minnesota wrote in 1934:

> The former distinction between bailments for the sole benefit of the bailor; those for the mutual benefit of both bailor and bailee; and those for the sole benefit of the latter, in respect to the degree of care required of the bailee in order to protect him from liability for negligence, has long since been pretty much discarded here as elsewhere. "It is evident that the so-called distinctions between slight, ordinary and gross negligence over which courts have perhaps somewhat quibbled for a hundred years, can furnish no assistance."

> or less logical deduction from some postulated major premise. It might be well, therefore, if we could abandon the search for the definitions and elements of bailment, and confine ourselves to a consideration of the various rights and duties which arise when one person has possession of goods, which belong to another.

Id. at 226 (internal footnotes omitted).

[51] JOSEPH STORY, COMMENTARIES ON THE LAW OF BAILMENTS, WITH ILLUSTRATIONS FROM THE CIVIL AND THE FOREIGN LAW § 23, at 27 (9th ed. 1878).

> Defendant's liability, if any, is for negligence. In that field generally the legal norm is a care commensurate to the hazard, i.e. the amount and kind of care that would be exercised by an ordinarily prudent person in the same or similar circumstances. The character and amount of risk go far, either to decrease or increase the degree of care required.[52]

As we have seen elsewhere, a general standard of reasonableness tends to emerge, rather than more particular or categorical standards announced by judges in advance.

The existence of bailments in which the bailee receives no benefit but still has duties to the bailor suggests a new category of promises for which consideration is not required: promises to take care of someone else's property when it is in one's possession. The law is effectively that such promises are enforced by their (typically implied) terms, rather than only by reliance damages.[53] More precisely, damages for lost or destroyed goods are measured by the market value of the goods or their replacement cost.[54] The justification for this departure from the usual rules of contract law is unclear, but reliance is quite likely in these cases, and the promisee's (bailor's) reliance interest may be difficult to satisfy confidently except by awarding damages equal to the value of the property.

Overall, the relative rarity of bailment cases today suggests, perhaps, that US society has grown out of the need for the overcomplicated rules in this area of law. Bailments may simply be less important as a factual matter than they used to be; goods might be more durable overall (requiring less care by others when owners decide to travel, for example), more easily transported, and so on. More commercial services—such as storage lockers and safe-deposit boxes—have arisen, and they structure the activity of storing and maintaining personal property with fairly elaborate contracts. Customers therefore have a menu of services to choose from and probably rely more on customer-service organizations (and their reputations) than they would have been able to do a hundred years ago. The decline of a legal field is nothing to mourn, however; it

---

[52] Peet v. Roth Hotel Co., 253 N.W. 546, 548 (1934) (quoting Trs. of Elon Coll. v. Elon Banking & Tr. Co., 109 S.E. 6 (N.C. 1921)).

[53] *See* Detroit Inst. of Arts Founders Soc'y v. Rose, 127 F. Supp. 2d 117, 136 (D. Conn. 2001) ("[A]ctual consideration is not required for a bailment to be enforceable. As stated above, gratuitous bailments are generally not supported by actual consideration, but are still binding on the bailee.") (internal citation omitted).

[54] *See* B&Y Heavy Movers, Inc. v. Fluor Constructors, Inc., 570 N.E.2d 777, 784 (Ill. App. Ct. 1991) ("[D]amages for breach of a bailment agreement is the market value of the goods at the time of the loss. . . . However, . . . when market value is difficult to ascertain, for example, where the property converted is unique, a court may award damages using some other reasonable calculation of value, such as replacement cost.").

simply suggests that a recurring problem may have gone away or at least is of sharply diminished importance as a result of technological and social change.

4.6 Property Torts

The subjects of property law and tort law overlap in a variety of torts that affect property. Most of these torts can, in the end, be analyzed using straightforward tort principles, but it may be helpful to provide a quick guide to them. This section focuses on the torts that protect interests in *land*; there are also torts called *trespass to chattels* and *conversion* that protect interests in *personal property*, like goods and intangible property—and, like the law of bailments, the general law of negligence covers damage to personal property (see section 2.6). The tort of *conversion* is a label applied to, among other situations, those where a good-faith buyer loses a claim against an original owner of property (see section 4.1); it therefore can be conceived as a strict-liability tort.

4.6.1 Private Nuisance

The tort of *private nuisance* is extremely similar to the tort of negligence; we might think of it as negligence that harms someone's *use* or *enjoyment* of land rather than negligence that threatens only property *damage*. As a comment to the *Restatement (Second) of Torts* puts it, the difference between negligence and nuisance is not in the *conduct* of the defendant but simply in what it *harms*: "Failure to recognize that private nuisance has reference to the interest invaded and not to the type of conduct that subjects the actor to liability has led to confusion."[55] As the comment further notes, though the history of nuisance is complicated, "an actor is no longer liable for accidental interferences with the use and enjoyment of land but only for such interferences as are intentional and unreasonable or result from negligent, reckless or abnormally dangerous conduct."[56]

It would be far easier, and probably not change the law in this area significantly, simply to say that the general background duty of reasonable care (see section 2.2) applies to physical injury, property damage, and people's use of their land. Indeed, even the choice between strict liability and negligence for those types of harms follows similar patterns; for example, nuisance liability arises for "negligent or reckless conduct, or for abnormally dangerous conditions or activities"[57] (compare section 2.8.4). Instead of following a simpler, unified view, however, analysis of nuisance has proceeded

---

55 RESTATEMENT (SECOND) OF TORTS § 822 cmt. b. (1979).

56 *Id.*

57 *Id.* § 822(b).

in different jurisdictions with different particular elements that tend toward the same general result but in a more complicated fashion.

The leading Torts treatise largely agrees with my analysis here: "So far as a supposed nuisance rests upon proof of the defendant's negligence, the case proceeds largely as would any other negligence case, and the nuisance label adds little or nothing to the analysis."[58] The treatise notes several specific doctrinal parallels and concludes, "To put it bluntly, a nuisance claim based on negligence is merely a negligence claim with harm to interests in use and enjoyment."[59]

4.6.2 Trespass to Land

The tort of trespass to land, by contrast, is commonly treated as something new as compared to the analysis of torts in chapter 2. Trespass involves, at its core, an intentional entry onto someone else's land. The tort is said to retain a significant element of strict liability; at least, the reasonableness of an entrant's decision onto the land isn't formally judged in processing the tort. That said, there are a number of *privileges*—a term used in the law of intentional torts that simply means *defenses*—that move the law of trespass much closer to that of negligence.

For example, entering someone's land, even intentionally, does not lead to liability "if it is or reasonably appears to be necessary to prevent serious harm" to persons or property[60] or if a traveler "reasonably believes" that a road is blocked and entry onto the land is necessary to "continue" their "journey."[61] And trespass requires a "tangible" entry, so that traditionally "penetration of the land by smoke, noise, or light, might affect use and enjoyment (thus constituting nuisance), but it would not affect possession" and therefore be a trespass.[62] The supposed intangibility of smoke or even light isn't grounded in physics but instead in the harshness of trespass liability: any intentional intrusion is a trespass even if it causes no harm, so that if smoke or light counted it would be extremely difficult for even ordinary and unobjectionable activities to avoid being trespasses onto others' land. So the tangibility requirement, like the other limitations to trespass just described, move the tort back somewhat toward being a simple negligence tort.

---

58 DAN B. DOBBS ET AL., THE LAW OF TORTS § 400 (2d ed. 2011 & Supp. 2022).

59 *Id.*

60 RESTATEMENT (SECOND) OF TORTS § 197 (1965).

61 *Id.* § 195.

62 DAN B. DOBBS ET AL., *supra* note 58, § 53.

Even more importantly, the law recognizes consent as a privilege—defense—to trespass, and consent may be implied by custom:

> In determining whether conduct would be understood by a reasonable person as indicating consent, the customs of the community are to be taken into account. This is true particularly of silence or inaction. Thus if it is the custom in wooded or rural areas to permit the public to go hunting on private land or to fish in private lakes or streams, anyone who goes hunting or fishing may reasonably assume, in the absence of a posted notice or other manifestation to the contrary, that there is the customary consent to his entry upon private land to hunt or fish.[63]

So, for example, a neighbor making a friendly inquiry and knocking on someone else's front door has probably not trespassed if the neighbor reasonably expected, based on the customs of the community, that such an entry was consented to. Once told that they're not wanted, the neighbor would be trespassing if they remained for an unreasonably long time[64] or if they came back without any justification.

Given all this, while trespass is often taught and tested as if it contained significant elements of strict liability, just like nuisance it is unclear what is added by treating it as a separate tort. Courts could simply say—but haven't—that *unreasonably* entering onto someone's land is a tort; that would extend the general duty to avoid unreasonable conduct beyond victims' interests against bodily injuries and property damage (see section 2.6), and beyond their interest in the *use* of land (see section 4.6), to their abstract right to exclusive occupancy of the land they own. That would still add something new—an extension of the duty of ordinary care to a new type of interest—but it would be considerably less complicated than having separate rules about smoke, light, subsurface entries, entries over the air of land, the details of privileges, and the multitude of other rules that remain in the law of trespass.

4.7 Conclusion

Property courses are very different from each other—so much so that this chapter couldn't easily try to match all of them. Much

---

63 RESTATEMENT (SECOND) OF TORTS § 892 cmt. d (1979); *see also id.* § 167 (1965) ("The rules stated in §§ 892–892D as to the effect of consent to the actor's conduct apply to entry or remaining on land."); RESTATEMENT OF TORTS § 167 cmt d. (1934) ("[A] general or local custom may confer a consent").

64 *See* RESTATEMENT (SECOND) OF TORTS § 171 (1965) (allowing "reasonable egress" after consent terminates).

material taught in Property courses in JD programs is more mechanical than the material found in Torts or Contracts courses. For example, much of the material on the law of landed estates involves a kind of formalistic interpretation of language in conveyances, and it is taught today perhaps just as an exercise in understanding the historical property structures.[65] Some material, by contrast, is extremely theoretical, focusing on abstract explanations for the role that property plays in society. Some courses introduce material on intellectual property; others emphasize the regulation of "land use" and its environmental effects.

This chapter has covered some of the basic rules of property law that are similar in structure and scope to the sorts of basic, intrapersonal puzzles that arise in tort law and contract law—that is, basic questions of how individual people live with each other, which are in many respects the core questions for the common law. Indeed, sometimes the problems are susceptible to the same sorts of analyses we saw in the previous chapters. For example, the law covering good-faith buyers of stolen property exercises the same principles of negligence and strict liability that we saw in tort.

---

[65] Much of the material in the area of landed estates is so formal that it has literally been the subject of computer programs that do a decently good job of encapsulating the legal material. *See* Shawn J. Bayern, *A Formal System for Analyzing Conveyances of Property Under the Common Law*, 23 JURIX 139 (2010); Shawn Bayern, *Conveyance Interpreter*, https://essentially.net/property/; Shrutarshi Basu et al., *A Programming Language for Future Interests*, 24 YALE J.L. & TECH. 76 (2022).

Chapter 5

CONCLUSION

Contents

This book's coverage of tort law, contract law, and property law has built an understanding of the common law from the bottom up rather than the top down. That is, it has walked through particular problems that arise in disputes between people, trying to explain and develop the best rules to govern those disputes based on their specific features, rather than trying to derive legal rules from a single unified theory. Common law resists grand theoretical conceptions because it wrestles with the nuances of human affairs. Legal academics frequently try to put the common law into particular boxes, but those efforts tend to fail. For example, you'll sometimes hear that the common law is "libertarian," but there is nothing in the rules that this book has covered that suggests an impulse in that direction; if early English common law was libertarian, that may reflect its institutional difficulties in regulating anything. Common law has not developed in a vacuum; the development of the law reflects the values of different times and changing institutional features of courts.

To conclude the book, this short chapter surveys the book's coverage to draw some lessons about potential errors to avoid when learning and thinking about the common law.

5.1 Pitfalls to Avoid in Learning and Analyzing Common Law

5.1.1 Reliance on Grand or Political Ideologies

The law relies on principles. Those principles inevitably rely, in turn, on abstractions—or generalizations about and social interpretations of the physical world. Indeed, nearly all human activities do; otherwise, what we call *facts* would just be shapes and colors without meaning, or physical processes so complex and formless that they would be impossible to describe.

Determining the right principles and the right level of generality for any endeavor requires judgment. In law, a particular tendency among scholars and other analysts has been to select levels of abstraction that are far too general. Again, some generalization is always necessary; principles that achieve goals of fairness and policy may well, for example, need to distinguish between sellers and buyers in contract law, or between innocent and at-fault parties in a world where any party is unlikely to be wholly innocent or wholly blameworthy. The challenge is to avoid generalizing too far. As Grant Gilmore put it: "the lesson of the past two hundred years is that we will do well to be on our guard against all-purpose theoretical solutions to our problems. . . . When we become too sure of our premises, we necessarily fail in what we are supposed to be doing."[1]

There are several missteps that cause courts and commentators to overgeneralize their legal analysis. One mistake, as I've suggested at least implicitly throughout this book, is to take the legal "subjects" too seriously. Courts often describe a claim as "sounding in contract rather than tort" or the like, but that alone is not a reason or an argument. It is just a label, and it may not be a helpful one.[2] Moreover, as we've seen, different legal subjects often have many features in common.

Another mistake is to try to decide legal questions without regard to the real facts on the ground, ignoring such features as business customs and the reasonable expectations of parties. As Lon Fuller, one of the leading legal theorists of the 1900s, once wrote: "It is remarkable how many people in this world . . . go about deciding things with only the slightest notion of what it is they are really deciding."[3] He was referring to those who try to make decisions about law without understanding facts or their context. Often, straying too far from facts leads to abstract, unworkable decisions. For example, in all the analysis of this book, I haven't justified any rules in terms of grand generalizations like *rule-of-law values*, any other kinds of *essentialism* about law ("law is necessarily *X* because . . ." where *X* is some appealing adjective not tied to any operational proposition of morality or policy), or any particular strand of general political philosophy that happens to be in vogue. I also haven't tried to reduce the common law to some singular process, like "reasoning by analogy."

---

[1] GILMORE, *supra* ch. 3, note 73, at 109–10.

[2] *Cf.* EISENBERG, *supra* ch. 1, note 13, at 45–46 ("Deep doctrinal distinctions that are not themselves supported by applicable social propositions usually originated in periods in which they were socially congruent. Distinctions that lose the support of applicable social propositions tend to dissolve over time, because they provide only an impoverished justification for different treatment of socially comparable transactions. For example, a well-known trend in modern law is the gradual dissolution of the deep doctrinal distinction between real estate contracts and other contracts.").

[3] Fuller, *supra* ch. 1, note 12, at 279.

Instead, in discussing particular doctrines of tort law, contract law, and property law I've tried to demonstrate the sort of principles that lawyers and judges use to structure, analyze, and improve legal rules. I sometimes call that level of generality *mid-level theory*, in that it is less abstract than grand political theory but more abstract than case-specific reasoning, analogies, or formal empirics.

To be clear, however, one of the pleasant features of common law is the recognition that legal rules and even the level of generality at which to analyze them are often sharply in dispute among courts and commentators. The approach I've outlined fits with the modern approach to the common law that has arisen over the last century or so, but I don't ever mean to say it's the only approach. The point in learning the common law is to become comfortable with the different possible modes of analysis.

5.1.2 Credulity

This may sound like a crass marketing statement about competing books, but if you're evaluating any book on contract law, you might check whether it repeats the illusory-promise rule (see section 3.1.4) uncritically or whether it presents it skeptically and with enough context to understand how and why courts have eroded it. Similarly, in evaluating books on tort law, you might consider whether they state the assumption-of-risk defense (see section 2.7.2) without suggesting that it doesn't add anything new to negligence law. It is impossible to understand those two particular doctrines deeply without understanding the criticism they have faced.

Avoiding a credulous view of the black-letter law is an important job for any US common lawyer. Learning lists of outdated rules that are under pressure probably does more harm than good. A typical Wikipedia page about the common law, or a typical undergraduate textbook on US legal studies or business law—and even the pages on law firms' websites that try to explain particular areas of an individual state's law to potential clients—often present the law with exactly that sort of credulous view. Just because courts say something doesn't mean they do it (see section 1.5.1), and doctrines do not always do what their names suggest (see section 1.5.2). They often have exceptions and limitations that have developed in response to real-world concerns, and as a result the law changes.

The only way to be sure what the law is is to read cases and then to analyze them using approaches broadly like those in this book: to determine and then evaluate the results of cases in view of doctrine, social morality, and social policy; to figure out if the cases fit into a pattern; and to chart the development of those patterns over time. Often cases outright contradict one another, even in the same jurisdiction—or two lines of cases develop rules that could both apply to the same sets of facts, setting up potential conflicts that courts need to resolve. One of the skills of a lawyer is to understand how those conflicts are likely to be resolved and to know where the weak links in the doctrine are—what is outdated and what can be pressed on to change. If a student asks me the state of the law on some topics, the best answer might be, "A good lawyer could convince a good court that one particular result is proper. But without good lawyers and good courts, the cases suggest several possibilities." There is then no further resolution without litigation, applying the sort of legal reasoning this book has tried to demonstrate. Of course, the law is not always so unsettled—but even in more settled areas, the answer to the student's question might be, "The legal-duty rule still exists here and could theoretically govern this case of contract modification. But it is very unlikely that a good court would apply it to these facts." For the reasons discussed in section 3.1.5, the proper answer is *not* an uncritical statement of the legal-duty rule.

A related sort of credulity to avoid is to accept existing doctrinal categories as rigid rather than to look to simplify and organize them in ways that suit the law's development. For any doctrine you learn, you might ask what the law would look like without it. For example, does *res ipsa loquitur* (see section 2.2.3) really add anything to tort law? Do the rules of offer and acceptance (see section 3.5) provide a useful gloss on the general rules of contract interpretation, or will they just tend to get in the way of correct interpretations of parties' communications? Does a doctrine exist just because it helps courts erode a rule that is a poor fit with propositions of morality and policy, or does it have an independent justification based on such propositions? In developing an understanding of doctrine and organizing it for themselves, students should do the same kind of work that the American Law Institute does in writing Restatements.

5.1.3 Maxims and Oversimplification

Lon Fuller wrote in 1930 that "maxims"—short sayings about the law taken to embody some deeper wisdom—were the hallmark of unthoughtful legal systems:

> "Equity regards that as done which ought to be done." "The law often regards money as land and land as money." Happily such "short, dark maxims" are not so common as they once were. When they are used today, it is for the sake of their flavor of antiquity, rather than because of any

> notion that they are actually explanatory. Undeveloped systems of law have a decided penchant for such brocards.[4]

Almost a hundred years later, many US law schools have first-year courses focused on statutory interpretation that inculcate and apply these sorts of maxims—now often called *canons*—largely because the Supreme Court of the United States has tended to overemphasize them in the last few decades in the context of statutory interpretation. Generalities like these are an exceedingly poor way to analyze law and an equally bad way to analyze language, such as the language of statutes. Anyone learning the law should approach this kind of generality with a healthy dose of skepticism.

Apart from historical and more formal legal maxims, legal commentators sometimes have a tendency to try to reduce principles of social morality or policy to short bits of supposed verbal wisdom that have the ring of truth. (We saw this in section 3.1.4 in the historical notion of mutuality in contract law, where the dictum that "both parties need to be bound or neither is bound," which might sound nice in theory, works terribly in practice.) Often, these attempted bits of wisdom sound like they come from dull adults providing overly vague life lessons for children. Such sayings aren't even successful on their own terms: "You get only one bite at the apple," but that's not even how apples work. "You've made your bed, and now you have to lie in it"; that's usually meant as a statement of the harsh consequences of some action, but it actually sounds delightful. At their best, these sayings do little more than capture a sort of pseudo-folksy wisdom that works in a limited range of situations, and that level of generality is not a helpful one when the goal is to determine appropriately sensitive legal rules. To put it differently, not all grand and misleading legal maxims are pretentious, historical, or in Latin. Regardless of their origin, their excessive application tends to reflect laziness or brittleness of thought.

Often, as Karl Llewllyn famously pointed out, maxims even directly contradict one another.[5] As many have observed, so do folksy sayings—for example, "look before you leap," but "he who hesitates is lost." As one writer put it more than a century ago, "All maxims

---

[4] L.L. Fuller, *Legal Fictions* (pt. 1), 25 ILL. L. REV. 363, 368 (1930) (later published in LON L. FULLER, LEGAL FICTIONS 33 (1967)) (internal citations omitted).

[5] Karl N. Llewellyn, *Remarks on the Theory of Appellate Decision and the Rules or Canons of About How Statutes are to be Construed*, 3 VAND. L. REV. 395 (1950); see also, for fun, Patrick M. McFadden, *Fundamental Principles of American Law*, 85 CAL. L. REV. 1749 (1997) (listing a variety of often contradictory general propositions so that law-review editors can have something to cite in formal scholarship—e.g., "The law, however, has not adapted. The law has adapted more slowly than we might have wished. The law wisely resists every transitory change in the social wind.").

have their antagonist maxims; proverbs should be sold in pairs, a single one being but half a truth."[6]

This sort of antagonism is true even of sayings that are commonly accepted as legal doctrines, or at least proto-doctrines. For example, it's commonplace for courts to say that people shouldn't be able to profit from a wrong, but it's also commonplace for them to say that damages shouldn't make plaintiffs better than they would have been without a wrong. This is all clearly an unhelpful level of generality at which to analyze, for example, the proper availability of disgorgement of profits from breach of contract (see section 3.6).

There is another way to think of maxims, particularly when lawyers rely on them to figure out the meaning of textual communications, like contracts or statutes: *Large language models*—GPT-4 and so on—have developed over the last decade and, while astounding in their capabilities, still don't always get the interpretation and generation of language right despite considerable complexity and training on extremely large sets of data. The kind of maxims that some judges and professors use today are, by contrast, essentially *tiny language models*—extremely simple and mechanical ways of trying to construct language. They contain only a tiny amount of information, like "the expression of one thing is the exclusion of another." We got through all of chapter 3 on contract law without relying on this type of canon or on other mechanical approaches toward language. At least in the common-law subjects, their use should be sharply restricted because they lack the necessary sensitivity of the common law.

5.1.4 False Certainty

One particular type of grand theory that the analysis in this book has avoided or rejected is the notion that law must be absolutely certain. Legal uncertainty is not usually desirable for its own sake, but legal theorists often make several mistakes about certainty (see sections 1.2 and 3.1.6). First, they implicitly assume that certainty in legal rules is important principally for professors and theorists, rather than for actual parties who are subject to the law. (For example, the rules of classical contract law were perhaps more "certain" for students to learn and for professors to teach than those of modern contract law, but because they mapped poorly onto business practices they did not increase the law's certainty for contracting parties; they often in fact did exactly the opposite of what reasonable parties expected or thought was fair.) Second, they treat certainty as an end in itself, rather than as a proxy for some other

---

6 TRYON EDWARDS, A DICTIONARY OF THOUGHTS 338 (1906) (attributed to "W. Matthews"). Of course, this too is a maxim.

value that is directly important in terms of morality or policy, like the unfairness of changing a rule that people have relied on. Third, they overestimate the value of certainty. The world routinely deals with significant social and technological change, and indeed one of the things businesses are great at doing is planning in the face of uncertainty; a significant amount of what is taught in business schools today involves that sort of planning.

Legal rules that are too formal, harsh, or unbending contain the seeds of their own destruction, because there will always be a tendency to avoid their harshest effects in the cases that demonstrate why the rule needs to be expanded or changed.[7] Students new to the study of law—or lawyers from other legal systems first encountering US law—often wonder why the law can't be more mechanical or why it takes a book of this length rather than a simple statement of rules to cover routine disputes that arise among small numbers of people. Indeed, some legal theories and some other legal systems pretend, at least on the surface, that legal rules are simple and don't require much skill to apply. Whenever a more formal system is genuinely tested, however, it immediately begins to erode. Judges use whatever discretion they have to avoid results that are absurd, immoral, or deeply inefficient—and lawyers are expert at pressing the boundaries of the rules in such systems. The result, as we have seen throughout this book, is an array of inconsistent exceptions to bad rules that are eventually replaced. In other words, one answer to the question "why can't law be more mechanical?" is simply that such systems don't work and don't last.

We could try to develop a system of laws administered entirely by robots, but very few people think that would be a good idea—at least across the range of the common law. (Maybe it's all right for parking tickets.) There is a persistent fiction in US political thinking that our system, or desired system, is a *government of laws* rather than a *government of people*, but the sharp division between those two concepts is an illusion.[8] No legal system is in fact mechanical and made up only of simple rules, even if commentators pretend that that is the case. We have yet to come up with a workable system of justice that doesn't require judges, and we probably never will.

5.1.5 Limiting the Role of the Lawyer

In a common-law system, the obvious roles of a lawyer—for example, arguing and planning on behalf of private clients—are deeply connected with a sort of thinking that lies beyond those more specific tasks: common lawyers need to envision solutions to social

---

7 *See supra* ch. 2, note 71.

8 *See* ALFRED WHITNEY GRISWOLD, IN THE UNIVERSITY TRADITION 9–16 (1957).

problems, holding up possibilities for decision makers (either in the documents they draft or in the litigation positions they adopt) to accept. The decision makers accept these positions based, as we have seen (see particularly section 1.2), on both existing rules and on the ability to adapt or change rules to suit new circumstances. Therefore, even on a day-to-day basis—not just when participating in law-reform efforts like statutory-drafting committees—lawyers often need to work as social engineers. Lon Fuller described part of the skill of the modern common lawyer as follows, comparing it to working out a physical puzzle that involves fitting irregular shapes into a circle:

> with patience, with insight, with hard intellectual labor, one will find that there is an arrangement that will avoid the overlapping or conflict of the pieces or will reduce it to negligible proportions . . . . [For example, in the context of labor relations, workers] can be protected against indignities in ways that do not reduce, too much, industrial efficiency; there are ways of promoting industrial efficiency which do not involve pushing the worker around.
>
> This is the kind of job in which the lawyer, properly trained, excels. He it is who has the detachment that is the first essential for the task. With this he combines the imagination and the capacity for analyzing the factors in the situation that are equally indispensable. Lawyers representing both management and labor have made important contributions to this task.[9]

Too often, lawyers and law students ignore the generative capacity of legal work—and of the improvements to law that imagination and intellectual effort make possible. Lawyers should not readily accept that they are in a zero-sum game but instead look for improvements whenever possible.[10] To deny the need for that improvement is to cut off possibilities for growth—for greater fairness and efficiency in the law, for example.

The reference in this book's title to both principles and possibilities is not an accident. Lawyers and law students should always be on the lookout for creative ideas, drawn from the full range of disciplines and experience that inform human affairs. For all the reasons we have seen, law is an imaginative endeavor.

---

9 Fuller, *supra* ch. 1, note 12, at 279.

10 *Cf.* ADRIAN TCHAIKOVSKY, CHILDREN OF TIME 588 (2015) ("The idea of two prisoners [in the *Prisoners' Dilemma* well-known in game theory] incapable of communication would not be an acceptable status quo for them, but a problem to overcome: the Prisoners' Dilemma as a Gordian knot, to be cut through rather than be bound by.")

Table of Cases

Index

References are to Pages